Last of t...

Andrew Vine is an award-winning journalist and assistant editor of the *Yorkshire Post*. His next book is about the liner *Canberra*'s role in the Falklands War, to be published by Aurum in 2012 on the thirtieth anniversary of the conflict. He lives in Leeds.

Last of the Summer Wine

The Story of the World's
Longest-running Comedy Series

ANDREW VINE

First published 2010 by
Aurum Press Limited
7 Greenland Street
London NW1 0ND
www.aurumpress.co.uk

This paperback edition first published in 2011 by Aurum Press Ltd.

A catalogue record for this book is available from the
British Library.

ISBN 978 1 84513 711 3

10 9 8 7 6 5 4 3 2 1
2016 2015 2014 2013 2012 2011

Typeset by Saxon Graphics Ltd, Derby
Printed by CPI Bookmarque, Croydon, Surrey, CR0 4TD

In memory of my parents, Jeffrey and Sheila Vine

'You can't help getting older, but you don't have to get old.'
George Burns

'It takes a long time to become young.'
Pablo Picasso

Contents

Prologue

THREE MEN ARE pausing for a breather at the top of the hill, silhouetted against a moorland skyline of tough green grass and thorny yellow gorse and springy purple heather. The sunny day stretches before them yet to be filled, but for now there is time enough to dawdle, to find a rocky outcrop to sit upon, or lie in the brush with their toecaps pointing at a cloudless sky and talk, remembering and reminiscing on schooldays, wartime, friends half-forgotten or newly recalled, even unlikely loves past and still hoped for. Summer is still here, but its best days are past, and so are the best days of these men who nevertheless still dream and plan and adventure, mindful that winter's chill will soon draw on, but preferring to turn their thoughts to prolonging this golden, balmy moment while ever the sun is still high in the sky. They are an ill-assorted lot: one tall, authoritarian, even pompous, convinced of his own superiority and earnest in his desire to improve his companions; the second is endlessly self-effacing, shy, nervous, cowardly, cautious, yet redeemed from ineffectuality by a sly wit and an acerbic view of the world. The less said about the third, the better; he is an utter disgrace, uncouth, unshaven, unkempt, his trousers barely less horrifying than the unspeakable thing kept in a matchbox among the bits of string and pencil stubs that fill his pockets, a short, animated, skipping, perky, compost heap of a man, ageing but still with the mischievous spark of the naughty boy of the form, in wellington boots and knitted beanie hat, whose innocence lingers, even when his thoughts turn to towards romance with one whose charms are unfathomable to all but him.

This is a landscape that invites reflection, and for these three its tranquillity is filtered through their own preoccupations. For the tatty one, that means betting on the horses and cadging cigarettes: 'Do you know, it's so quiet up here, you could hear the rustle of a fag packet being handed round.' For the timid and thoughtful one, it is the existential insignificance of man in this terrain, which was born long before he existed and will survive him when he has gone, allied to his capacity to annoy while he remains: 'When you come up here, you realise how small a creature man is, and you wonder why he's standing on other people's feet.' For the third, relentless in his desire to remake an inglorious military career in retrospect, all is viewed through the prism of the great commander of fighting men he never was nor ever could have been: 'Every time I come here, the spirit soars. You can't help thinking what a wonderful place it would be to set up a machine gun. Give me a small squad of hand-picked men, and I could defend this place indefinitely.'

Chatting and bickering, they range far and wide over these summits and valleys. Time is of little consequence; life has passed by, relinquishing its claims on them. All are single, unmarried, widowed or abandoned by a wife who gave up in exasperation, and if there is perhaps the faintest undertone of loneliness in their friendship, the hills where they amble are an ideal place to be alone together. These are the Pennines, the great range of peaks running through the north of England, that in late summer are among the most glorious landscapes in the world, and these men's corner of them is Yorkshire, a feisty, plain-speaking, sometimes dour, more often generous, honest and hospitable county in which grim vistas of mills, mines and manufacturing give way to this beauty.

Up here on these high moors, they are the masters of their own fate, even heroic in their own small way, inventors of schemes that will see them shrug off the years and slide down the hillsides on tin trays or in barrels, or career along a road on a runaway sofa or a three-seater bicycle as they resolutely refuse to grow old. That will change when they descend in search of a cup of tea in the café they frequent, or return to the scruff's reprehensible home. There, they run the gauntlet of a category of woman to be feared and obeyed, large, bustling and possessed of a tone of voice that brooks no insubordination in the ranks of mere men. These doughty northern wives, veterans and unquestioned victors of domestic trench warfare, are as much the backbone of their world as the Pennines are of this part of Britain, and no less flinty or immovable; indubitably the stronger sex, they fume at the idiocies of husbands: 'Why is it that a million years of natural selection has produced a breed of men in these parts perfectly adapted to uselessness?' Here is a hopelessly unequal battle of the sexes. All the weaponry is with the women; if withering put-downs and barked commands will not do, a sweeping brush or tin tray are there to shoo an undersized lecherous ratbag away from stone steps or café door back to his ferrets. The heavy armour is pinnies, curlers or stockings more wrinkled than a Chinese lantern, and in the face of its advance, the men's only options are surrender or retreat. The skirmishes stretch across decades; the combatants pass from their fifties into their eighties, yet still take the field with undiminished vigour.

This was the landscape of a unique, absurdist, make-believe comic world through which these three mismatched friends journeyed, as far over the hill from real life as Shangri-La or Oz, even though its peaks and country lanes and cobbled streets were there to be found in Yorkshire by countless thousands who came looking for them. The imaginations of millions more were caught by it, not with the cloying nostalgia or soft-hearted sentiment of old men maundering on the past, but with laughter born of an utterly distinctive, pathos-free humour that thumbed its nose at conventional notions of ageing as it encompassed the most delicate linguistic subtlety and uproariously knockabout slapstick. It made its own land, its own era, and its own surreal reality, all of them offbeat. Even its title, *Last of the Summer Wine*, was offbeat.

The story of *Last of the Summer Wine* is one of the most extraordinary in the history of television comedy. No other series, in Britain or elsewhere, has come close to rivalling its longevity – 37 years from its first screening to its last, spanning 295 episodes, all of them penned by a single writer, Roy Clarke, who would still, in his eightieth year, be looking up from his desk and out of the window at a stretch of Yorkshire countryside very different from the landscape of his imagination, dreaming up new adventures for three men on a hill. It is a story of a unique comic vision, of a slow climb to success, of how fame and adulation came knocking late for a faded film star struggling for work and two journeymen actors, of how on-screen chemistry was mirrored by off-screen antipathy, of innovation that changed the face of television, of how a show outlived fads and fashions to stand alone as the sole survivor of a golden age of entertainment. It is also the story of a place, of how the fortunes of a dilapidated mill town that nobody much noticed were transformed in a manner its people could never have imagined.

The long shot of the trio silhouetted against the skyline is the quintessential *Summer Wine* scene, but it was a longer shot still that the series Clarke invented would develop into the national institution it became. He disliked its premise, struggled to make it work and did not rate its chances of developing into anything. There was opposition to casting the actor who would bring to life one of the most beloved of all comic characters, and the show faced trial after trial as ageing cast members died or became too frail to carry on. As the years passed, it endured indifference and even hostility from its masters at the BBC, suffering the fate of being rendered invisible by its omnipresence, its excellence and individuality resolutely ignored by executives and critics who lavished praise on shows that came and went in what was, by comparison to *Summer Wine*'s run, the twinkling of an eye, even as its audience stuck by it.

Despite its travails, *Summer Wine* not only survived, but prospered, along the way pioneering quietly. It was the first to liberate situation comedy from the confines of a studio, taking it outside with extensive location work that created a broader, richer backdrop against which to play for laughs. The scenery had a starring role in *Summer Wine* and the countryside in which it was filmed became a key part of its appeal. It was also the first to produce a feature-length special, a radical departure that opened up new possibilities for writers and producers, bringing about a sea-change in programming as television realised it did not have to buy in feature films to draw huge audiences to peak slots at Christmas or Easter, but could instead make an event of established favourites.

And in its heyday, there was no bigger favourite than *Summer Wine*, as a third of Britain's population tuned in from the humblest of homes to the royal palaces. The public held it in a degree of affection reserved for only a small, select handful of shows. It continued to triumph after all its great contemporaries – *Dad's Army*, *Fawlty Towers*, *The Good Life*, *The Liver Birds* among them – born of the same glorious era and culture of BBC situation comedies, when Television Centre had no rival in producing shows that united tens of millions in laughter, had faded into fond memory. But *Summer Wine* lived on, a bedrock of BBC family entertainment, the starring trio of its best years, Bill Owen, Peter Sallis and Brian Wilde as Compo, Clegg and Foggy, seeing their careers transformed, as its humour took a great British tradition of mismatched threesomes and built on it. There were echoes of *Just William* and *The Wind in the Willows* in these ageing adolescents, but the originality of Clarke's wit took them serenely into comedy as madcap as another immortal comic trio, the Marx Brothers, ever achieved with a poker-faced calmness that made even the most lunatic exchange sound plausible. An undercurrent of subversiveness pushed what sounded like everyday conversations about the humdrum over the line into comic fantasy.

Compo: He's doing all right is Charlie. I know he's doing all right, 'cos I asked him. Can't complain, he said. He's got his pension and a bit tucked away in a eunuch's truss.

Foggy: A eunuch's truss? Don't you mean a unit trust?

Compo: That's what he said.

Clegg: No, I like it. If ever I have any spare money, it's going to go straight into a eunuch's truss. I don't care how many thieves there are about, nobody's going to go poking round there.

'I thought it was Badger, Ratty and Mole,' said Peter Sallis, the only actor to appear in every episode. 'I still do, I said to anybody that was interested that this is *Wind in the Willows* all over again, only with grown-up people.' To the great humorist Alan Coren, it was much more daring and inventive than that: 'It is *Winnie the Pooh* recycled through Samuel Beckett, with Pooh, Piglet and Eeyore emerging as Compo, Clegg and Foggy ... the joke goes up towards surrealism and down towards music hall in the same split second.' Commentators who did occasionally take notice commonly labelled *Summer Wine*'s humour 'wistful' or 'gentle'; it certainly possessed both those qualities, but there was much more besides. It was knowing, wryly observant, had a streak of anarchic silliness, poked fun at authority and was underpinned by just a touch of melancholy on the part of three ageing men who knew they had more to look back on than look forward to. It also came to relish visual gags, whether Compo's relentless pursuit of the forbidding Nora Batty or the stunts and set pieces which became an increasingly important part of the show.

Clarke's singular comic vision grew more expansive over the years, as the show matured from three talking heads around a table into a seamless ensemble piece with the trio at its heart, partly out of necessity because ageing principals could not carry the show by themselves and new characters were needed to sustain it. More often than not, newcomers – and the guests who followed their lead for occasional appearances – had a long and affectionate history with the television audience, and *Summer Wine* developed into a comfortable berth for comic actors of a certain vintage. So it was that the likes of Thora Hird, Jean Alexander, Brian Murphy, Burt Kwouk and Russ Abbot found themselves tramping the hills, to be joined occasionally by other old favourites, such as Norman Wisdom, Warren Mitchell and Eric Sykes.

This was the most timeless of shows, and that kept it fresh; the present day hardly ever intruded. 'It has its own world, a nonsense world,' said Clarke. 'That's why it's survived fashion changes, plus it's not real, though funnily enough some people think that's how life used to be.' The Britain of the early 1970s in which *Summer Wine* was conceived and made its debut was a different country to that same land nearly forty years later. Everything had changed: work, technology, music, politics, entertainment, the make-up of society. What Sallis always termed Summer Wine Land, though, was a better place to be than any of the decades through which it passed and mostly ignored, except in its very earliest days. Its world was a funny, eccentric, quirkily individual patchwork of dreamers, battleaxes, downtrodden husbands, and flat-capped romantics, who played out their stories against an alluring backdrop that seemed all of a piece, even though stitched together from disparate locations. This was an eternally optimistic place and attitude of mind, life-affirming in its refusal to acknowledge that age should be a barrier to anything, whether it be racing headlong down a field in a giant pigeon outfit, walking the Royal corgis or scheming how to woo the siren of the wrinkled stockings. Here, it was possible to shrug off the years and climb even the steepest hill to sit and ponder awhile on weighty matters such as rustling fag packets, how parents took a wrong turn when they stopped naming sons Herbert, the ordeal of a schoolboy whose trousers were full of beetles, or even Hitler's hitherto-unrevealed links to the Isle of Man, and in doing so to create one of the greatest of all television comedies.

PART ONE

A Breath of Fresh Air

CHAPTER ONE

The Library Mob

ROY CLARKE'S POLICE helmet tended to sink over his ears, which rather detracted from the air of authority needed by a young bobby trying to keep the peace amid the rough-and-tumble of a Friday night in a Yorkshire pit village where the men were thirsty and their women treated hangovers with a stiff dose of shouting.

Pounding the beat in a black-and-white 1950s world of faces grimy from coal dust scrubbed clean for the evening's boozing was an unlikely apprenticeship for a man who would become the most prolific solo author of situation comedy that Britain ever produced, whose output of hit series could only be rivalled by the gag-factories of the USA, where brittle laughs were hacked out by teams of writers.

There was nothing brittle or artificial about Roy Clarke's humour. It was drawn from the people he found on patrol, or in the places where he lived, and even when it scaled hilarious heights of whimsy, his dialogue was so rooted in the rhythms of real life that his audience laughed not only because the lines were funny, but also because they might have been spoken by friends or neighbours. These were laughs cultivated from the seed of everyday conversations, a heightened and fantasised vision of them certainly, but as natural and unforced as anything that Ray Galton and Alan Simpson wrote for Hancock or David Croft and Jimmy Perry gave to Captain Mainwaring.

It all came from what he heard; the trio of ageing juveniles who refused to grow old in *Last of the Summer Wine*, the stuttering shopkeeper Arkwright in *Open All Hours*, the desperately genteel Hyacinth Bucket in *Keeping Up Appearances*, the officious retired mint magnate in *Potter*, the gauche young policeman in *Rosie*; all of them hugely popular characters, all of them drawn from the people Clarke saw around him, all of them given a life of their own thanks to his ear for the absurd.

Observation was everything. 'I like some point of reference between real people and the characters I write about. If I can't see a real person doing something, then I know it's not right for the fictional,' he was to say. Indeed his wife, Enid, would later tell actors and producers that she had become used to hearing conversations at home turning up on television the following year.

Success, though, was hard-won. Roy Clarke was no bright-eyed kid in his twenties who made it big at his first attempt. He was a family man in his thirties before he achieved any professional success and then it seemed his forte was for drama; he'd hit forty before his talent as a comedy writer really flowered. The beginnings of an extraordinary career that would eventually see him grow into one of the greatest of all situation-comedy writers lay in what this natural and compulsive observer of humanity's capacity for daftness saw and mentally noted during two years as a policeman in a tough industrial area. He encountered battleaxe women and henpecked men whose lives would eventually be filtered through a remarkably fertile mind to emerge as gloriously funny comic characters.

Clarke said: 'It came from the police force for me, I only did a couple of years, this young bobby with his helmet falling over his ears, thrown into the fringe of Rotherham, a fairly lively area for policing, and you'd go to these houses and meet these people, and the men were feckless, absolutely irresponsible, and you could see why. If they're working down this awful hole all day, what else are they going to do but have a drink, but their lives would have been in much more chaos if not time and time again there was at their house a woman who would be tearing strips off them. They kept the whole bloody show on the road, magnificent, and I do admire them. They're tougher than men, and I admire them. They're maybe better from a distance sometimes, but there's a strong streak of admiration in these comedy women of mine.'

Not that Roy Clarke really wanted to be a policeman, any more than he'd wanted to be a suit salesman, or a factory worker, or a teacher. He dreamed of being a writer, and eventually he would make it, producing an astonishing body of work that included not only comedy, but drama, films and novels. The road to getting there would be longer than he could have imagined. His laconic entry in *Who's Who* reads: 'Educ: badly during World War II. Soldier, salesman, policeman and teacher until I was able to persuade people I was actually a writer.'

But for now, a policeman it would have to be. Apart from the descending helmet, which made him resemble one of the comic coppers that would later spring from his imagination, PC Clarke looked every inch the keen young officer of the West Riding Constabulary, as he patrolled Dalton, close to the industrial powerhouse of Rotherham with its collieries, steel mills and heavy engineering works. Six-foot-one tall, and a wiry fourteen stone, he'd arrived in the police by way of National Service in the Far East and dead-end jobs.

He'd known this patch, and its people, all his life. Clarke was born on 28 January 1930 into a farming family just a few miles to the east, in the hamlet of Austerfield, where the heartland of Yorkshire's coalfields around Doncaster gave way to flat grasslands and quiet villages that sheltered behind screens of woodland from the winds that whipped in from the North Sea. It's a forgotten corner of England, not noticed by the drivers hurtling past on the A1, not passed through because it isn't really on the way to anywhere, not giving the outside world much reason to intrude, and even if it did the twisting roads and secluded lanes help preserve its privacy. 'Even the people who live round here get lost,' observed Clarke.

Few other comedy writers have evoked such a sense of place in their work as Roy Clarke, whether it be the dramatic grandeur of the Pennines, in *Last of the Summer Wine*, a tatty corner shop on a terraced street in *Open All Hours*, or manicured suburbia in *Keeping Up Appearances*, yet the environment that nurtured him and remained his home ever afterwards differed from all of them. The Pennines are only forty miles distant from the village where he was born, but might be another world, so utterly opposed are the landscapes. He'd never heard of the mill town he would make famous, and didn't really know the hills and valleys against which his humour would be played out. He was content where he was.

So PC Clarke was at home in Dalton, and soaking up the quirks of life on the beat, such as the night when he had to ride a skittish runaway racehorse back to its stables behind a pub, or the days when he became involved with fearsome wives mopping up after their husbands who'd had a skinful. 'I'd recommend any writer be in the police force,' he said. 'Your eyes are opened to areas of life a normal citizen never gets a look at. Households exist you'd never invent.'

Not only his eyes opened. So did his imagination. Years later, Rotherham and its environs would once again float to the front of his mind as he embarked on the pilot episode of *Summer Wine*, but for now there were other things to think about, like slogging away on a correspondence course that would lead to a job teaching English in the pit towns of Goldthorpe and Thorne, consigning police work to the list of his ex-professions. Every spare hour, though, was devoted to what really drove him – writing. 'It's what I do, it's all I ever wanted to do is write. I love it, I hate it, but I can't leave it alone. I don't go on holidays; if I was on holiday, the second day I'd be writing, bored to death with where I was, I don't care how many churches and paintings there were, I'd be bored to death.'

Those who came to know him well, like *Summer Wine*'s long-time producer and director Alan J. W. Bell, attested to that compulsion. 'He can't not write. His wife told me once, she said to him, "Look, we're going on holiday. Put your pencil and pad away, you're not going to write, you're going to have a holiday with me, talk to me, we're going to have a nice break together." So they went away and one day he went for a walk. He was very restless and he came back from the walk and she went to see what he'd bought, and he'd bought a writing pad from Woolworths and a pencil and was writing something else, he couldn't stop.'

Clarke was as prolific as he was compulsive, but he suffered the curse of all tyro writers: nobody wanted what he was producing. Nevertheless, he persevered, and eventually the breakthrough came, thanks to a young radio producer called Alan Ayckbourn, then working for the BBC in Leeds. Ayckbourn would go on to become one of Britain's most admired playwrights and turn the Stephen Joseph Theatre in Scarborough into a centre of pilgrimage for audiences who adored his comedies of sharp social observation, but between 1964 and 1970 his brief was to find and develop regional talent and get new drama on the air.

Clarke had reached back to his days in Dalton for a police thriller called *The Big Bite*. At the age of thirty-five, his career as a writer was under way. 'I did a couple of plays and a serial for them and got an agent which was the magic key because they won't accept stuff if you haven't got an agent. Catch 22, you can't get an agent until you sell some stuff, so that was a big move for me and she got me straight away into television and again it was drama.'

The drama was a BBC series called *The Troubleshooters* – known as *Mogul* in the United States – about an oil company with operations around the world. But with a wife and two children to support, it took guts for Clarke to break with the security of teaching. 'I got a four-script contract, but no sooner had I packed in teaching than my agent said, "It's not enough money, I'm turning them down." It was a fearful moment.'

Fearful or not, Clarke pressed on and began to garner a reputation as a writer to watch. Other dramas followed, including one of the BBC's prestige productions, *The Power Game*, set against an industrial backdrop, but it was a change of channel for a spin-off from *The Troubleshooters* that was to set him on the road to the hills. As the 1970s dawned, Clarke resurrected *Troubleshooters* figure Basil 'Badger' Allenby-Johnson for ITV and created a series around him. *The Misfit* was comedy with undertones of sadness as it followed Badger's return home from a rubber plantation in Malaya. He was beautifully played by one of Britain's finest character actors, Ronald Fraser, whose gift for portraying wounded pride was exactly right for the role. Badger was an old-school Colonial figure, who found in his mid-fifties that modern Britain was a baffling place with no place in it for him. If Fraser was a perfect fit for the part, *The Misfit* was also a perfect series for its times. Britain was changing, industrial unrest was rife and the traditional industries that held so many communities together were crumbling, leaving men who had thought they had a job for life on the scrapheap. Nowhere was immune. Less than an hour's drive from where Clarke was writing *The Misfit*, the woollen mills of a town called Holmfirth were closing down.

The two series of *The Misfit*, in 1970 and the following year, were a huge critical and popular success. The thirteen one-hour episodes caught the public's imagination and Badger became a focal point for middle-aged men uncomfortable with the uncertain times. They began writing to Clarke and Fraser in their droves. Sackfuls of mail were delivered to their homes and, more importantly, Clarke won the Writers' Guild Award for Best Series. The ex-policeman had not only arrived; his writing for *The Misfit* had caught the attention of one of the most influential men in television, Duncan Wood.

What Wood didn't know about situation comedy wasn't worth knowing. That was because he pioneered the format, taking Tony Hancock from radio on to television in 1956, and for the following five years steering The Lad Himself through his definitive performances. *Hancock's Half Hour*, with Sidney James retained from the radio days as his foil, and then *Hancock*, in which that most restless and troubled of comics went it alone, remain a high-water mark in British television comedy, and set a template for how shows should be made, thanks to Wood's intuitive feel for bringing the best out of performers and writers, as well as technical innovations that did away with the often hair-raising ordeals of broadcasting live. In tandem with Galton and Simpson, Hancock's greatest writing team, Wood went on to produce another classic, *Steptoe and Son*, as well as less successful series with Spike Milligan, Sidney James, Benny Hill, Ronnie Corbett and Harry Worth. Even after he left the BBC for Yorkshire Television in 1973 after twenty-five years, Wood had one great sitcom left in him, providing the guiding hand behind *Rising Damp* with Leonard Rossiter.

Three years before his departure, Wood was appointed Head of Comedy at a time when the BBC was unrivalled the world over as a powerhouse of light entertainment. It was on his watch that *Some Mothers Do 'Ave 'Em* began and Eric Sykes embarked upon his finest television years, and he presided with genial authority over a department whose established favourites included *Steptoe*, *Dad's Army*, *The Liver Birds*, *Up Pompeii* and *Till Death Us Do Part* as well as the innovations of *Monty Python's Flying Circus* and *The Goodies*. The nation looked to the BBC to make it laugh, and it didn't let them down, producing shows of the highest quality, nurturing talent, and keeping faith with promising projects. Besides the sitcoms, there were gems under the Light Entertainment banner; Morecambe and Wise in their pomp, and *The Two Ronnies*.

He saw potential in *The Misfit*'s author and invited him to a meeting to discuss possible projects. Wood, who died in 1997, never explained his thinking about what happened next to Clarke, or anybody else. What he suggested made the writer's heart sink.

Clarke said:

He was a big name in those days, he'd done just about everything you could think of, and I went in to see him because I liked the idea of trying a sitcom and he said, 'We want something with three old men.' That was the extent of the brief, I promise you, nothing else. Even today, where the hell it came from I have no idea. And I thought, what a dreadful idea. I was about forty years old then, what did I know about old men, or want to know about old men? And I figured there'd be no audience out there who'd want to know about old men, so I thought it was a terrible idea. Whether there was some kind of primitive audience research and they figured there was some sort of age gap not being satisfied in their audience, I don't know, but that's all it was. They must have realised before me, because I never thought this would go, I really didn't. Three old men? No. I couldn't see it getting a big audience.

Clarke had been fired up by the chance of a BBC sitcom, his confidence buoyed by the success of *The Misfit*, but this idea seemed terrible. He embarked on a dispiriting and unsuccessful struggle to make it work.

'So I came home with this brief for three old men and played about with it for a couple of weeks, very much keen on trying a sitcom, but hopelessly out of love with this idea. I wrestled with it for about a fortnight, which was a very long time for me in those days because I used to crack on, continually on the point of turning it down because I just couldn't get any joy out of it.'

The breakthrough came when the thought struck Clarke that just because his protagonists were old, they didn't have to behave like they were old. That same thought also held the glimmer of a title.

'It's got to entertain me first, or else I've lost. If it's not going to entertain me, it's not going to entertain anybody else, and I couldn't get a smile out of this at all until, and I don't know why, it occurred to me that if they were all footloose and free, no ties, either work or family, they're in the same position as adolescents, or kids even, and as soon as I saw them as kids, I was away. That's what they are; they're not three old men, they're kids. They weren't that old, they still had some life in them. And that was the title, trying to suggest that, all right, it's late summer, but it's still summer, there's still some life around.'

Once he had got over the hurdle about making three old men funny, Clarke cracked on as usual, and in short order had a deceptively simple half-hour comedy that he called *The Last of the Summer Wine*, in which nothing much happened. The story was about three old school friends thrown together in their later years. Cyril Blamire, Compo Simmonite and Norman Clegg had all the time in the world to fill, so they went for a walk in the countryside, took refuge in the library, café or pub when it was time to sit down, mused on the workings of the world, detoured via a stream to catch a tiddler, and then went their separate ways at the end of the day.

Clarke created a trio that was in perfect balance. Blamire was a self-appointed leader of men, a strait-laced ex-water board official and Royal Corps of Signals RSM who prided himself on his neatness and correctness of manner. Compo was everything that Blamire despised – a scruffy, workshy waster only interested in fags, booze and the horses, his name drawn from slang for industrial compensation for the bad back he proclaimed, the 'compo'. Between them stood Clegg, the former Co-op lino salesman, cautious, timid but nobody's fool. There was an undertone of melancholia to the situation. Misfortune, missed opportunities long past and loss left these three wondering on their place in the world and thrown together for company as a shield against loneliness. Blamire had never married and in the autumn of his life found himself adrift and alone, a paying guest in a private house; Clegg was widowed and met his friends while visiting his wife's grave; and Compo's wife had run away with a Pole.

Clarke was satisfied with his trio, the elements of which had fallen neatly together in his imagination. 'The first character in my mind was Compo, this layabout, this rough stuff, and we wanted three, so the rest of the elements were fairly necessary. You had to have one who in most circumstances loathed him – Blamire – and those two were so far apart that if you didn't have the third one – Clegg – in the middle, they'd never survive, but the three of them together could hang together because of Clegg in the middle, so that took care of the dynamics. My wife came from Thorne, and in those days there were loads of characters about in those small mining communities and Compo was based on a guy who used to work on the dustbins, enormously strong, a gentle giant sort of guy.'

The script – subtitled *Of Funerals and Fish* – was notably individual in its tone and dialogue. The humour was essentially quiet, yet robustly earthy; the characters were at once childlike, yet worldly; their philosophising yearned for past certainties of an age lost to them but implied a stoic acceptance of their fate. Clarke was staking his place in a grand tradition. Trios were the most solid of bedrocks on which to build comedy; the more at odds they were with each other, so much the funnier. Badger, Ratty and Mole had formed an awkward alliance in *The Wind in the Willows*; so had George, Harris and J in *Three Men in a Boat*. The format was durable and ageless, a formula for creating laughter from contrasting characters thrown together, as potent on stage or screen as it was on the page. The set-up remained as effective in the second half of the twentieth century as it had been in the first. In Clarke's childhood, a trio with faint echoes of Blamire, Clegg and Compo had ruled British comedy: the great film and variety comedian Will Hay exemplified the preposterous authority figure as hopeless schoolmaster or station-master, his pomposity pricked by two irreverent sidekicks, the porky, sardonic youth, Albert, and the aged, decrepit Harbottle. Eight years after *Summer Wine* began, another top-drawer sitcom, *Only Fools and Horses*, would again depend on the antics of a trio.

Compo, Clegg and Blamire exemplified mismatched, but devoted, friendship. Their conflicts, wildly differing attitudes and cautious trust offered Clarke a rich seam from which to mine laughs. There was something else, too, that marked this half-hour as out of the ordinary. Clarke had set large parts of his script outdoors, so this would be no studio-bound show, unlike the majority of sitcoms. This would, literally, be a breath of fresh air for all concerned.

It was now early 1972. Clarke had his opening episode, but no guarantee of a series. *The Last of the Summer Wine* was a one-off project that would go out under the banner of one of the BBC's most productive strands, *Comedy Playhouse*, which presented a different show each week in the same slot. Since it had started in 1961, as a showcase for Galton and Simpson, it had broadened into a vehicle for trying out promising ideas, allowing established writers to explore new directions and giving newcomers the chance to prove they were up to the mark. *Comedy Playhouse* served the BBC well, premiering some of its finest sitcoms, notably *Steptoe and Son*, *Till Death Us Do Part*, *Are You Being Served?* and *The Liver Birds* as well as some less enduring series which were nevertheless hits in their time, including *All Gas and Gaiters* and *Meet the Wife*, a key element of which would much later play its part in the *Summer Wine* story. Almost every year since its inception, *Comedy Playhouse* had delivered at least a couple of shows that had the legs to run. Three months after *The Last of the Summer Wine* aired, a similar selection box of seven programmes tailored for Ronnie Barker would give that peerless comic actor – and the BBC – his two classic, career-defining sitcoms, *Porridge* and Clarke's *Open All Hours*. Dozens of shows, though, failed to make it beyond the pilot.

Duncan Wood loaded the dice in Roy Clarke's favour. He handed the show to one of the BBC's elite and most senior producers, James Gilbert. Gilbert – Jimmy to those who worked with him – had a glittering track record at the BBC. The early 1960s had seen him work with Jimmy Edwards and Stanley Baxter, as well as on the innovative *It's a Square World* with Michael Bentine. He had been a driving force behind David Frost's *The Frost Report* and produced Peter Cook and Dudley Moore's *Not Only ... But Also*. He had also been entrusted with the production of Cole Porter's musical *Kiss Me, Kate*, which launched BBC2 in 1964.

Ever afterwards, Clarke would credit Jimmy Gilbert with turning his vision of what *The Last of the Summer Win*e should be into reality. He set the tone and style for the programme that stayed throughout, and was a crucial factor in its popularity. Equally crucially, Gilbert embraced Clarke's desire to open up situation comedy, to take it outside the confines of the studio. If Gilbert was a gift to Clarke, in turn the script was a boon to the producer when it landed on his desk in the spring of 1972. Gilbert had just arrived back from Australia, where he had directed a feature film, *Sunstruck*, starring singer and comedian Harry Secombe, who wintered there every year. It had been a happy project, a warm-hearted family yarn about a Welsh teacher who moves to the outback and, feeling homesick for the singing of his native valleys, forms a children's choir. Gilbert said: 'I'd been directing a film out in the bush and was feeling totally liberated by this, and not having to do the whole thing in a studio with three walls and so on, and here was something which would let me film and use the same sort of directing as I'd just done in Australia.'

He found Clarke's script tremendously impressive, and full of potential to develop into a series: 'When I read it, I was bowled over by the originality of the dialogue, the gentle, quirky characters and the atmosphere of the Yorkshire countryside. I wanted to direct it in the same way as I'd done in Australia, making the scenery an important part of the series. The script was brilliant and if we got the casting right, I felt we were in with a very good chance.'

Irrespective of the script's merits, the BBC were dead set against its title when Clarke sent it in. *The Last of the Summer Wine* simply did not sound like a comedy title, they said, so find something else. 'They told me so straight away, "This is no good," and, fine, it's a temporary title, we'll have to change it when we get down to thinking about producing it. I thought, well, my first sitcom, they know what they're doing. It came to the crunch finally and they said, "OK give us a title," and I tried several things, but nothing, and they kept *The Last of the Summer Wine* almost in desperation, because it was never a sitcom title.'

Somewhere along the way, the script acquired the title *The*

Library Mob, since the trio habitually ended up there, to the chagrin of the librarian. Peter Sallis claimed it came from him. 'When we knew we were doing it, he hadn't got a title and I came up with breathtaking things like *The Library Mob*. A real knock 'em for six title that was, *The Library Mob*.' Whoever came up with it, everybody hated *The Library Mob*.

Gilbert was among them. But he had a more serious reservation about the script. He worried that the central characters were too old, and his concern was rooted in an experience from seven years before that still smarted. In 1965, he had produced *The Walrus and the Carpenter*, written by the crack team of Barry Took and Marty Feldman. It starred two superb veterans, Hugh Griffith and Felix Aylmer, as Luther Flannery and Gascoigne Quilt, a pair of old men with nothing in common thrown together by loneliness, who meet in a graveyard and go off on adventures. It deserved to be a success; the writing was witty, the performances excellent. The critics loved the show, but the public was underwhelmed, and it did not go beyond a single series. Took later wrote of it: 'My own feeling is that the sight of two old men, however amusing, living out their few remaining years was rather depressing, because after all the only outcome could have been their deaths.'

Gilbert also detected unease within the BBC over the central theme. 'The only reason we could find out was that the front office thought that as they were old men in their seventies, that audiences were uneasy, they weren't really keyed in to what direction they should laugh, they shrank from laughing at old men, which is all nonsense in my opinion, something either is funny or it isn't funny, it's either well written or not well written, well acted or not well acted and *The Walrus and the Carpenter* passed all three tests on that. It was a series I was very proud of.'

Did Duncan Wood have *The Walrus and the Carpenter* in mind when he asked Clarke to write a comedy about old men? There were obvious parallels between the two projects. Did he gamble that a concept which failed to click with viewers in the mid 1960s might work with a trio instead of a duo in the early 70s? By then, of course, *Dad's Army*, which began in 1968, had demonstrated conclusively that audiences found the antics of old men, if presented with affection and warmth, hilarious. If this formed any part of Wood's thinking, Gilbert never knew, and he wasn't going to take the chance. He said:

> So when I got the *Summer Wine* script, with this ringing in my ears, and read the script of three old men in their seventies, I thought, now wait a minute, we're going to get into the same problem as we got into with *The Walrus and the Carpenter*, and I thought it was a lovely script and I was mad keen to do it. I said to Roy, 'Please can we not have them so old?' because I had had this problem. 'Can we not have them redundant so that they're out of work for one reason or another but they've still got at least ten years' good life?' When we started filming, whenever I was in doubt, I'd just get them to kick a can or something, behave like kids.

Gilbert was sensitive to Clarke's needs. 'He's a very private individual, excellent company if you know him but I knew at once that if I wanted to get really comfortable with Roy, I should go and see him at his home where he felt comfortable, because otherwise he's getting in a train, going down to Television Centre, going in the office, the whole thing is very formal, and then it ended up I used to look forward to going up and seeing him. He's got a very dry, very individual sense of humour. He came out with the most surprising things, which he does in the script, too.'

The two got on well, and tweaking the age of the characters was not a problem. Redundant instead of retired still left the trio footloose and unencumbered by responsibility, and did nothing to alter the basic premise of disparate characters thrown together by circumstances searching for things to do in a world that had left them behind. Being in their fifties instead of their seventies still left them plenty to look back on. It dawned on Gilbert that the writer had put a lot of himself into one of the central characters. 'I think

Clegg was the voice of Roy Clarke. I think that was his mouthpiece. I saw a lot of things that Roy felt strongly about used to come out of the mouth of Clegg, either sitting around or, especially in later series, on the hillsides, and then he'd argue against them through Compo.'

The first thing Gilbert and Clarke talked about, though, was the working title. 'The title, of course, I hated the title *The Library Mob*. They said nobody would ever watch a series called *The Last of the Summer Wine*, it's not a comedy title. *The Library Mob* was the most awful title and immediately said "trad sitcom", so I said to Roy, "I don't like the title," and he said, "Neither do I, the title was *The Last of the Summer Wine*, and they told me to change it." He used it as the subtitle on the opening episode. It was *The Library Mob* and then in inverted commas, "The Last of the Summer Wine".' Gilbert eventually put his foot down at the BBC, and Clarke's title stayed – even though the producer would later come under pressure from within the show to drop it.

If Clarke and Gilbert were going to take situation comedy outside, getting the location right was of vital importance. And Gilbert had an idea, thanks to his friend and collaborator, Barry Took, then working as a comedy advisor at the BBC. Took, who died in 2002, had a long and influential career in British comedy, not least when he acted as midwife to *Monty Python's Flying Circus* in 1969, bringing together the writing and performing teams of John Cleese and Graham Chapman, with Michael Palin and Terry Jones, before adding Eric Idle and Terry Gilliam to the mix and championing the ensemble to a reluctant BBC. Earlier in the 60s, he and Marty Feldman had written one of the greatest of all BBC radio comedies, *Round The Horne*. He was now to do *The Last of the Summer Wine* one of the best good turns it could have had.

The tall, gangling, bespectacled Took had served a long apprenticeship as a performer before moving into writing. He'd toured as a stand-up comic when variety was in its death throes during the 1950s, billed as 'Barry Took – The Lanky Look' or 'London's Longest Laugh', and found himself booked on the notoriously tough club circuit. One date took him to a mill town in Yorkshire called Holmfirth, where he played Burnlee Working Men's Club. London's Longest Laugh got short shrift from the hard-drinking northern audience, who regarded him with all the enthusiasm they usually reserved for empty pint glasses, and like many another comic who suffered the ordeal by silence, Took never forgot it.

Twenty years afterwards, he returned to Holmfirth to film an episode for a six-part BBC documentary series, *Having a Lovely Time*, which took a quirky look at how British people enjoyed themselves. His contribution was 'At the Club', which hadn't changed much since the night his gags hit the back wall and slid lifelessly to the floor. But Took wasn't in Holmfirth to do a hatchet job. His half-hour, which was broadcast in August 1972, took in the town's distinguished place in the history of entertainment, which was secure thanks to the work of Bamforth and Company, pioneers of early film-making. Between 1898 and 1900 and then again from 1913 to 1915, the firm produced a clutch of historically important films, and its head, James Bamforth, had ambitions to make the town an international centre for the new medium. The company had some success, notably with comedy shorts – including one in very dubious taste from 1913 entitled *Winky Starts A Smallpox Panic* – but Holmfirth was not destined to eclipse Hollywood. Unpredictable weather – seventy years later, also to plague Jimmy Gilbert and those who followed him – and the onset of the First World War put paid to any hopes of that. Instead, Bamforth's became famous for producing saucy seaside postcards whose cast of big-bosomed ladies, harassed husbands and men who looked down to find their feet hidden by their bellies were the essence of end-of-the-pier humour.

What struck Took was how picturesque this mill town was. It nestled in a valley, and its stone buildings huddled to the hillsides. It had cobbled streets, alleyways and a river, moss-covered steps worn down by the footsteps of generations, cottages and chapels, a lovely old church. Comedy could peep round corners here, or scarper for laughs. And in what countryside it lay – above it the great peak of Holme Moss from where hikers on the Pennine Way could look down to the town, or across to the wooded hillsides and heather-covered high moorland. There were reservoirs and rocky outcrops, lonely roads and viewpoints. In the late summer sunshine, no landscape in England seemed more beautiful, and in the depths of winter none was harsher. Film-makers scouted long and hard for backdrops as photogenic as this, and spent a fortune on creating streetscapes as quaint, and here it all was for real, minding its own business, getting on with its life, just another working town, five miles south of Huddersfield, the hub of Yorkshire's textile industry, at the heart of the Pennines, J. B. Priestley's 'knobbly backbone of England'.

Took told Gilbert about Holmfirth. 'He thought it would be perfect because I said I wanted a place where there was a centre surrounded by hills so when [the characters] went off on their daily adventures they were never far from the centre.'

Gilbert drove north once again. Clarke had suggested that his old police stamping ground, Rotherham, might be a good location, so they went to take a look. It just wasn't right. This was a big, grimy, metal-bashing town shaped and sooted by its factories. Gilbert said: 'I had had a completely different visual concept from Roy because nobody had told me that it was an urban comedy at all, I just saw it as something that was screaming out to be visual. When Barry told me about Holmfirth I drove up to Thorne, where Roy was living then, and we went off the next day in the car and we had a look at Rotherham, right up at the top and looked over the valley and the whole thing was just packed with houses, which was the opposite of what I had conceived it as, so I said, "Let's go to Holmfirth," and Roy was all for it. We went and we just stopped the car at the top of the hill coming into Holmfirth and saw the valley, and we both knew instantly. That was the end of the hunt, and we'd put up with the weather.'

Clarke, like most other people from outside the Huddersfield area, didn't know Holmfirth. 'I said, "Where's that?"' he recalled, but he saw its potential immediately. 'Choosing it made a hell of a difference. In those days, sitcoms were allowed about one-and-a-half minutes of location filming. We'd intended to be different and I'd written in these long-distance shots with characters in silhouette.' This was a comedy that needed wide-open spaces and room to breathe. It needed hillsides and heather. It needed Holmfirth.

There was another conversation left to have – the music. Gilbert recalled what Clarke said to him: 'I leave that to you, but nothing jokey, please. I'd just like a good tune.'

The script, the place, the vision were all set. Now the actors had to be found who could bring it to life.

CHAPTER TWO

❧

Left, Right and Centre

H E HAD A round, smooth, expressive, almost childlike face
that in middle age was softening into jowliness. Across it
could flit bewilderment, joy, slyness, concern,
compassion, fear and even menace. It was a face that could radiate
warmth or coldness with equal conviction, an ideal character
actor's face, in fact. And that is exactly what he was. Peter Sallis
was a character actor for all seasons, at ease in Chekhov or
Shakespeare or Osborne, the sort of player stars of the calibre of
Olivier, Orson Welles or Nicol Williamson valued for the
unstinting support and intelligence he offered on stage, the sort
prized by film-makers who needed his brand of solid professionalism
to lend the corny gravitas and the good the hope of greatness.

Sallis hovered just short of stardom, even though he was given
leading roles. He did not fit the ideal of tall, firm-jawed and
handsome that prevailed as his career got under way, being shortish
and equipped with a delivery more naturalistic than heroic. His
fellow actors knew how good he was, as did producers, who kept
him busy in theatre, in films, and on television. Both also admired
him for his laconic wit. Sallis was the best sort of journeyman, his
adaptability keeping him working steadily, taking him from
provincial tours of Britain to Broadway and, for a glorious year,
seeing his name in lights in the West End. He belonged to that
breed of actor upon which quality productions were built, the

strength in depth of whatever he appeared in. He'd been bitten by the acting bug early, in the RAF, for which he'd volunteered during Dunkirk, escaping the drudgery of a bank clerk's job and swapping it for a post as a radio instructor at Cranwell, where he spent the war.

A service production of Noel Coward's *Hay Fever* gave him a start on a road that led to a scholarship at RADA, a first high-profile role in *School for Scandal* at the 1948 Bath Festival, and on from there through the Old Vic, rep in Guildford, Chesterfield and Sheffield, and into the West End with Welles in an experimental production of *Moby Dick*, Ionescu's *Rhinoceros* with Olivier and a stint on Broadway in the ill-fated *Baker Street*, a musical evocation of Sherlock Holmes. Back home, Sallis found his name in lights outside the Strand Theatre for *Wait Until Dark*, a thriller by *Dial M for Murder* author Frederick Knott in which he terrorised archetypal 60s glamour girl Honor Blackman to packed houses. Film work ticked over, even if it was less fulfilling than the theatre, as Sallis appeared in *Saturday Night and Sunday Morning* and *Charlie Bubbles* before dipping a toe into the fake blood of the busy British horror-film industry with entertaining turns in *Scream and Scream Again* and *Taste the Blood of Dracula*, as a sort of Satanic Norman Clegg, embarking timidly upon debauchery.

His flexibility kept him busy on television too, and on 27 October 1970, viewers of BBC2 tuned in to one of the station's flagship drama series, and watched as it opened with a shot of an apparently trim, well-dressed woman walking with her back to the camera. She turned right, towards a front door, went inside, took off her hat, and then removed a wig. Only then did the audience see her face.

It was a very familiar one, especially to viewers with a longish memory and a taste for culture. Twelve years before, Sallis had become a household name when he starred in the BBC's adaptation of *The Diary of Samuel Pepys*, at that time one of the most ground-breaking productions mounted on television, and here he was, back on the box, only in a different sort of wig. The series was

Menace, which between 1970 and 1973 garnered good audiences and critical praise for its subtle and chilling thrillers, and this was episode five of the first season, called 'The Millicent Sisters, Edward de Bruno and Ruth – Where are They Now?' In it, Sallis played Sonny Waters, a transvestite who ran a boarding house where the atmosphere was heavy with menace. It was a deliciously offbeat chiller, shot through with dark humour, and its author was Roy Clarke, who, because the script was running short when it came to filming, wrote a five-minute speech for Sallis, now dressed as a priest.

Actor and author were mutually impressed. They had a second taste of each other's work about a year later, when Sallis guest-starred in one of five episodes written by Clarke for the ITV espionage series *Spyder's Web*. So when Clarke wound a sheet of paper into his typewriter and began the struggle to prise laughs out of the concept of three old men with nothing to do, unusually, he had Peter Sallis in mind. Unusually, because Clarke rarely made casting suggestions for his work, a habit that would remain with him, not least because he cheerfully admitted that from the tranquillity of his base in the Yorkshire countryside, his knowledge of who was available was very limited. 'I wanted him for it,' said Clarke. 'I don't usually have any suggestions for casting because I don't get to the theatre from here and they know far more than I do about who's available and who's suitable, so it's not often I make any suggestions, but I did want Peter. I had gelled with Peter initially, more than the others, and I used him for things I wanted to sneak out, things I wanted to say, and he was always known for years for having the best lines. It helped me a lot in the writing, having Peter.'

Sallis would later say: 'It happens sometimes in an actor's life, if you're very lucky, that something special turns up, and when I read *Last of the Summer Wine*, I thought, this is it.' It was to be years later, when *Summer Wine* was an established success, before Sallis realised that the part of Clegg had been written with him in mind. 'Somewhere along the way, I picked up the information from him. I think I'd done his first two television plays, "The Millicent Sisters – Whatever Became of Them?" and the other one was also a pretty bloodcurdling thing.'

As Clarke was submitting his script, Sallis had just celebrated his 51st birthday, having been born on 1 February 1921. Jimmy Gilbert concurred that he was exactly right for Clegg, having known him since RADA, but even though the two were near-neighbours in Richmond, they hadn't seen much of each other in the years since then. It was, therefore, a shock when this successful and busy West End and Broadway actor turned up dressed more like somebody who had not worked for years, arriving as he did at the BBC in a ropey old dark suit, cardigan and flat cap.

Clarke recalled the jolt that Sallis sent through the room when he entered to talk about the pilot. 'Peter came in in this awful-looking suit and we all thought, my God, he must be on his uppers, there can't be much work about. And right at the end, before he's going out the door, we'd been discussing wardrobe and Peter said, "I thought I might wear this, that's why I put it on, it's my demob suit."'

It had not occurred to Sallis that his eagerness for the part and the thought he'd put into Clegg's costume would be misconstrued as desperation for a job. Practicality played a part, too. His time in rep at Sheffield had taught him that the Yorkshire weather could be unpredictable, and up on the Pennines even summer could turn wintry, so on went a cardigan under a waistcoat, creating a look that was both practical for keeping warm yet emphasised the cautious nature of Clegg, a dowdy widower who would naturally guard against any eventuality of the weather turning nasty. 'Everybody looked at me and thought, poor old thing, he's really having it tough, and this has probably just saved his bacon. That was lovely, and it didn't occur to me that they would think I always looked like that, and it was the last thing I said as I was leaving, I said, "By the way, Jimmy, I just thought you'd like to see that this is what I'd thought of for the costume for Clegg." "Oh, I see," he said.'

Gilbert was impressed. 'He loved the script and he was determined he was going to get the part of Clegg and he came in dressed as Clegg, and never changed. He'd dressed as Clegg, and of course when he'd read the part, he was Clegg.'

If Clarke had been certain that he wanted Sallis as Clegg, Gilbert was equally certain who he wanted for Blamire. 'As soon as I read it I had Michael Bates in mind. He was a marvellous comedy actor, and he had this erect, bristling, extraordinary delivery, rather like Leonard Rossiter, he had this terrific timing in comedy. Of course, he was playing an ex-RSM in the Royal Corps of Signals. It would always be something like that with Roy, it would never be a traditional regiment. He was absolutely brilliant.'

He was also the best known of the trio in the early 1970s, an immensely popular actor familiar to radio, television, theatre and film audiences, whose career was at its peak. Bates had virtually cornered the market in playing the sort of stuffy, stiff-necked military, police or other authority figure incapable of recognising his own ridiculousness, or that of the rules he insisted on sticking to, usually to superb comic effect. He looked exactly right for such parts – tall, carrying himself with parade-ground correctness and with a clipped moustache that twitched with irritation or self-righteousness. The more serious he looked, the funnier he was. The real Bates was, of course, anything but stuffy, even though there were points of similarity with the characters he played, notably an uncompromisingly conservative view of the world. His background made him a British Empire man to the core, and unafraid to voice deeply unfashionable opinions about Johnny Foreigner. More importantly, he was a noted technician, an extraordinarily precise actor who, if he were playing a scene that involved him buying a drink, liked to have exactly the right amount of money in his pocket.

The military bearing he brought to his parts was for real. Bates, who had been born in Jhansi, in India's United Provinces on 4 December 1920, grew up in Derbyshire after his parents sent him back to England aged seven. He joined the British Army not long after the outbreak of the Second World War before transferring to the Gurkhas, with whom he served for four years, ending the war as a major. Hostilities interrupted his study of history at Cambridge, and after returning home from the Far East he fulfilled a long-held ambition to act by going into rep at Worthing, where he met his wife, actress Margaret Chisholm.

Shakespeare beckoned, and Bates worked extensively at Stratford-upon-Avon and the Old Vic before carving out a busy career in the West End, where his and Sallis's paths first crossed in 1960, when both played with Olivier in *Rhinoceros*. Bates's defining moment in the theatre was to come six years later, when he created the part of Inspector Truscott in Joe Orton's black farce *Loot*, to rave reviews. The role demonstrated how superbly he could evoke preposterous authority and led to a burgeoning film career. There were appearances in *Oh, What a Lovely War!*, *The Battle of Britain* and *A Clockwork Orange*. His finest hour on film came in 1970, when he appeared opposite George C. Scott in *Patton*, playing Field Marshal Bernard Law Montgomery, to whom Bates bore a passing resemblance. It was a virtuoso performance, in which Bates caught the spirit and arrogance of the great commander with uncanny accuracy, even down to the speech impediment that meant he could not pronounce his Rs. This mannerism was to give Bates the chance to indulge a mischievous sense of humour. The producers of the film worried that the revered Monty would complain about the dramatic licence that had been taken with his acrimonious exchanges with General George Patton, and Bates did nothing to calm their nerves when he telephoned them in character and announced: 'This is Monty here. I'm cwoss and I'm going to sue.'

There would be another fine film role for Bates that hit the screens as the cast of *The Last of the Summer Wine* were preparing to depart for Yorkshire. He appeared as Sergeant Spearman in Alfred Hitchcock's penultimate film *Frenzy*, offering the deftest support to Alec McCowen's henpecked police inspector in darkly comic interludes that provided some respite from a grim tale about a mass murderer.

Radio and television work were also proving rewarding for Bates. He served fifteen years in the hit radio comedy *The Navy Lark*, and after numerous supporting roles in sitcoms was given his own in late 1972 by Yorkshire Television, *Turnbull's Finest Half Hour*, in which he was naturally cast as the inept authority figure of a struggling television station.

For now, though, Cyril Blamire was uppermost in his mind, and everybody was happy. Bates loved the part. 'It's got a gentle sort of humour,' he said. 'More a smile than a belly laugh.' Sallis, who had after their initial meeting on *Rhinoceros* also worked with him in the theatre in *Look After Lulu*, was more than happy to have him aboard. 'We just got along very well together, we laughed at the same things and we made jokes at the same things, it was just very comfortable.'

That left Compo, and the casting could make or break the show. The anarchic imp would be the first of the trio that the audience saw, and his outrageously uncouth behaviour and scorn for authority would drive the interaction between the trio. It was a plum role and needed an actor of consummate skill to carry it off without descending into caricature. Once again, Jimmy Gilbert knew who he wanted, but this time Clarke was less than happy.

'I had qualms about Bill Owen, because Jimmy picked him and rang me and said, "What about Bill Owen for Compo?" and I thought, what a dreadful idea, because I'd only ever seen Bill in the films as Cockney other ranks, so I thought, how can this be?'

It was an understandable reaction, and filmgoers of Clarke's generation would surely have agreed. If Bates was typecast as coppers and soldiers, Owen was equally fixed in the public mind as a feisty Cockney, a brilliantined salt-of-the-earth, cheery everyman with a fast line in chat, always ready with a wisecrack. London seemed to run through his performances as unchangingly as the Thames through the capital. Owen as a northerner? Not likely. Duncan Wood did not like the idea any better than Clarke. Like Bates's military bearing, Owen's evocation of cocky Londoners was rooted in reality.

William John Owen Rowbotham was born in Acton Green, London, on 14 March 1914, the son of a tram driver whose fiery left-wing politics shaped his son's entire life. Until the day he died, Owen would view the world through spectacles not so much rose-tinted as shaded the brightest red. Argumentative and direct, he was always ready to take offence, quick to unleash a generalised anger about the world that always seemed to bubble just below the surface, and into old age still saw class war as the motivation of anybody who disagreed with his opinions, often alienating those around him, admitting few close friends, determinedly standing outside the mainstream of his profession, preferring to go his own way, jutting his jaw at what he deemed pretension and hypocrisy, and yet inspiring rare loyalty in those who managed to get beyond the prickliness and find the warmth beneath. Owen would prove to be a prodigiously talented, multi-faceted artist, so skilled an actor that for millions he would come to embody an archetypal northerner just as he had once seemed the quintessential Cockney, so full of ideas that he would charge headlong into new challenges reckless of failure, so driven by his convictions that he would devote his off-hours, even when worn out by work, to causes that mattered to him, notably the Boys Club movement, of which he was a tireless champion, believing that involving young people in drama taught them discipline.

He was the oldest of the three leading men, and had travelled the hardest road. Bitter disappointment had come knocking often enough, not least when he achieved stardom, only to see it fade. Owen was of poor but respectable stock, and after leaving school went to work in a dyers and cleaners factory. He had always shown a knack for entertaining, singing for the family, then palling up with another boy to sing in working men's clubs and later with dance bands. 'The cheek was all there,' he would say, 'I'd have a go at anything, did a little bit of music hall, had an act which I got together, not a very good act, but I liked entertaining people.' Before the 1920s were out, he had seen the effect that singing and a bit of comic dancing had on an audience. (Sixty years later, the same cheek and the echoes of that tyro entertainer, still clowning when most of his contemporaries were taking it easy, clad in woolly hat, scruffy jacket and wellies, would enchant television viewers in occasional set pieces where Compo would sing or dance.) A teenage crush on a girl led him towards amateur theatricals. The girl fell away, but the acting bug didn't. Characteristically, he saw his choice of career in class terms, as he told the *Yorkshire Post* in 1990. 'Nobody in my class, and I use the term class, thought about going into the theatre. I mean, how were you going to do it? You left school at fourteen and got what job you could, because you had to keep the home fire burning. If you didn't have a shotgun wedding you had a legitimate wedding, and then you moved as near to your parents as you could and that was the pattern. That was the routine of life.'

Not for him, though. 'I don't think I could have withstood the monotony of the life I saw in front of me. I was a good organiser, not a good employee.' A trip to a holiday camp in Devon in 1937 saw him spending a week entertaining and organising others, and led to a full-time job as a camp host. Once the summer was over his socialist views led him towards Britain's leading political theatre, the Unity, at Kings Cross, which staged a programme of left-wing productions that were much admired. Owen could not have had a better grounding; the Unity specialised in original work and, beginning with a small part in a satirical pantomime in 1938, Owen wrote, acted in, and staged plays and revues there for a dozen years.

The war intervened, and Owen was called up in 1940, joining the Royal Pioneer Corps, which recognised his intelligence and selected him for officer training, but during a battle exercise he witnessed an accident in which one of his men had a foot blown off by a grenade. Owen was severely traumatised and, after a spell in hospital and psychiatric treatment, had to be invalided out of the army. He returned to the theatre, playing Gunner Cohen in *Mr Balfry*, by James Bridie. By now, producers had noticed him and offers began coming in. He was much praised for his performance as Trooper Bates in Colin Morris's play *Desert Rats* at the Adelphi in 1945, and that same year Owen embarked on the film career that would define his public image, when he played Nobby Clarke in Anthony Asquith's *The Way to the Stars*, a drama set in the RAF, starring Michael Redgrave and John Mills, with an exceptional screenplay by Terence Rattigan. It remains one of the great films about men at war, sober, thoughtful and free from cliché or gung-ho mock heroics. Owen was ideally cast as a member of Mills's aircrew, and showed a gift for comedy in scenes with Stanley Holloway as a louche saloon-bar bore.

Britain's Rank Organisation was at its height, and had ambitions to create a home-grown Hollywood. It was signing up talent as fast as it could find it, and Owen got the call after two outstanding performances in the West End, as a simpleton in the thriller *Now the Day Is Over*, and as a chirpy young romeo in the Victorian social comedy, *Caste*. 'I was playing a little Cockney plumber called Sam Gerridge, and that's where it happened,' he told the *Yorkshire Post*. 'Bang! It was a big part and I took it and shook it and there was nothing more to get out of it, and all the critics went for it. To a working-class boy in those days, a film contract was the thing.' He signed on the dotted line and reported to the old Gainsborough Studios in Islington to star opposite Patricia Roc in the weepie *When the Bough Breaks*, about a woman trying to reclaim the illegitimate child she was forced to give up.

But before it came out, a change needed making. The surname Rowbotham was hardly marquee material, especially in the USA, and under pressure from Rank, he agreed to use one of his middle names. Bill Owen, film star, was born, and he behaved accordingly, embarking on a round of publicity and promotions for the picture, and even finding enough leeway in his man-of-the-people socialism to buy a second-hand Rolls-Royce, which he parked outside the Unity. *When the Bough Breaks* did well enough when it was released in 1948, but more than one reviewer noted that Owen was an odd choice as a romantic leading man, even though his performance was sincere, sensitive and dignified. He was short and blessed with a face more homely than handsome. On screen, he didn't so much smoulder as look mischievous, and it soon became clear that Rank was not quite sure what to do with him. They cast about for a label that would make him identifiable, an image they could sell, and as they did so turned to Hollywood, settling on two stars whose charisma more than compensated for both their lack of physical stature and absence of conventional good looks, coming up with the idea of billing him as a 'British James Cagney', or even a home-grown Humphrey Bogart, but neither idea stuck.

There could no more be a second Cagney or Bogart than there could be a copycat Laurel or a Hardy, and Owen was shrewd enough to realise that he wasn't going to make it big during his two-year contract, which when it was up was not renewed. He was that uncomfortable proposition, difficult to know how to bill, a star who had not made it. In 1994 he admitted, again to the *Yorkshire Post*: 'I wasn't ever a big film star. I was put under contract on the supposition that I would become a star, well, nobody knew what to do with me. I wasn't the average contract player, six foot, very good-looking, etcetera, etcetera; I was a short-arse and had none of the requirements needed at that time. There was talk of making me a James Cagney, but nobody actually did it. It was very frustrating and in a way I got my best film roles when I came out of contract.'

As the contract ticked away and Rank dithered over what to do with him, Owen turned back to the stage, scoring another major success as Touchstone in *As You Like It*, starring Katharine Hepburn, on a US tour in 1949. Back home, he gave his finest film performances, as a cocky boxer in 1953's *The Square Ring* and a disgraced jockey in the following year's *The Rainbow Jacket*. These flawed, corruptible characters offered him the chance to show the subtlety and depth of which he was capable, and marked him out as a character actor of rare skill. Stage work was rewarding too – he created the role of Macheath in only the second ever British production of *The Threepenny Opera*, and productions of his own plays *The Ragged Trousered Philanthropists* (adapted from Robert Tressell's novel), *Money for Nothing* and *Breakout* were modest successes. As the 50s rolled into the 60s, there were parts in four *Carry On* comedies, including the first, *Carry On Sergeant*, in which Owen played – inevitably – a Cockney NCO, and a defining radio performance from 1962 in which Owen originated the title role of Bill Naughton's *The Little Life of Alfie Elkins*, a part to be immortalised on film later in the decade by Michael Caine in *Alfie*.

But Owen's proudest achievement of the 1960s was his musical *The Matchgirls*, based on the first recorded industrial dispute by women, at the Bryant and May factory in London in 1888. The women went on strike because they were being poisoned by the phosphorous in the matches, and the dispute was the subject of a play by Robert Mitchell, which was staged at the Unity during the Blitz. The subject matter chimed with Owen's politics and he was captivated by it, re-staging a modified version, again at the Unity, in 1948. In the early 60s, Owen met composer Tony Russell and came up with the idea of a musical version. He was already a prolific writer of songs and would eventually have more than seventy published and recorded by stars including Cliff Richard – who had a hit with Owen's 'Marianne' – Sacha Distel, Engelbert Humperdinck and Harry Secombe. The libretto and lyrics to *The Matchgirls* were of a very high calibre, and the musical opened at the Globe Theatre in the heart of the West End on 1 March 1966 after a successful out-of-town tryout in Leatherhead, Surrey. The audience was enthusiastic, and the songs, notably Secombe's recording of 'I Long to See the Day', were getting a lot of radio play. But *The Matchgirls* was to close within three months, a victim of its subject material. The story it told of the strike was essentially a harrowing tale of poverty and illness, hardly the stuff of musical entertainment. Here was another bitter blow, but Owen would eventually have the last laugh; *The Matchgirls* took on a new life, gradually becoming one of the most popular musicals in the amateur theatre, performed all over the world. In a strange twist of fate, thirty-three years later the musical would provide the most poignant of soundtracks as Owen's life drew to its close.

For now, though, the late 60s were dispiriting. Owen was no longer the in-demand young actor of *The Way to the Stars* or *Caste*, with everything before him. He seemed like yesterday's news; the film star who hadn't made it, the author of a musical which hadn't made it. In his fifties, everything seemed to be on a downward spiral: his marriage had collapsed and so had a subsequent serious relationship, there was not much work coming his way, and nobody seemed quite sure what to do with him, even if he crossed their minds. He was just another middle-aged actor, touting for voice-over work for commercials and picking up what he could.

The pendulum began to swing back in his favour as the end of the decade approached, thanks to the great director Lindsay Anderson, who cast him against type in a new play by David Storey, *In Celebration*. Anderson wanted Owen to play the patriarch of a Yorkshire mining family, a plum character role. The cast featured a trio of outstanding young actors, Alan Bates, Brian Cox and James Bolam, and the production opened in April 1969 to rave reviews. It was the shot in the arm Owen's career desperately needed, and shortly afterwards Anderson gave it a booster jab, casting him again in another Storey play, *The Contractor*, in which he played a tough father-figure who ran a company supplying marquees. Suddenly, the faded star was showing his mettle as a powerfully effective character actor.

Jimmy Gilbert had seen Storey's plays and been impressed. He'd already worked fruitfully with Owen on the production of *Kiss Me, Kate* that launched BBC2, casting him as one of the two gangsters who performed 'Brush Up Your Shakespeare', and capitalised on his northern character of *In Celebration*, using him as the irascible father-in-law of Rodney Bewes in *Whatever Happened to the Likely Lads*, a role Owen embraced with relish. And there was another performance pushing Gilbert towards offering Compo to Owen. In the autumn of 1964 he had appeared in a theatrical oddity. *Oblomov* was an adaptation of a Russian play that starred Spike Milligan as an idler who saw no reason to do anything except lie in bed. It was intended to show that Milligan's talents as an innovative comedy writer and performer could extend to being a leading man. Owen was cast as his decrepit and disreputable manservant, Zakhar. Soon after opening night, the restless Milligan became bored with the constraints of the role and started improvising. The play became a huge hit as word of its anarchic unpredictability spread. No two performances were the same, all pretence of sticking to the script was thrown to the wind by Milligan, who delivered some inspired clowning as Owen lived on his wits to avoid being steamrollered.

'I saw him in *Oblomov*, where he virtually was Compo,' said Gilbert.

> He played this scruffy servant in welly boots terrifying Spike the whole time who was bedridden, and he was almost playing the part of Compo then. Then I saw him in David Storey's play, *The Contractor*, where he was playing the tough Yorkshire boss of a gang who were assembling a big tent. I'd used him in *The Likely Lads* as a northern dad, father of Thelma, father of the bride, so it all seemed to point to Bill playing Compo. I had seen all these things, and I knew he could play it, but other people remembered him as Bill Rowbotham, a typical Cockney actor especially in wartime movies. How he dressed was obviously important, the scruffy hat and unshaven, filthy-dirty welly boots and socks, you felt that he would stink within thirty yards. Absolutely the opposite of Bill. Bill the actor was the most dapper, the most elegant performer, the most graceful performer. I'd worked with him in *Kiss Me, Kate* with Howard Keel and he moved with great elegance, not like Compo.

Clarke went along with Gilbert, though he remained unconvinced. 'We read around the table, but you can only judge so much from that, and I was very dubious about Bill being suitable until I saw the pilot.'

Owen recognised the quality of Clarke's script as soon as he saw it, not least because of his own extensive writing experience and a miserable recent job. A year earlier, he appeared in a dismal ITV sitcom, *Coppers End*, about a bunch of lazy policemen, which had been a dispiriting experience as it staggered through its thirteen episodes. The script from Clarke that arrived at his home was in a different league. Shortly after his 58th birthday, out of the blue had come a television role rich with promise. 'I'd been in some right doffos, like *Coppers End*. All you could do was keep your fingers crossed someone would laugh,' he said to the *Yorkshire Post* in 1990. But this script made Owen laugh. 'I read the script in bed, I got about halfway through and I rang Jimmy Gilbert, the director and producer. "What do you think?" he said. I said, "It's pure gold, count me in."' Gilbert had his trio.

There were five supporting parts to cast, and for two of them Gilbert turned to a bittersweet comedy drama, *The Fishing Party*, that was broadcast on 1 June 1972 as part of BBC1's *Play for Today* strand. Peter Terson had written a charming, touching story about three Yorkshire miners who go on a sea-fishing trip to Whitby and book into a guest-house whose landlady is puffed up with self-importance and social pretension. She regards fishing parties as beneath her, but takes them in nevertheless, not least so that she can cheat and short-change them. The miners make friends with a down-to-earth stallholder on the seafront, and even though seasickness blights their trip, their indomitable optimism sends them home happy. *The Fishing Party* was beautifully played by the entire cast and proved popular with both the public and critics, with particular praise being lavished on Jane Freeman as Audrey, the landlady. She was exactly right for the role as a big, buxom, harridan who bridled and bristled. Freeman was working at Birmingham Repertory Theatre, but also making increasingly frequent and telling appearances in one-off television dramas. The tea-stall holder was John Comer, a beefy stand-up comedian turned character actor who had been a familiar face to audiences since his appearance as one of the workshy trade unionists in the 1959 Boulting Brothers satire on British industrial relations, *I'm All Right Jack*.

Gilbert immediately recognised that Freeman and Comer would be perfect for Ivy and Sid, the argumentative couple who ran the café where the trio took refuge, seeing in their performances the seed of a classic love-hate relationship. 'I was very impressed with *The Fishing Party*. Casting was never far from my mind, really, same as you're keeping an eye open for any likely locations. We went to the theatre a great deal, which is how we saw Bill, and we watched television as well and that was what sparked off John Comer and Jane.'

Not that Freeman and Comer knew each other. 'We never met,' she said. 'It was some time into *Summer Wine* before we both realised we'd been in *The Fishing Party*, because all his scenes were outside and I was inside, running the boarding house.' Comer's tenure only ended with his death; thirty-seven years on from the pilot, Freeman and Sallis would be the only surviving members of the original cast. Clarke had written a pair of illicit lovers into his half-hour, the librarian, Mr Wainwright, and his assistant, Mrs Partridge, who would be introduced surfacing from beneath the front desk. For them, Gilbert turned to a couple of familiar sitcom players, Blake Butler and Rosemary Martin, who were ideally cast. They were funny and touching, but their characters would not endure.

That just left Gilbert to find the battleaxe who would deliver the opening line of *The Last of the Summer Wine*, whom Clarke had called Mrs Batty. On one of his trips north, he decided to see who was available in Manchester. Gilbert had a clear idea of what he wanted – a big, fat, plain woman hanging out washing who would look on disdainfully as two men repossessed her scruffy neighbour's television and exclaim, 'They're taking his telly again,' as a couple of other women looked on. There would be another element in her scorn and disgust of him, that he lusted after her:

Compo: Hey up, love! I wish you'd stay inside, Mrs Batty – tha knows it only excites me.

Mrs Batty: That's all he can talk. Filth.

Compo: But fluently. And your Harold's that wrapped up with his pigeons. Give us a word of encouragement, Eunice, else stop flaunting tha laundry where I can see it. Washdays are purgatory.

Woman: No wonder his missus went off with that Pole.

Younger woman: It's no fun being lonely.

Mrs Batty: He's not lonely. There's a gang of them. Hang about that public library. They've nowt else to do.

Younger woman: Poor old soul. What does he do when the library's closed – without his telly?

Mrs Batty: Her next door says he exposes himself.

And that was it, just a few lines, but essential in setting up the shiftless, lecherous character of Compo and announcing the appearance of Clegg and Blamire. But Gilbert wasn't having any luck in finding his Mrs Batty. The actresses coming in for audition neither looked nor sounded right, and the one who turned up at 4 p.m. for his last appointment on 5 June appeared no better. For starters, she wasn't the big woman he had in mind, but a perfectly normal size 14 dressed in an elegant black velvet trouser suit. Gilbert was unimpressed. 'Oh dear me, no, I'm sorry,' he said. 'You're nothing like the part we're looking for.' But since she had arrived back from a family holiday in Spain that morning and dropped everything – including the washing, which she'd been doing when the phone rang – to attend at short notice, Gilbert let her read. It was the luckiest afternoon for them both. Before him was Mrs Batty to the life. When she'd finished, he exclaimed, 'That's it! That's her!' Then he realised the irony: 'But we were looking for a really big, fat woman, because we don't know whether or not this scruffy, dirty little man really fancies her, or if she's so dreadful nobody could fancy her.'

Gilbert was ecstatic. 'The delivery – big, rich voice. She'd dominate every scene that she was in. It was perfect with Bill, the little fellow scuttling away back down to the cellar. She had that great face. It was written in the stage direction of that character that she looked pretty formidable, a bit of a hatchet face, and a big woman, which she wasn't, but she had a great face and a marvellous voice and she just was the character, so we just dressed her up, made her up, and there she was.'

Kathy Staff took the idea of being too dreadful to be fanciable in her stride. She had been cast as plain Janes ever since she first stepped on to a stage, and had no problem in transforming her customarily kindly, smiling demeanour into a scowling, humourless visage as hard as the stone steps her character scrubbed and swept with a vigour that threatened to wear them away. She was distilled disapproval given human form, all slab-like face, fearsome temper, foghorn voice and air of outrage. The reading of the bit part that so impressed Gilbert would prove to be her fortune, and she cheerily embraced what was asked of her. 'I never mind how ugly they make me,' Staff told the *Yorkshire Post* in 1982. 'I love it. I always have, even when I was young. I never had any wish to look glamorous.' She was only forty-three when she was cast, much younger than Owen, with whom she would bond to such unforgettable comic effect in the years that followed. Staff could not have guessed at what was to come; this was just another one-off job in a workaday, stop-start acting career that showed no signs of bringing her fame, let alone fortune. She was the most down-to-earth and grounded of performers, staying close to, and drawing strength from, her roots throughout her life. She was born Minnie Higginbottom on 12 July 1928 in Dukinfield, Cheshire, to a working-class family. Like Owen, she made her way into acting via an amateur company and went professional at twenty-one, calling herself Katherine Brant, simply because she liked the first name and thought it should be counterbalanced by a short surname, which was provided by a shop called Brant's that she saw while on a bus to Oldham repertory theatre. Stage work followed, but marriage to a teacher, John Staff, in 1951, marked the start of a professional hiatus for the next decade as she worked as a shorthand typist to help the couple buy a house and devoted herself to bringing up their two daughters. Gradually, she made her way back into acting as an extra, and then on to bit parts in the venerable soap *Coronation Street*, small but telling roles on film in *A Kind of Loving* and *The Family Way*, and then, in 1969, a substantial part opposite Roy Barraclough in a Yorkshire Television drama, *Castle Haven*, about a couple who ran a ramshackle block of flats. The series was not a success, but it made enough of an impact to see Staff considered for the role of the matriarch in the company's new soap *Emmerdale Farm*. She got down to the last two, and then lost out. So she was clear of commitments, and glad of Mrs Batty, which she thought may or may not lead to anything. One thing was certain; it was handy for home, only a twenty-minute drive across the moors from Holmfirth. She'd be back in time for tea with the family, and the following day she'd look for the next job.

CHAPTER 3

A Talking Show

THEY SET OFF by minibus from BBC Television Centre on a bright, sunny morning in midsummer's week and headed for the M1, about a dozen in all, Jimmy Gilbert, Peter Sallis, Bill Owen, Michael Bates, plus crew. Four hours and 190 miles later, they arrived in a grey, sodden Holmfirth where the rain was bouncing off the cobbles. It was the first taste of the trials Gilbert and the producers who followed him would face. Lunch had been booked at a pub, the Elephant and Castle, but it was delayed because the landlady had failed to put a joint of meat in the oven soon enough, and it was mid-afternoon before they had eaten and the weather brightened enough for the men to get into costume and Gilbert to start filming. He began as he meant to continue, making the scenery a vital element in the action, shooting the trio in long and medium shot as they walked along a road and through a field, where one of them had to stand in a cowpat. After some discussion, Bates said he would do the deed, and production wrapped for the day. The dialogue would be dubbed in later. So far, so good. The day was about to go horribly wrong.

Headquarters was over the hill to the west of Holmfirth, in a large pub on the edge of the moors near another mill town, Marsden. The Coach and Horses was, in Clarke's words, 'Wuthering Heights with strippers'. Gilbert said: 'It was well run, the food was excellent, but a bleaker place would be hard to find in

England. Although convenient for our chosen locations and very popular with walkers on the Pennine Way, it was highly unpopular with our actors, who wanted somewhere more congenial to relax in after a hard day's shooting, especially at the weekend when the pub became a strip club and large ladies strutted their stuff on the saloon bar.' Gilbert and his stars retreated for dinner to a tiny private lounge, which quickly proved too small to accommodate the tensions that sprang up when the conversation drifted on to politics. It had been a cold afternoon, and a few stiff whiskies were taken against the chill. Wine followed with the food, and Bates, all twitching moustache, started to vent some very trenchant opinions with an air of certainty that brooked no disagreement. 'Michael Bates was born in India, a lovely man, but had very strong Tory views on the Empire, patriotism and pretty much everything else,' said Gilbert. 'For example, he thought that India was mad to let the British leave, and that no good would come of it.'

That was the red rag for Owen, who exploded with anger. He would try the patience of colleagues over the years by holding forth long and loud on his own politics, and it may have unsettled him to find in Bates a through-the-looking-glass mirror image of himself. Sallis, stuck in the middle, did his best to joke them out of it, but to no avail. Voices were raised and the atmosphere began to turn ugly. 'With Bill Owen, you had somebody who was slightly to the left of Lenin, and with Michael Bates, you had somebody who was slightly to the right of Margaret Thatcher,' said Sallis. 'So to put the two together was really asking for trouble and that first night's suppertime, they got started until eventually we couldn't really eat, and Jimmy said, "Come with me, you two," and he took them outside and they must have been gone the best part of half an hour before they came back and they were very quiet, neither of them spoke.'

Gilbert felt he had to impose some order or the production would become impossible. 'They were both very extreme in their views, and Peter was making droll remarks to drop the temperature, and it got really quite heated, and it was something I felt that had got to be stopped instantly or there'll be blood on the carpet. I told them that if it was going to be like this I'd have nothing further to do with it and I'd just go back to London and tell them "Forget it", and so it apparently had the desired effect because Peter said there was never any more trouble after that. I wouldn't have walked out on it, but it was a jolly good threat. They thought that maybe he is so pissed off he really will, they weren't prepared to take a chance on it, so they behaved themselves.'

Sallis, as he would find it necessary to do down the years, especially with Owen, saw the value of providing a sympathetic ear to all sides. 'I've never been political, I could no more give a talk on the Conservative Party than I could on the Labour Party. We were all having such a nice time, why ruin it with politics? It was as simple as that. I could guess what was going on, and much later Jimmy said to me, "I said to them we've got a jolly good script here, we've got every chance of a series, and if you two play around with this political-debate attitude towards everything we do, we're going to pack it all up and take it back to London." He didn't say he would re-cast it, but the implication was there.'

What was left of dinner passed off uneasily, and the following morning Gilbert did what he could to ensure that the week's filming would not descend into a nightmare of personal conflicts. 'I put them in separate hotels. Bill was in some boarding house on the edge of the moors. Peter was in the George Hotel, in Huddersfield, right by the station, in the room that Harold Wilson used to have when he came up from London, and Michael Bates was in the brand-new motorway hotel at Huddersfield. They'd be picked up and they'd come together and then they'd go back to their hotels, and peace reigned. They couldn't have got on, certainly not over thirty years, because they used to get into terrible political arguments.'

Bates and Owen did establish a good working relationship, both perhaps recognising a little of himself in the other, and moved beyond purely professional contact. Owen later wrote: 'We never had a cross word again. We became good friends and, with our wives, shared many a social occasion. My friends will be amazed to have me admit that I'm not the most orderly and diplomatic participant in discussion, but it was Michael's bloody-minded and forthright refusal to come to terms or even consider my point of view that got me going.'

Sallis recalled that after the two had slept on the argument, they put it behind them and went to work in high spirits on the scene in which Blamire is introduced. 'It was a joy to watch them doing their scene together, two experts at it.'

With his three stars settled, and filming under way in earnest, Gilbert found that the BBC in Manchester had laughed at his choice of Holmfirth as a location with some justification. One of the major headaches was the light, as clouds scudded across the Pennines. A few lines of dialogue would begin in bright sunlight and end in gloomy darkness, which was unacceptable as it would make a scene look odd to viewers and destroy continuity. He had to wait for one or the other to last long enough to film a complete scene. 'It was perishing cold. The wind was blowing and what made it worse was that it was alternate sun and cloud, sun and cloud, so we were continually waiting so that there was some sort of consistency.'

Gilbert had to be fast on his feet when the light was right.

We were in a steep wooded glade and this was the last shot of the day. It had been a long one and everyone was tired and looking forward to packing up and going home after the final scene was safely in the can. This looked increasingly unlikely in the gathering gloom. The camera crew were looking down at us from on top while I waited with the three actors. We were standing in a stream, hoping against hope for a change in the weather when suddenly a shaft of sunlight came through a gap in the trees above, lighting the scene as if by magic. 'Stand by, everyone,' I shouted. Then seconds later, 'Action'. We were only able to shoot one take before the sun went back in again for the day, but it was enough. It was perfect. 'OK, it's a wrap,' I called. A voice came from the trees high above. It was Enid, standing beside her husband, the writer Roy Clarke. 'I think God is looking after you, Jimmy.'

His good fortune held in finding the location for the key opening shot. Gilbert needed Mrs Batty in a setting where she could look down on Compo with scorn as his television was repossessed. He picked a house and set his crew up. 'When we went to film it, I realised I'd made a mistake as far as the sun was concerned, it was dark and it really wasn't right at all, and I literally had to go and look for somewhere else while the film unit were hanging about.' After a search, Gilbert and his assistant, Bernard Thompson, arrived at 28 Huddersfield Road, close to the town centre. It was a stone-built terraced house overlooking the river, with a steep flight of steps to the front door and a small yard. Beneath the steps was the cellar entrance to the adjoining property. It would do nicely. The occupants, though, were reluctant to co-operate. 'We had to negotiate that place being used, and I think they weren't all that keen on us coming, but somehow we persuaded them and we just moved across the other side of the valley and plonked ourselves down in there, which became a central part really. And that location was a mistake, a sheer bit of good luck, where Kathy was upstairs and he was downstairs, in the cellar underneath.' It would become *Summer Wine*'s most recognisable location, and one of the best-loved settings in all television comedy, the potential for laughs of the battleaxe shooing her scruffy suitor away from her immaculate steps with a sweeping brush never palling.

The week's filming passed quickly and with no more arguments between Bates and Owen. Gilbert was pleased with the results, and now it was back to London. 'It was going to be a very expensive production. One third shot on location and the remainder in front of an audience in Television Centre.' Now it was time to edit the footage from location and studio together, and add the finishing touch – the music.

Clarke had asked for a good tune, and Gilbert turned to a trusted colleague who was synonymous with music for comedy shows.

Ronnie Hazlehurst hailed from Kathy Staff's home town, Dukinfield, and had served time as a trumpeter in big bands before doing his National Service, during which he studied at the Royal Military School of Music. Dance bands claimed him again after he was demobbed in 1949, but by the mid-50s he was busy at the fledgling Granada Television where he moved away from playing and into orchestration. A decade later, he was a staff arranger at the BBC and began a long career writing some memorable sitcom themes. *The Likely Lads*, *Some Mothers Do 'Ave 'Em*, *Are You Being Served?*, *The Fall and Rise of Reginald Perrin*, *Yes, Minister* and *To the Manor Born* were all his, as were the themes for *The Two Ronnies* and the game show *Blankety Blank*. The corporation recognised that his was a very special talent and would eventually promote him to Head of Music for Light Entertainment. It wasn't just a job to him; Hazlehurst was a witty man to whom laughter came easily, and an ardent student of how music could enhance and enrich comedy. He was a long-time member of The Sons of the Desert, the Laurel and Hardy appreciation society, and a devoted admirer of Leroy Shield, the uncredited composer who wrote much of the background music for the peerless double act's films, even using some of the themes to accompany the hapless antics of contestants struggling with potter's wheels and cake-decorating on the hugely popular *Generation Game* on BBC1 during the early 70s. Hazlehurst would later record a couple of albums of Shield's music, and even sneaked a snatch of one of his tunes into the first *Summer Wine* episode proper, 'Short Back and Palais Glide'. Another hero was Scott Bradley, who composed the manic music for the Tom and Jerry cartoons.

Hazlehurst went to see Gilbert during the editing, talked about the show, and departed to write a theme. On his return, Gilbert was underwhelmed. 'About a week later, Ronnie gave me a tape of what he'd written and I didn't like it at all. Ronnie was usually brilliant at getting the mood of a show right, but the music here seemed very conventional and opposite to what Roy wanted. "Can we have something more atmospheric?" I asked. "Something with a haunting tune, maybe a harmonica in it somewhere?" Ronnie nodded and went off, apparently disappointed at my reaction, but ten minutes later came back and said, "Is this the kind of thing you want?" and whistled the tune, note-for-note of what has been the theme music of *Last of the Summer Wine* for over thirty-seven years. "That's not a good tune," I said. "It's a great tune." Ronnie beamed. "Well, that's that fixed then."' Gilbert was overjoyed. Hazlehurst had caught exactly the feeling he was looking for. 'Again it was the film in Australia. I'd had a very outdoor feel to the music using harmonica and orchestra, and I asked him if he could do the same, which he did and of course that typifies the programme more than anything. That tune has never outstayed its welcome.'

Hazlehurst's orchestration, using harmonica and a small string section, brought out the beauty of his tender little waltz. This was a sitcom theme unlike any other. Most comedy shows from *Hancock's Half Hour* onwards had rumpty-tumpty, jaunty tunes that announced the laughs to come, but this was different. Its strength lay in its simplicity. The melody was so memorable and felt so right that the wonder was nobody had ever thought of it before. It was a new tune that immediately felt like an old friend, and captured to perfection the mood of Clarke's writing, his characters' fond remembrance of times past, their touch of sadness at the passage of time, the leisurely feel of a late summer's afternoon stretching ahead. It was music that chimed perfectly with Gilbert's vision of spaciousness. Here was a theme exactly in accord with a programme that sought to lead its viewers along unhurriedly and allow them time to bask in its humour. Everybody loved it. Clarke said: 'Sitcom music was funny music, more or less declaring itself, "Watch me, this is going to be funny." Who would have expected a sitcom to come up with a kind of a beautiful melody that Ronnie came up with?' Sallis felt the same: 'It isn't a comedy tune, it's just a lovely waltz.'

Alan Bell, who would work closely with Hazlehurst for twenty-six years, said: 'It's a classic piece of music. It just caught the right feeling. It was elderly people enjoying a leisurely life that they hadn't had except in their past as teenagers.' Bell believed Hazlehurst was guided by the show's title. 'What Ronnie does is like most songwriters – they take the words and the music is guided by the words. So if you think *The Last of the Summer Wine* – but it's *Last of the Summer Wine*, and he changed it later, subtly – it follows The-Last-of-the-Sum-mer-Wine, and that's why the notes are where they are. That's how songs are written – the lyricist gives the composer the first line. That's where I thought Ronnie got it from, the title.' It was a tune that cried out for words to match its mellow mood, and over time, at least three sets of lyrics were written for it, by Clarke, Owen and Ronnie Taylor. Bell said: 'The only good lyrics are Roy's, but Mike Sammes, the choirmaster we had, said they weren't easy to sing. They are lyrical and they are sentimental, because they are talking about the past, but they aren't sickly.' Clarke's lyrics would see very occasional service, but it was Hazlehurst's instrumental that insinuated itself into the public's affections, becoming one of the most popular and familiar of all television themes, irrespective of genre.

Its first airing would be at the studio recording, scheduled for 1 July, where the scenes in a chapel, a café, a pub and the library would be played live. All went smoothly, and Gilbert was reasonably happy. The performances by Bates, Owen and Sallis had matched their excellence on location, but the reaction of the studio audience had been fair rather than ecstatic. They had been slow to latch on to Clarke's highly individual humour, and there were moments when the trio tried to force the pace and squeeze out the laughs by delivering the lines more loudly. As the half-hour progressed the audience began to get it and the laughter started coming longer and louder. The pilot was ready, and a broadcast date was set for Thursday 4 January 1973, at 8 p.m. on BBC1. *The Last of the Summer Wine* would follow the police drama *Z Cars*. It was up against the 1964 comedy thriller *Murder Ahoy*, starring Margaret Rutherford as Miss Marple, on ITV and a serialised adaptation of *War and Peace* on BBC2. Viewers saw an opening shot of a wet mill town as Hazlehurst's waltz played and the credits rolled, then a couple of children running down an alley before the camera followed a small van as it pulled up outside a cellar door under the disapproving gaze of a stern-looking woman in a pinny. Compo's exchange with the television repossession men drew the first big laughs: 'Why don't you let me have one of them little portables? Save a lot of bother. Tha's going to be sweating when I get colour. And while tha's got it, have a look at that vertical hold.' It was up and away, and the audience was seeing the first of three expert comic performances as Owen sketched Compo with extraordinary deftness. He presented a picture of near-total dereliction: unshaven, unkempt and unconcerned at either; the greasy salt-and-pepper hair poking out from beneath a dark-green woolly hat; the grimy, collarless shirt with a ratty old tie knotted round a neck everybody knew instinctively was a stranger to soap and water; and the grubby jacket, shapeless trousers and battered wellington boots. There was no trace of the dapper Cockney characters here; the voice with its flattened vowels sounded as if it had sprung from the earth of Yorkshire, its delivery cocksure and bantering. Compo leered at Mrs Batty, dissolved into laughter at his own baiting of her, his neck hunched into his shoulders with mirth, and when he jammed the hat on his head and walked away, it was with the slouching gait of a couldn't-care-less schoolboy who made it a point of honour to ignore all instructions to stand up straight and tidy himself up. Within a minute of being on screen, Owen had summoned up a characterisation so vivid that it obliterated every image the audience had held of him for the preceding thirty-five years.

Blamire was next, bringing with him the contrast at the heart of Clarke's script. He appeared on a street in a smart private housing estate as dapper as Compo was flea-bitten. The trilby sat dead centre on his head, the blazer, regimental tie and spotless shoes were all beyond reproach; Michael Bates was the image of middle-class rectitude as he walked a tiny Yorkshire terrier and bumped into a none-too-clean little boy who wants to stroke the dog, and duly does so after spitting on his hand to make sure it's clean enough for Blamire, who, after sending him on his way, spots Compo approaching.

Compo: Mornin', Cyril.

Blamire: When I became a paying guest in this quiet little backwater, nobody said a word about it being in the path of migrating hordes of the proletariat.

Compo: What's up, Cyril?

Blamire: Let's have a bit less of the Cyril. Suppose the neighbours hear?

Compo: Old schoolmates, aren't we?

Blamire: Shut up. I'll deny it.

Compo: I saw where you were scarred once in the penalty area. I can quote details, me old love.

Blamire: Have less of the Cyril. I prefer the more rounded tones of Mister Blamire.

Compo: Don't mind me telling you, but …

Blamire: Spoken respectfully while clutching your tatty hat.

Compo: … Thee dog's crapping all over the pavement, you know that, don't you?

Blamire: That's funny. He usually sews it up in little bags and sends it by post.

And there it was. Blamire, his nose resolutely in the air, clinging to a tiny amount of dignity in the face of a crumbling foothold on respectability, trying desperately to keep himself a cut above the tatty old schoolmate, who prods him with sly facetiousness. The contrast between the two was delicious; Bates, straight-backed, not a hair out of place, trying not to look at Compo, pursing his lips in prim disapproval, rolling his Rs and elongating his Os as he tries in vain to emphasise his superiority even as they walk away together.

> Blamire: Five paces behind, if you don't mind, Simmonite. I drag me way up by the boot heels out of Hardwick Street and now, at the end of life's journey, here you are again. Undermining me rising confidence. There's not only me City and Guilds – there's this social chasm between us.

> Compo: Lend us a fag and I'll give thee a sniff at me socks.

If Blamire's entrance did not have quite the impact of Compo's, it was because the character was a variation on a familiar theme for Bates, who nevertheless played it superbly. As did the man in the middle, who rode into view by bicycle to give the programme its first visual gag. Clegg labours up a hill, and then grabs the back of a passing hearse to take him smiling to church, where he meets the vicar. Close by is a grave, whose headstone bears the name Edith Clegg. Peter Sallis, in his audition outfit of flat cap, old suit, cardigan and mac, sits down with him on a bench and takes his first chance to wonder at the world: 'This feller picks up this tiny bird in his hands and carries its quivering little body across this busy junction and feeds it to his cat. Life's like that. A complex texture of conflicting moralities.'

The vicar leaves to conduct the funeral, and Clegg starts making notes in a pocketbook as Blamire and Compo approach, and the trio comes together.

> Blamire: He's still calling for me in broad daylight.

> Clegg: Tell the neighbours he doesn't belong to you. You're just looking after him for somebody.

> Compo: They've taken me telly again.

> Clegg: Only because you haven't paid. It's nothing personal.

Compo: What are you writing now?

Clegg: Just catching the passing thought.

Blamire: I don't know why you bother.

Clegg: Somebody's got to think about things. And who's got more time than we have?

They move into the church, and it is here that the dynamics really click, as they get into a discussion about politics and religion, and Clarke fleshes out the characters, notably Clegg, who comes into his own with: 'You've got to remember, Compo, that Cyril's a Tory, and Tories can't stand it if you're filthy and obscene. That's what the Labour Party's for.' The wry observation that would become Clegg's trademark is already fully formed, and Sallis is wonderful as the flat-capped philosopher, his timing razor-sharp.

Clegg: If God's omnipotent, with all that choice available, what could he possibly want with my old woman?

Compo: Even if you don't believe in God, he'd take her just for spite. They're all alike, the bosses.

Blamire: What do you know, you tatty heathen?

Compo: I'm entitled to my opinion.

Blamire: Not exactly an expert opinion is it, considering how much experience you've had of either church or full employment.

Compo: It stands to reason that God's a boss, even if you don't believe in him.

They move on to the library, where the shared background of the trio is explored, and cigarettes are scrounged. The whole episode is wreathed in smoke; it is a running joke that Compo constantly scrounges fags from Blamire, who delivers more than a few of his lines with a cigarette clamped between his lips. The librarian throws them out, and they end up in a pub, via a detour to a stream where a tiddler is caught and put in a jam jar.

> Compo: Do you reckon angels wear underpants?
>
> Blamire: You what?
>
> Compo: Under their overcoats. It never shows in the pictures. 'Ere, do you reckon they've got parts, you know, to hide?
>
> Blamire: He's a scruffy peasant. They don't need them, do they? There's no mucking about like that.
>
> Clegg: You see, no variety even in the heavenly chorus. Just rank after rank of sopranos.

By now, the studio audience was fully in tune with Clarke's humour, and the laughter is often uproarious. After visiting the café, where Sid and Ivy are seen shouting at each other, the trio gets back into the library after spotting Wainwright and Mrs Partridge having an assignation. The dialogue is glorious, and the audience shrieks with laughter.

> Blamire: Do you know how he started his romantic career? Stuffing broken biscuits down Susan Anderson's knickers.
>
> Compo: Yeah, but that were research. That were just an excuse to see if it were true what Doggy said.
>
> Blamire: Rubbish!
>
> Clegg: No, shut up a minute, what did Doggy say?
>
> Compo: Well, Doggy reckoned they'd got a trap door.
>
> Blamire: A trap door?
>
> Compo: Yeah, he said that's how babies were born.
>
> Blamire: Through a trap door?

Clegg: Think about it, Cyril. Is it any weirder than the truth?

Blamire: Oh, it's a queer world for those of us brought up to believe in God, the Queen and the superiority of British bicycles.

Clegg: Sometimes, Cyril, I could swear that your idea of orgasm is a quick flick through Burke's Peerage.

The half-hour was almost over. The last sight of the trio is in a square where they bid farewell and go their separate ways, the final line going to Clegg: 'I think I'll get a bit of sausage for me tea.' It was a homely touch on which to close, as the three split up, at least for the day, underlining that none was going home to very much. Hazlehurst's waltz played over the closing credits as Gilbert gave his audience a last glimpse of Holmfirth, at least for now. He had his fingers crossed that the pilot for which he had so much affection would develop into a series.

The omens were good. Critics liked the show, with one, Stanley Reynolds of *The Times*, praising the originality of its concept in a comedy landscape of stereotypes including 'girls who share flats, parents who cannot cope, neighbours who cannot keep up, workers who hate work and workers with odd work'. This, though, was different: 'Roy Clarke's particular gift, as seen in his ITV series with Ronald Fraser, *The Misfit*, is for capturing human grotesquerie in an objectively comic style and for sketching in as background the society which has made his characters. *The Last of the Summer Wine* rang unnervingly socially true.' More to the point, the BBC liked it, which was hardly surprising since its Head of Comedy, Duncan Wood, had come up with the idea. A series of six episodes was commissioned, one of only two shows from that season's *Comedy Playhouse* to make it beyond the pilot. (The other, a sitcom starring comedian Gordon Peters, ran for only a single series.) Gilbert would be back in charge, and he was delighted. He'd proved that he could take a sitcom outside and now had the chance to extend the concept over the course of a series. The only reservation that the BBC had was over cost.

Gilbert explained:

> It was a very expensive series to do, because you had to take your unit all the way up to Yorkshire, where the weather was pretty awful, so you had to allow a lot of extra time, so you had all those filming costs, but then you had to come back and there were all the studio costs as well, so you had no more than a quarter of the series, but you'd done three weeks' filming in Yorkshire. Also, they were still thinking of comedy as studio based with an audience and you only used a film camera when you had to show outside, not to gain benefit from using film. I was fairly senior by then anyway and they loved the pilot. Pilots are always expensive because you are putting all that investment into design and filming and one thing and another, and if it doesn't become a series that's it, a very expensive one-off programme. Fortunately they'd seen the pilot and thought it was a real quality show and after that I had no problem at all, they just told me, 'Keep it down as much as you can.'

Clarke and Gilbert talked about the new series, which had a slightly amended and neater title, *Last of the Summer Wine*, and both agreed that there should be an addition to the regular cast – Kathy Staff. She had made such an impact with her few lines that the character demanded to be retained. The sheer force of her performance had burst off the screen. 'I think it came as a surprise to Roy,' said Gilbert. 'It was very much just another member of the cast as far as Roy was concerned, until he saw her in the pilot and then he realised what I realised – we'd got sheer gold there with her.' Clarke recalled how he too had been bowled over. 'It happens sometimes that you think you've got just another member of the cast, and then you see it and it hits you that this is worth keeping. She was so right for it that she had to stay.' Mrs Batty was equipped with a new first name, Nora instead of Eunice, and Clarke had a great comic foil for Compo.

Sid and Ivy would be retained and developed, and Wainwright and Mrs Partridge would also stay. Clarke pressed on with the writing, heartened and inspired by the performances of Bates, Owen and Sallis in the pilot. 'It comes as a huge lift when you've got your casting done, and you've got your actor in it, and once I've seen it and got that voice, even on a read-through, I can hear that voice speaking when I'm doing the dialogue, and that keeps you on the straight and narrow, because you wouldn't write anything he wouldn't say in that way, so it's a safety valve and a huge bonus. The minute I can hear their voice, I'm away, and until I can I'm tentative about a character. And then when you've got a voice, you can go anywhere.' Some voices resonated more loudly than others. 'The big help for me was Bill fell totally, one hundred per cent, in love with that character. Bill just adored Compo, so that made things very easy for me. I was always very impressed by Bill's physical ability, his clowning, which was a huge bonus.'

The writing went well, each episode taking about two weeks. 'I could do it comfortably in a fortnight, but the process is mainly getting something out of fresh air. That's the tortuous bit, and that produces a draft that I would never dare show anybody because it's so awful because it's so rough, but it's got a kind of structure and it's got pointers in it, so it's an entity, I've got something. The next bit is not so much a writing job as an editing job. That second stage I really enjoy, polishing it, getting it right. Once I've got that I can relax. I've got thirty minutes, it might be rubbish, but I've got thirty minutes, I've got something I didn't have, and I play with that until it suits me.'

Gilbert, meanwhile, was making his preparations for several weeks of location filming in and around Holmfirth when he was taken aback to find the old argument about the show's title resurfacing from the cast.

I had a delegation after the pilot, and before the first series started, I had the three actors, Michael Bates, Bill Owen and Peter Sallis, come and see me in my office to ask me to change the title because they didn't think *Last of the Summer Wine* was right. They said it was a shame because it was such a brilliant series and it had a title that would put people off from watching, and I said, 'I'm sorry but I love the title.' Maybe it was Bill that instigated it. They genuinely felt that it might stop it from becoming as popular as it deserved to be, same thinking obviously that the BBC had that we were starting with one arm tied behind our backs. I said, 'We'll have to differ on that one, because that's the title,' and they said, 'OK, fine, just thought we'd mention it.' It never became a big issue, but they obviously felt strongly about it and talked about it before they would have come and made this request.

Holmfirth beckoned earlier this time, in May, and once again Gilbert and his cast had to put up with unpredictably foul weather. However, one change made life a lot easier: a new resident had moved into the key address of 28 Huddersfield Road. Sonia Whitehead (who would become Sonia Lee when she remarried), far from being reluctant to let the exterior of her home be used for filming, welcomed both cast and crew, marking the start of a long and cordial relationship. There were new locations to be found, notably what would become Sid and Ivy's café, in reality an evil-smelling fish and chip shop in the centre of town. That would be Jane Freeman's domain, and it was a trial. 'I could barely go into the chip shop, which was my café, because it smelled so awful. We only used it for the exterior shots, but of course I had to go in there and change and then come out and shout.' But before she confronted the horrors of stale fat, Freeman had to find the location. Her role in the pilot had been entirely in the studio, and she was fitting the Holmfirth scenes around her theatre work in Birmingham. 'I had to film on Sunday. The car came for me at five o'clock in the morning, and I staggered out bleary-eyed and the driver asked where to and I said, "Well I don't know, I thought you knew," and at five o'clock in the morning there were not many people up who could tell us where we should be going. All I got was the script, not a shooting schedule or anything, so I read the script and I said, "Well, it's in the north," so we headed up north and he shot into Sheffield and found some taxi drivers and said, "I think they're filming up near Halifax or Huddersfield, somewhere like that," and eventually we got to Holmfirth, and somebody said to me, "Ah, there you are, Jane. Glad you're on time."'

There were no arguments this time, Bates and Owen working together smoothly, and together with Sallis developing a deeper, more believable on-screen relationship. The longer shooting schedule inevitably threw everybody together more than the pilot had, and the atmosphere was amicable. 'There were only six of us and we were all in a minibus, and we would do the crosswords,' recalled Freeman. 'The strength in the cast went right through. There wasn't a weak one anywhere. That was Jimmy's casting. He watched drama. It gave Bill's career a shot in the arm. He'd not made any films in a long time. He'd done some marvellous stuff on the stage at the Royal Court, but this gave him a tremendous rebirth.'

Freeman got on well with the three principals, and found in Bates a vastly experienced comic actor keen to help her make the best of her role. 'In those days he seemed much older than me, and he was a great comedian and he was often trying to help me, and he was so nice that I didn't mind. He used to give me long lessons on hitting people on the head with tin trays and things. He was sweet, very nice. Michael was a very precise actor, and that's why he used to give me technical hints about comedy: "Hold the tray like that, don't shield your face with it." He saw me doing something, and he would think that we would get the better laugh if we did this, that or the other, and I was very happy for him to tell me because I admired him as a technician.' The chemistry with her on-screen partner, John Comer, was good as well, and over the course of the first series they developed into a formidable comedy duo, her barking at him, him responding with insults, as the trio looked on and reflected that the single life wasn't so bad after all. 'The warm-up man always used to call us the Elizabeth Taylor and Richard Burton of Huddersfield. We weren't sort of friends off the set, but he was a skilled comedian, and that I admired. He wasn't an actor born and bred, but he was very good at acting. He was really a stand-up. He used to write all his lines out in an exercise book, and he learned them like cues. It was never a script to John. He'd have a typewritten script and he'd write it out in longhand into a schoolbook and he learned it like a stand-up. He was perfect, the way he delivered the lines. We got on very well and we worked very well together, I think.'

They returned to London with some hilarious footage, and went into the studios to rehearse the scenes that would be recorded in front of an audience. Gilbert was already an avid admirer of Clarke's writing, but the skill and flair for comedy he was to show under pressure was to leave a lasting impression.

Come Thursday, and we're doing the show on Friday night, and I want rewrites, and they come in at white heat and it was pure gold. Peter Sallis used to say that. 'Comedy pure gold, Jim,' he'd say when I'd come back from the phone and get the rewrites from Roy, and they nearly always were. He'd been used to writing twenty-five minutes for ITV, so the scripts for *Summer Wine* initially were always short. Enid was very funny about that, because I used to go up and see him to discuss script and what not, and she knew that the script needed two full-length scenes to make up the thirty minutes, and she said, 'You let me know, Jim, if Roy's selling you short.' With Roy, I would know that if we rang up, what we would get would certainly be of comparable quality and sometimes the best stuff in the whole script.

The reaction from the studio audiences was better than for the pilot, which would be repeated on 5 November 1973 as a curtain-raiser for the new episodes, beginning a week later at 9.25 p.m., immediately after the BBC evening news.

The opening scene of that first episode, 'Short Back and Palais Glide', immediately made it clear that something special was happening. The dialogue between the three men is crisp and assured, the relationship sharply defined. Bates, Owen and Sallis have relaxed into their roles, and the trio truly feel like old friends with a long, shared history. There is physical humour, as Compo is turned upside down in the library to rid him of evil spirits but, like the pilot, the first series concentrates on dialogue rather than action. In the opening episode, the trio barges its way into a dance in search of the librarian, finding Sid and Ivy on a night out. The second, 'Inventor of the Forty-Foot Ferret', sees Blamire trying to get Compo to attend church, while the third, 'Pâté and Chips', finds them on a day out to a stately home, pondering class as well as politics. The fourth, 'Spring Fever', gives Kathy Staff her first substantial contribution, when she is panicked by Compo cleaning his house before he advertises for a housekeeper to satisfy his romantic longings. The fifth, 'The New Mobile Trio', foreshadows the *Summer Wine* of a few years later, where physical comedy would play an increasingly important part. Clegg buys a car so that the friends can get out more, only to crash it into a tractor and scarper on foot away from the scene. Undeterred, he buys another, and crashes it again into the tractor, to roars of laughter as they leg it away for a second time. The final episode, 'Hail Smiling Morn or Thereabouts', was a wonderful closer as the trio go camping so that Blamire can photograph the sunrise, only to oversleep and miss it. This was comedy to savour, funny, literate and intelligent, that gave its audience credit for having a brain, did not talk down to them, but invited them into a skewed world of hare-brained ideas and little schemes that loomed large in the world of three middle-aged men with time on their hands, who for all their ruminations about sex, religion and politics remained essentially childlike, as Blamire and Compo demonstrated while visiting a photographic exhibition.

Blamire: It's marvellous what you can do with a close-up lens.

Compo: Well hurry up and do it and let's go and get Clegg.

Blamire: You've no cultural interests at all, have you?

Compo: I've got me ferrets.

Blamire: Didn't you take advantage of the army's further education schemes?

Compo: Well, we had this army film show once about social diseases. My mate fainted. Well, it's all a lot of rhubarb this, innit? Look at this – a tatty bit of wood. Who wants to take a photograph of a lump of wood?

Blamire: It's a study in texture.

Compo: I bet that bloke had a dolly bird sitting on there.

Blamire: So what?

Compo: And he clicked his shutter and she fell off.

It's all there, the pretension and determined gentility of Blamire in the face of all the evidence of his own life, the resolute refusal of Compo to be improved and, in the middle, Clegg, who had the best lines of the whole series in the opening episode, when he spelled out what amounted to a manifesto for the battle between wifely dictatorship and male efforts to escape it that would be a mainstay of *Summer Wine*: 'I don't care where you go, this is God's number one area for unpleasant women of strong character. Just what a man needs, it's the toughest training in the world, it breeds a sort of matrimonial guards division, wedlock's finest.'

Gilbert thought it a fine series, and viewers seemed to agree. 'It started with an audience of about five million and the last episode got about ten million, so it had built and built and built.' It was, though, some way short of the BBC's top sitcom, *Dad's Army*, which was pulling in twelve million, and there were those within the corporation's upper ranks who were less than impressed. The Television Weekly Progress Review meeting of 14 November (two days after the first new episode had been aired) was chilly, with comments including, 'not found as funny as the original pilot programme', 'found some of the dialogue difficult to hear', '10 minutes too long', and 'started to meander'. Gilbert, who had been promoted to Head of Comedy, diplomatically replied that, 'it had been the first occasion on which the characters had had an audience and this had undoubtedly had an effect on their style'. The criticism bordered on stinging at the following week's meeting, as it was suggested 'viewers were not yet ready for comedy with so little story to it'. By 12 December the mood among the top brass had thawed a little, and the comments were kinder: 'all along the series seemed to have been improving'. Even so, it was faint praise. The public, though, took a different view. The BBC's audience research report on the first episode found that well over half the sample audience responded 'very favourably', adding: 'Indeed, there was a good deal of appreciative comment, together with evidence to show that both performance and script were mainly rated quite highly.' This was something different in the way of television comedy, they remarked, with '"really true to life characters" and a form of wry humour that was "earthy enough to be convincing" but not offensively vulgar and at the same time appealingly subtle and whimsical.' The audience also liked the scenery, a point picked up by the research report on the last episode. 'Clearly most of the viewers reporting had relished the series, and many felt it was absolutely first class ... The three old cronies were finely characterised and quite exceptionally well cast ... The charming village and countryside in which the series was filmed provided an added pleasure.'

Gilbert prodded, and a second series was commissioned. It had always been one of the BBC's strengths to keep faith with talented writers and promising projects, and it did so now. Clarke said: 'The only good thing in those days was that they would play with a series, they would give it a bit of time. That's gone, of course. It was worth it to them because they got *Summer Wine*. We were a slow starter, *Dad's Army* was a slow starter, but they survived, whereas these days they'd never get past the gate.' This time, there would be a series of seven, and a new producer, Bernard Thompson. Even had he not moved up, Gilbert would have been reluctant to take charge again. 'I never liked doing, if I could help it, second series or third series. What gave me a buzz was getting things off the ground and moving on. What I had a lot to do with was the look of the whole thing, the little figures and the post-synch sound, using film technique really. I felt that the scenery was part of the cast, that was the whole point of going up there. They were totally indivisible. If you think of *Last of the Summer Wine*, you think of what it looked like as well as what the actors were talking about.'

Moving on gave Gilbert the chance to give his assistant a leg up. 'When I gave up directing and took the job of Head of Comedy that was the opportunity to push him forward. He did the next series of *Whatever Happened to the Likely Lads* and then he virtually took over my output. He was an excellent director and a very nice chap. He had been an actor, so he got on very well with the actors, having been one himself.'

Thompson, who died in 1998, had plenty of time to prepare. Industrial action at the BBC delayed production of a whole raft of programmes, and it would be the spring of 1975 before the audience had a fresh taste of *Summer Wine*. Once again, Clarke was coming up with new ideas, two of the best revolving around Nora Batty. The first was to become a talisman for the character – her wrinkled stockings, at which Compo grimaces in disgust for the first time in 'Who's That Dancing with Nora Batty, Then?' The second was a husband for her, not Harold, as referred to in the pilot, but Wally, acme of the henpecked little man whose only release from domestic tyranny was his pigeons. In the café, Sid gave as good as he got; Wally had long been battered into quivering submission. Casting the veteran character comedian Joe Gladwin as Wally was an inspired choice. He was tiny, with a wizened face like a scolded spaniel, whose gargling voice was known to millions from the Hovis bread television adverts. Nobody ever looked so lugubrious. He'd been around comedy since the late 1930s, first as the straight man in a double act and later working with Staff on the ITV sitcom

Nearest and Dearest, starring Hylda Baker. The physical contrast with Staff, who seemed twice his size, was delicious, and Gladwin's mournful exchanges with Owen about Nora added a new dimension to Compo. Clarke had written another unforgettable character, and in doing so brought a symmetry to the cast; his central trio was now bracketed by two feuding couples and the balance added richness to the mix.

There was a new vein of visual humour emerging in Clarke's scripts, as he gradually moved away from long scenes in the library. He said: 'It was a very talking-heads thing at first. There were longish scenes in those days. The funny thing was it had a good critical reaction initially until it started getting popular, then the critics all bailed out. It staggered on with a small but faithful audience.' Thompson embraced the physical humour, and so did the trio. Stand-ins were already being used for some of the long shots, and a stuntman brought in for a scene where Compo was dropped from a bridge into a river. Sallis remembers Thompson's enthusiasm for action. 'I think it was Bernard Thompson who was the most gung ho and hell-raising of our directors. Looking back on it now, I just get the feeling that Bernard was very physical.' That feeling stemmed from almost being drowned in the penultimate episode of the series, 'Ballad for Wind Instruments and Canoe', in which Thompson took everybody north from Holmfirth to a beauty spot at Bolton Abbey, in the Yorkshire Dales, for a sequence in which they paddle a canoe down a river. Sallis couldn't swim, and the River Wharfe is deep, fast flowing and very, very cold even on the sweltering August bank holiday when the filming took place. He began to worry. That brought out the Gurkha officer in Bates, who announced that he was very familiar with canoes, he would take charge, and nobody should worry. The moustache twitched, and they got aboard. Clarke could not have written a more quintessential scene for Blamire than Bates's command. He was in the stern, Owen was in the bows, and Sallis sat shaking in the middle. Thompson called 'Action' and off they went, paddling under a bridge as a crowd of sightseers out for a day by the river looked on. They shot the bridge successfully, and the canoe started to wobble. Then it shuddered. And then it went over. Sallis went under, and somehow managed to put his foot on a hard object which allowed him to lever himself out of the water. It was Bill Owen's head. 'Looking back on it, nobody would have gone out to film a scene in a river which in some places is as deep as this room and in other places as deep as a fireplace,' said Sallis. 'To have us row a canoe and shoot the bridge and come out the other side into this choppy water, there's no wonder the bloody thing turned over and no wonder that I nearly drowned. You couldn't have done that nowadays. It sounds funny, but it wasn't funny at the time.' Sallis lay on the bank, spluttering and giving thanks for being alive, and then one of the sightseers approached, with a question. '"Excuse me, weren't you Samuel Pepys?" And I'm all covered in water and weeds.'

The visual humour in the other episodes was less hazardous. 'Forked Lightning' saw John Comer riding a bicycle to wonderful effect and 'Northern Flying Circus' climaxed with some superb comic business involving a motorbike outside a pub. Another delight was the deepening relationship between Owen and Staff in 'Some Enchanted Evening', where Clarke teased the audience with the possibility of romance between Compo and Nora. He and Thompson had delivered a fine second series that had justified the faith put in *Summer Wine* by the BBC, and the public was starting to latch on. Gilbert said: 'We thought for the second series we'd start at ten million and build, but we started at five again and built up again to ten, and I suppose it wasn't until it became broader and they got up to a lot of visual comedy, that it became more popular.' BBC executives were starting to latch on, too. There was none of the grumbling of eighteen months earlier, the verdict from the Television Weekly Progress Review on the opening episode of 12 March being 'a strong, well-handled and hilarious start to a new episode'. The following month, the meeting was almost ecstatic over the antics on the river that had so shaken Sallis: 'A gem of an episode, beautifully done, one of the best ever.' Audience research agreed, with a report on 5 May delivering a glowing verdict from the public: 'The series had reached or exceeded the best standards of situation comedy, a number declared, the scripts being "original, clean and very funny".' There was not a moment's hesitation in commissioning a third series. Blamire, Clegg and Compo appeared to have a rosy future.

PART TWO

The Vintage Years

❧

CHAPTER 4

That Eccentric Look

MICHAEL BATES HAD every reason to feel happy. Professionally, life had never been better. The years of supporting parts as coppers and soldiers were past; top billing was now his due and he had it in not one, but two shows. As he approached his 55th birthday, he was one of the most popular and visible actors on television, thanks to the growing success of *Last of the Summer Wine* and *It Ain't Half Hot Mum*, another wartime series from the *Dad's Army* writing team of David Croft and Jimmy Perry. It was a lesser effort than the pair's masterpiece, broad stuff about a concert party in the Far East under the command of a bellicose sergeant major, that was packed with stereotypes – camp entertainer, ineffectual officers, endearing little private – but audiences loved it. Bates played Rangi Ram, an Indian bearer who introduced every episode with a monologue, blacking up for the part and jovially dismissing accusations of racism by pointing out that he had been born in India, a response that did nothing to mollify critics but did at least wrong-foot them, if only temporarily. The first series had aired in the winter of 1974, and the second went out the following year, just a few weeks before the second series of *Summer Wine*, which meant Bates was hardly off BBC1 between January and April. Much as he loved Rangi Ram, Blamire had the first claim on his affections, principally because Clarke's writing was in a different league, but also because his background in films had given him a taste for location work. 'You really get into the part with the wind in your hair and the sun on your face,' he told the *Yorkshire Evening Post* in 1977.

> That was one of the things I enjoyed so much about *Last of the Summer Wine*, for the greater part of the series is shot around Holmfirth. They are marvellous people around there, and I believe the series so accurately portrays the Yorkshireman's character. It was at Holmfirth that films were pioneered, and they had their own studios more than fifty years ago. One old chap came up to me while we were filming to remind me of Holmfirth's film history. I will always remember him telling me, 'Do you know, Mr Bates, but for t'climate we'd have been another Hollywood up here.'

Bates was sincere in what he said; he genuinely liked working around the town, and its people liked him in turn for his bluff cheeriness. It was his habit to relax and keep in trim by walking, and the hills gave him plenty of scope to stretch his legs. The show was happy, too. He'd got on well with Bernard Thompson, and he and Owen, having long put their early clash behind them, were rubbing along amicably by staying off politics.

Success and a high profile brought offers of work flooding in, and Bates accepted a pantomime, the first he had played. It was to shatter his happiness. Jimmy Gilbert said: 'It was really due to the success he had in *Summer Wine* that he was offered a job in pantomime at Bristol, and he was having a jousting match. They had these poles and he got struck, and it seemed it triggered off a tumour. He went to the doctor, the hospital, he went to the physio at Bristol City football club to see whether they could do something about it, but it never went away, it got worse and I think it spread then. It was a great shame.' The seriousness of the injury to Bates's groin was not immediately apparent, but it rapidly became clear that he could not cope with the rigours of location work he so loved, being able to walk only with the aid of a stick, and even then with difficulty. One of the strengths of the second series had been Clarke's increasing quota of visual gags, to which the audience had responded with delight; the humour was moving away from three talking heads gathered round the library table, and making ever more use of high jinks set against the Yorkshire countryside. The seven new scripts were more ambitious than ever, and called for some vigorous activity by the trio that could not be covered by the use of stand-ins.

Gilbert was both saddened and concerned. He bought as much time as he could in the hope that Bates would recover sufficiently to appear, but his condition grew steadily worse. 'I had to be very diplomatic about it and point out to him that we would keep it open for him, but I knew that it would only get worse. I had to point out to him, and also to his wife, that it was a very strenuous shoot up in Yorkshire, that you had to be running about doing fun and games on the moors in all weathers and you had to be really fit. Michael didn't want to give it up. No actor would want to give up a successful role in what was obviously going to be a successful series. He was a lovely man, too.'

Bates's loss potentially jeopardised *Summer Wine* at a point when the show was developing into one of the BBC's strongest comedies. Its entire premise was based on the relationship between Blamire, Clegg and Compo, which had deepened and developed throughout the first two series. Audience research made clear that viewers had taken Blamire to their hearts, and Bates's performance as that irascible, stuffy, yet kindly mug had been the best he had delivered on either film or television. Clarke's talent for tailoring scripts to the talents of the actors meant the part fitted like a glove, and Bates relished it. The public had an image of the trio already fixed in their minds, and it included the straight-backed, crabby figure with the moustache and trilby. Bates had been the only choice for the part, and his rapport with Sallis and Owen was growing ever stronger; he sensed that the best was yet to come but, desperate though he was to continue, increasing discomfort forced him to acknowledge that he simply wasn't up to it.

Thompson was moving on, and there would be a new producer for the series, Sydney Lotterby. He recalled: 'When I started, Michael was going to do the programme, and the scripts came in, and I sent one of them to him. There was a seaside scene and Michael had to go into the water with a swimming suit on. After a little while, before we actually started, he rang me and said he didn't think he could do it, which was a disappointment. He pulled out before we started the series.' Bates's only consolation was that he could continue in *It Ain't Half Hot Mum*, where he was able to play Rangi Ram seated as his condition grew worse.

Here was a problem that the new producer did not need. Lotterby was one of the BBC's most experienced comedy men, with a string of hit series to his name, notably *Porridge*, Dick Clement and Ian La Frenais's superb starring vehicle for Ronnie Barker as the old lag Norman Stanley Fletcher. Lotterby would go on to work with Barker again in his other great sitcom, Clarke's *Open All Hours*, as well as producing further fine series including *Yes, Minister*, *Butterflies* and *As Time Goes By*. As he prepared to take on *Summer Wine*, he had enough on his mind without the loss of a leading actor. 'I was asked by Jimmy Gilbert if I'd like to do it, and I must say I was a bit fearful to start off with. The scripts were lovely, but the thing that worried me was that a lot of it was on film and the thing about filming is that it's expensive.'

Using another actor as Blamire was out of the question; there would have to be a rethink, a new third man. The winning formula would remain; he must be the self-proclaimed leader of the trio, a man with an immovable sense of his own destiny, superiority and abilities, and, above all, a barmpot.

Clarke had much to do; the series had been written and now it would have to be substantially changed. Some scenes could be adapted, but there would have to be a new opening episode to explain Blamire's absence and introduce the new man. 'I was worried,' said Clarke. 'Michael had been such an important part of it. If you lose a major player, it forces you to think in new terms, and sometimes it's emergency and desperation.' Out of that worry came his greatest outlandish authority figure, and the impetus that propelled *Summer Wine* into the ranks of classic sitcoms. Once again, the third man would be an ex-soldier but, as with Blamire, no conventional military man; calm, competent command, a keen strategic sense and a knack for expert planning would simply not do, and former corporal Walter 'Foggy' Dewhurst was innocent of those virtues.

Foggy was not even a conventional NCO; he was an ex-corporal signwriter, clinging to the rules, routines and above all the minutiae of army life, an under-achiever who was unshakeably self-delusional over his abilities as both a leader of men and master of unarmed combat. Military manuals were his Bible, parade-ground discipline his comfort; the army had long left him behind, but he was unable to forsake it. For all his insistence that life should be governed by the ascetic code of the warrior, he was essentially a dreamer, by turns stern, petty, parsimonious, nervous, pedantic, cowardly, earnest and wounded. He was a more rounded comic figure than Blamire and, for all his quirks, more believable within the context of a series evolving from its beginnings as a story of three redundant men discussing sex, religion and politics into an increasingly idiosyncratic world of its own. Corporal Dewhurst (or Dewhirst – the spelling would vary over the years when it was glimpsed in written form on screen) with his occasional descents into a trance-like state as he contemplated a new, entirely foolproof, plan of action was a monument to failure, eternally redeemed by his refusal to recognise it and determination to press on with irrepressible optimism.

Gilbert continued to watch over *Summer Wine* like a favourite child and, as he had when the pilot was cast, knew exactly who he wanted for the role, finding his Foggy in Lotterby's own work. 'It was Brian Wilde that took over. I remember thinking at the recasting, because I was then Head of Comedy, that it was plain as a pikestaff that he was the one. He was playing Mr Barrowclough in *Porridge* and everything he did, he did well. He was a quite quirky sort of actor. He was brilliant, but very, very individual. He had a marvellous sort of eccentric look at his characters. He had a very personal view of everything.' Everybody liked the casting. Lotterby said: 'Jimmy cast Brian and said, "What do you think?" and I said, "Excellent idea".' Sallis was even more enthusiastic. 'Jimmy came to my house and he described this person called Foggy Dewhurst, and he said, "Who do you think could play it?" and I said, "Brian Wilde", because I'd already thought it before he'd asked the question. That was a lovely moment. I knew Brian, we'd done a stage play together.'

Clarke didn't know Wilde, but came to admire him immensely. 'I loved him, loved him. I never knew him put a foot wrong, say a line wrong, absolutely spot-on at all times. A lovely character to write; I enjoyed writing Foggy.'

Wilde was an actor of consummate delicacy and subtlety, who cut an extraordinary figure. He was a gangling, bony six-foot-three with a Mr Punch chin, gentle, expressive eyes and an unexpectedly boyish smile of immense charm, a more physical player than Bates, using his height to convey awkwardness, which, allied to a gift for wearing an air of injured pride, gave his performances depth and realism. The eccentric look at characters that Gilbert had noted was mirrored in the personality of this quiet, reserved actor with his passion for cricket and fondness for real ale, who could be fussy, pedantic, stubborn and tetchy. He was the youngest of the trio, forty-nine when the invitation came to join, and like Sallis already had a long and honourable career as an expert supporting actor behind him. Wilde was born in Lancashire, about fifteen miles west of Holmfirth, on 13 June 1927 and grew up in Hertfordshire, before attending RADA at the same time as Sallis. The traditional route into repertory followed, and he started to land parts on radio, proving adept at playing downtrodden characters. Film and television work began to trickle in during the 1950s, and there was an outstanding early performance in the supernatural horror film *Night of the Demon* in 1957 as a simple-minded farmer driven to suicide by fear, which came as his career gathered momentum. Wilde's distinctive looks became increasingly familiar to audiences, even if they were not quite sure of his name, especially on television where his quiet expressiveness and underplaying kept him busy, a long list of credits including *The Avengers*, *Dixon of Dock Green* and *The Troubleshooters*. Bigger roles arrived as the 1960s progressed, mostly in comedy, starting with a part as a harassed personnel manager trying to keep a bunch of maintenance men in order in the sitcom *Room at the Bottom* in 1966. Four years later, he landed another good middle-management role as the depot manager in the comedy series *The Dustbinmen*. Wilde could turn his hand to drama with equal skill, as he demonstrated with his chilling portrayal of Topcliffe the royal executioner in the prestige BBC drama, *Elizabeth R* in 1971. Two years later, he made the leap from familiar face to recognisable name, when he was cast as a soft-hearted prison officer in *Prisoner and Escort* opposite Ronnie Barker, an episode of *Seven of One* that developed into *Porridge*. The role made Wilde; his portrayal of Dudley Barrowclough was masterful. He created a beacon of human kindness and victim of a miserable home life, who in a delicious comic twist escaped into jail for some peace, a man who tried to see the best in the prisoners, but so gullible that he was easily manipulated by Barker's wily Fletcher. Clement and la Frenais readily acknowledged that the excellence of Wilde's performance brought Barrowclough to life more vividly than they could have hoped; he looked as startled as a gazelle, a fidgety bag of nerves whose own decency was his downfall. It was a sharply delineated, deservedly praised characterisation that in middle age propelled Wilde into the front rank of comic actors and set the stage for his most enduring role.

'*Porridge* was going strong and getting very good viewing figures, and I was enjoying playing Barrowclough,' he told Alan Bell.

Then, out of the blue, I received a call from Jimmy Gilbert telling me the shocking news that Michael Bates was dying of cancer. Jimmy then said he wanted the series to continue and felt I would be perfect to play the third man, which Roy Clarke would write as an entirely different character from Blamire. As you can imagine, I had very mixed emotions about the proposition – here was the challenge of creating a new character, Foggy Dewhurst, in a major series, but then there was the risk that he would be unfavourably compared with Blamire. Needless to say, there was a great feeling of sadness for Michael Bates, struck down after only thirteen episodes. Well, a little reluctantly I must admit, I accepted the challenge and in early 1976 travelled to Yorkshire to be in the first episode of that year's series.

Compo and Clegg were filling out as characters, and Foggy was exactly right for a new era. The challenge of losing Bates and introducing Wilde spurred Clarke towards a new, elevated level of comic characterisation; there were nuances in Foggy absent in Blamire. He had all the pompousness and the same misplaced confidence in his superiority and talents, but it was underpinned by a vulnerability and childlike innocence that attracted the sympathy and affection of the audience. In Bates's hands, the essentially abrasive Blamire was immensely likeable; in Wilde's, the unworldly Foggy made the leap into being loveable. Even that first name, the sort of daft moniker bestowed in playgrounds of a certain vintage, invited viewers' warmth. Clarke's admiration for Wilde's realisation of the role would inspire him into some magnificent flights of fancy; Gilbert could not have made a better choice. His arrival, and the chemistry that developed between Compo, Clegg and Foggy would herald the golden years of *Summer Wine*.

Amid sympathy for Bates, there was an enervating sense of a new beginning in the air. New producer, new third man, and seven scripts that were ringing the changes. For the first time, Clarke had written a two-parter, 'The Great Boarding House Bathroom Caper' and 'Cheering Up Gordon', which would take the cast to the coast, and be linked to a third episode, 'Going to Gordon's Wedding'. The writing was expertly judged, not just for the new trio, but for the supporting roles, which were growing as Clarke exploited the potential of his feuding café owners to superb effect, and gave Kathy Staff more opportunities to bounce laughs off Joe Gladwin as well as Owen.

Clarke also put in place another *Summer Wine* staple gag, bestowing on Owen a gift as precious as any finely wrought piece of jewellery in that third series – a matchbox. Its appearance would become one of his most familiar and beloved bits of comic business, an audience favourite that guaranteed a huge laugh every time for the next twenty-three years, a small but iconic part of the show. The matchbox, with its undefined horror within, first appeared in the final episode, 'Isometrics and After', and would become as invaluable to Owen's character as Nora's wrinkled stockings, as he sidled up to an unsuspecting woman, produced it from a pocket, held it up with great solemnity and extended a single grubby finger to push it open with the utmost delicacy, provoking a scream of disgust and the collapse of Compo, and the audience, into hysterics. The changes would be rung now and then, as its contents were shown to a wincing Clegg, or Compo, brow furrowed with concentration, salted it from the café's cruets, but it worked every time. It was not only a great comic device, it added to the audience's warmth towards Compo as the superannuated schoolboy, part of whom had never grown up beyond the stage of wanting to make the girls cry.

The cast were as delighted by the new scripts as Lotterby, recalled Freeman. 'I was very thrilled with them, but then after a bit I got very worried and thought, oh my God, they're so chauvinistic, and of course I was a very earnest young woman in those days and I wasn't sure whether it would be fitting to promote this myth about women. I can remember talking to Enid, Roy's lovely wife, about how awful Ivy was, and she said, "Oh love, Ivy's me."'

Lotterby was already familiar with Wilde's excellence at dialogue, and now he came to appreciate his prowess as a physical comic. A scene at Scarborough, on the Yorkshire coast, when he charged headlong into the sea and hopped about, grinning and whooping with manic cheerfulness as he tried to hide his anguish at the icy coldness, and a round of golf where he flailed at the ball with a club bent hopelessly out of shape were both executed with pinpoint timing and flawless judgment. The combination of his lanky frame being subjected to indignities while his eyes told a tale of desperately trying to hang on to his shredded pride was irresistible. Wilde brought Foggy alive, just as he had done with Barrowclough. Any fears that the loss of Bates would compromise the success of the trio were rapidly vanishing, as everybody pitched in to make the new set-up a success. Most thrilling of all was how the strengths of the leading actors complemented each other. 'Bill really was a comedy man,' said Lotterby. 'He was perhaps of the old comedy school of actors. I think both Brian and Peter were more serious types of actors. Peter was very good. If something didn't work and we sat down and tried to work out how we could make it work, Peter was extremely good at that. He was the one I could go to and say, "Help, Peter, I need a hand here."' Back in London, the studio recordings went well, and the series was ready to go out, beginning with 'The Man from Oswestry', which would introduce Foggy Dewhurst.

Lotterby opened the episode according to Gilbert's template, his camera panning over Holmfirth's rooftops with the hills in the background, before moving down to the café, where Compo finds the door locked and starts banging it with his hip. Sid opens up, and it's time to tackle the subject of Blamire.

Sid: I thought to myself, I've been jack-knifed into by some huge articulated vehicle. Imagine my surprise when I opened up and found it was just some undersized scruffy little twit.

Compo: I thought tha'd be open.

Sid: Well, that's a natural assumption if you ignore the drawn blinds and a forty-foot sign that says closed.

COMPO SITS DOWN AND OPENS CIGARETTE TIN.

Compo: It's times like this when I'm getting low on fags I miss old Cyril Blamire.

Sid: Have you heard from him?

Compo: Not a postcard.

Sid: Listen, it'd be more appropriate if he sent thee a cigarette card.

Compo: It was just a game, I used to cadge his fags, he used to make a fuss, he didn't really mind, he knew he could always have one of mine.

Sid: Very true, provided he had a pin to hold it with. Is he going to marry this woman?

Compo: I wouldn't be surprised, he were off like a shot when he heard she'd become a widow.

Sid: I never thought I'd hear the day when you'd admit to missing Cyril Blamire.

Compo: Well, it's so quiet. There's no one to shout at me any more. It's been weeks since I've had a right rollocking. We used to argue every day, you miss things like that.

Sid: You ever thought of getting married?

Compo: That's not funny.

Owen is regretful and thoughtful as he talks about the friend who has gone off to marry, but he is bested by Sallis, who arrives with a letter from Blamire telling them what he is up to in Wales and introducing Foggy, who will be arriving on the eleven o'clock bus. Sallis captures Bates's brisk delivery to perfection as he reads from the letter.

Clegg: Oswestry, Saturday. Dear all, weather remains mixed, wind variable. By the way, if you should see my former landlady, please inquire if the blue socks are back yet from the laundry. I have acquired decent accommodation in one of the better residential areas. Several persons of good standing are eager to propose me for membership of the Conservative Club.

Compo: The poor demented capitalists!

Clegg: The social circle is grateful for new blood now that the barracks are closing. It's very sad to see this once proud military establishment guarded now by this person with dandruff and an apparently Welsh-speaking Alsatian from Securicor.

In those few deft lines, Clarke has re-located Blamire and now builds up Foggy's appearance.

Clegg: You'll be interested to hear that among the last few people to be employed at the barracks was old Foggy Dewhurst. It says here, you remember Foggy Dewhurst.

Compo: I do. He were always sick every playtime at school. He were in the Specials before he went into the army. Great long, gormless streak from Arnold Crescent. His mother wore brown boots. He were always on traffic duty, blue uniform, white flares, he looked like a pencil with a rubber on the end.

Clegg: I thought he was dead. I had this feeling that he'd either died or something unspeakable had happened to him, but I never imagined anything as morbid as this.

Sid: What's that?

Clegg: Well, he's been in Wales all this time. Cyril says, Foggy has been employed at the barracks here in a civilian capacity since he retired from the army. We were stationed here together for several months in 1947. As you can imagine, he was delighted to see me, and we held a small, but thoroughly depressing reunion. So many of the old faces are gone, and it gave us no comfort to recognise thanks to this Labour government, when the Russians finally come, practically all we shall have left to throw at them is one Welsh-speaking Alsatian, on top of which, he's a reedy tenor, who bursts into song at the slightest provocation. Oh no, that's the guard, I thought he meant the Alsatian. Old Foggy's returning home, to an empty house in Arnold Crescent, with all his relatives passed on or moved away. It would be a friendly gesture if you could meet him and show him that comradeship which will help him over this difficult transitional period. It is with confidence that I commend to your care old Foggy Dewhurst, one of the finest corporal signwriters with whom it's ever been my privilege to serve. A master of the Gothic script, and a keen leader of men.

The great long gormless streak duly arrives, and it is a marvellous entrance. The warrior is back at war, this time with a bus conductor who throws his bags off, as Foggy bristles. The costume of cap, military-style field jacket with multiple pockets, regimental tie and scarf, highly polished shoes and cane speak volumes about the character as the man of action ready for any eventuality. His opening lines capture the spirit of this befuddled military reject: 'Clegg? Simmonite? Take that bag will you? Now keep your eye on that, it's a lifetime collection of army office door signs, narrow format.'

Just as during 'Of Funerals and Fish', the studio audience takes some time to attune itself to the new character, as he goes into the bus station and tinkers with his luggage. Clegg scored the best laughs as he regards Foggy with wonderment when he briefly sinks into a trance-like state: 'He's doing all right. You get depressed sometimes and begin to believe that there aren't any old-fashioned idiots left. And then, out of the blue, comes a genuine, fourteen-carat, gilt-edged barmpot like this.'

Only when the trio move on to a pub did the audience really begin laughing at Foggy as he flies into a rage with Compo and raises his fist: 'Don't you provoke me like that. I'm all right now, it's just I get these murderous tempers, but no, on the whole, you shouldn't say anything to me you couldn't say to John Wayne.'

Wilde, wide-eyed and panicking, displays his gift for clowning in the final scene as his scarf becomes wound round the wheel of the cart on which he, Compo and Clegg are hauling his luggage, dragging him down a hill. It is a wonderful introduction of the new third man, and serves notice of the glories to come, not least because the tempo of the show has risen by several notches, thanks to Wilde's extraordinarily animated performance; he is never still except when in a trance. Foggy is an overwound clockwork toy of a man, a bundle of nervous energy, emphatically jabbing a hand to make his point, eyes darting, thoughts flashing across his face, endlessly bombarded by ideas and impulses to action. Suddenly, *Summer Wine* has new impetus.

It was the best series yet, and not just because of the writing for the trio; Clarke gives full rein to his take on domestic disharmony in a priceless exchange for a frustrated Ivy and a resigned Sid, as they sit in deckchairs.

IVY HITS SID WITH MAGAZINE AS HE DOZES

Sid: What's up?

Ivy: Talk to me.

Sid: What?

Ivy: You never talk to me, not even when we, well, you know … not even when we make love.

Sid: There's not much to talk about, the rate we go at it. You still do it as if your mother's watching.

Ivy: It's you, you're not thoughtful enough.

Sid: Thoughtful enough? I do far more thinking about it than actually getting it.

Ivy: That's your fault, you should … you should try and rouse me more.

Sid: Rouse you more? You've been playing roasting hell with me all day as it is.

Ivy: Will you shut up shouting, that's all you're good at, barging in with two feet. It's the same when you get that look in your eye. I always know when you feel like messing about.

Sid: Messing about, that's a lovely way of putting it, isn't it? That puts it on a high spiritual plane, doesn't it?

Ivy: Oh, where do you put it with your smart sophisticated romantic approaches? I get a smack across the backside, a dig with your elbow, one boozy wink and that's supposed to throw my senses in a whirl.

Sid: Well, it's a waste of time trying it gentle. Do you remember the last time I decided to give you a squeeze in bed?

Ivy: Will you keep your voice down?

Sid: Not quite, but something very similar.

Nobody can predict with certainty when a series will come of age, when the elements find an ideal balance and the comedy attains a weightless, magical quality, but it was clear that this had happened with the introduction of Foggy. Lotterby said: 'The relationship between Brian and the other two proved to be a little bit greater, I think, than perhaps it had been with Michael. Roy had written a stronger character for him, and that helped make the audience enjoy it more. The other characters, Nora, Wally, Sid, Ivy, seemed to fit in with the whole thing, and Roy seemed to find his feet somehow. I think suddenly it all worked better. Roy got his second wind.'

The series went down well with audiences, who took to Foggy, with viewing figures again hovering around the ten million mark. One viewer, though, watched with sadness. Michael Bates saw 'The Man from Oswestry' at his home in Twickenham when it was broadcast on 27 October 1976. 'When I had to be written out of the series because of this damned leg, in the first programme they read a letter supposed to be from me and introducing Foggy. I must admit that when I saw the programme and heard the letter, I had tears in my eyes,' he confessed to the *Yorkshire Evening Post*. A few months later, he would be back in Yorkshire for the last time, only a few miles from Holmfirth, appearing in pantomime in Bradford as the Emperor in *Aladdin*. A stroll in the hills was by now completely beyond him; he was able to accept the role only because he was carried on and off stage in a litter. As 1977 wore on, he defied increasing pain to push himself through a last series of *It Ain't Half Hot Mum*, and then backed out of the limelight. Among his visitors towards the end was Bill Owen. The man whose expert comic acting had been such an important factor in the success of the fledgling *Last of the Summer Wine* died in the Royal Marsden Hospital on 11 January 1978. He was only fifty-seven.

There were unmistakeable signs that *Summer Wine* was capturing the imagination of viewers, not least the increasing attention paid to its most immediately identifiable figure. The year of that third series had been gratifying for Owen. He had been awarded the MBE for services to the National Association of Boys Clubs, and not long after would be lured to Trafalgar Square in full Compo get-up by Lotterby, ostensibly to record a promotional film to sell *Summer Wine* overseas, only to be ambushed by Eamonn Andrews disguised as a policeman and whisked off to a studio where he was the subject of *This Is Your Life*. Both accolades were acknowledgements that he was becoming one of the most popular figures on television thanks to the scruffy, aged urchin created by Clarke. It was starting to feel like the best of the Rank years all over again; he was in demand for profiles and interviews, and adept at playing the publicity game, which he invariably used for the show's benefit. Owen had been taught some hard lessons by his ups and downs, and was shrewd enough to know that without *Summer Wine* his work for the Boys Club movement might have gone unrecognised; however good his performances in *In Celebration* or *Caste* had been, his standing with the public depended on the woolly hat and wellies. He basked in the attention, and gave thanks for the turn in his fortunes that brought stardom knocking at his door for a second time as he approached pensionable age. His eagerness for success burned as brightly at sixty as it had when he had agreed to change his name so it could fit on a marquee. The hook for much of the coverage was the gulf between the elegant Owen and the decrepit Compo, a total transformation that was testament to his skill as an actor. The short, incorrigible character that slouched and shrugged, kicked at stones and hopped on and off the kerb was a world away from the straight-backed bantam of a man who stepped out in good tailoring, never dreaming of leaving his front door unless immaculate. The mane of hair he kept all his life was always beautifully coiffed, his suits of the finest cloth and cut, the tie knotted dead centre, the cuffs shot from the sleeves to perfection, the trilby he wore as he boarded the train north from Kings Cross at exactly the right natty angle. The public who approached for autographs during breaks in location filming could be disconcerted to find Compo in mucky wellies and ripped jacket smoking a cigarette with a holder and thanking them for their interest not with thee's and tha's but in beautifully modulated Queen's English delivered in firm tones trained to be audible in the back row of the gods in a packed house. There was none of Compo's wonderment in his manner, either. Owen was assertive and direct, brisk and self-confident.

'He was always beautifully turned out, always well dressed, quite snappy, wearing very well-cut suits,' recalled Gilbert. 'After he played Compo, he made certain he looked straight out of the bandbox.' Alan Bell found the same refusal to take any trace of the character beyond the confines of the set. 'He had this strange thing. When we finished filming a scene, say at eleven in the morning, and he wouldn't be wanted until three in the afternoon, I'd say, "Bill, do you want to go off home?" "Yes, fine," and he'd take off all this costume and put his normal day clothes on, and I'd say, "Why don't you keep them on, you're coming straight back?" and he'd say, "I'm not leaving the set dressed as Compo."' Sallis spent more than a quarter of a century admiring how the actor submerged all trace of himself: 'I remember in particular one evening, we were on location, and Bill and I were having supper and thinking while we were chatting – he did most of the talking – "This guy's poles away from the character he plays." I couldn't find anything that they had in common. He was a true, real character actor.'

Owen was as fastidious about Compo's appearance as he was about his own. The overall look had been worked out over lunch with Gilbert, Sallis and Bates when they were discussing the pilot in 1972, and Owen steadily refined it over the years until it arrived at the definitive image that stuck in the public's mind. Compared to what it became, Compo's outfit was initially disreputable but just about salvageable; his jacket was scruffy but free of holes, his trousers shabby but not yet disgraceful. Being unshaven was a starting point, and an irritation to the well-groomed Owen, as he told the *Mail on Sunday* in 1985. 'The stubble is kept trimmed with an electric razor so it's always the same length. It feels like having a dirty face all the time. I'm always glad to get rid of it.' As time passed, pullovers were knitted for Compo to patterns that specified where gaping holes should be, and he got a new-old outfit of tailor-made scruffy jackets with bespoke tears in the cloth. He let the *Yorkshire Evening Post* in on the secret in 1985: 'They are deliberately made badly – which upsets the tailor who does them – and then they have holes cut in them. The thing is though that they all have to look the same, both for me and my stunt stand-in, so you can't just go out and buy one from a junk shop.' The dark-green woolly hat of the first three series would go, to be replaced by one of three light-green knitted models sent in by an elderly fan of the series. Owen thought the colour more suited to the character and found the hand-made hats more comfortable to wear. A length of string originally kept the trousers up, later to be replaced by a piece of window sash cord Owen had cut to measure. The tie, which was worn around his collarless neck, would be supplanted by a kerchief. The wellies, of course, remained throughout, though they were broken in by a dresser before Owen put them on. Sallis noted with interest how completely he got into character when the outfit went on and he assumed the childlike mantle of Compo with more than a touch of the Method actor. 'Bill was a Stanislavskyite, although he probably didn't admit to it. He would go about in costume with his pockets full of matchboxes and cigarette ends and old pennies. I've seen him do it on location, because everybody used to go and watch him, and with the children, he was very good with them, chatting and showing them his little bits of this and that. It came naturally to him, whereas I was quite different. I don't mean that I didn't like children, but I've never been very good with them, I didn't know what to say to them, but Bill did.'

It was that childlike quality of Compo that won the nation's hearts – and was soon to win *Summer Wine* a new audience – and Owen had an extraordinary ability to evoke the spirit of a naughty schoolboy. Hands stuck in pockets, whistling between his teeth, he did become, as he put it, 'Just William with a pension book'. 'He's a cheeky little sod for a start,' he reflected in 1994 to the *Yorkshire Post*, 'and he's never quite grown up. He isn't aware of it – the other two are, but they've sort of given up. If he walks along a street and there's a kerb, he'll walk with one foot in the gutter. If he's walking along a country lane, then he'll walk on the stone wall, and everything is spontaneous with Compo. He lives for that minute.' Acting the aged schoolboy made some serious physical demands on Owen, and he met them, even into old age. He did walk along the walls and fall off gates and stand on his head; he did climb ladders on to the roofs of buildings, and get up trees, and remained remarkably game into his eighties, though as the years passed increasing use was made of body doubles and stuntmen as Clarke's scripts demanded more visual comedy. Whatever was asked of him, he delivered, even if he ritually grumbled about doing it. 'Bill had his problems,' said Lotterby. 'He wasn't a particularly fit man, and in nearly all the programmes, he had to come a cropper. He had to fall off a bicycle, or fall in the water. It was always Bill.' That suited Sallis and Wilde, who were happy to let him get on with it. 'I think that Brian and I would stand back and allow him to do his turn, safe in the knowledge that he was going to be all right and we wouldn't have to do it,' said Sallis.

Doing it would become increasingly necessary over the next two series. Seventeen episodes would be spread over 1977–79, including a first Christmas special, a sure sign that it was becoming an audience favourite. The quotient of visual humour was growing, but the dialogue Clarke was giving his trio was becoming ever funnier. Having seen Wilde inhabit the role of Foggy, Clarke homed in on the actor's qualities and speech patterns to create a masterful portrait of lofty ideals and ambitions that were doomed to fail because of congenital incompetence. Wilde once remarked that the difference between his two classic sitcom characters was that Barrowclough knew he was a failure, but Foggy did not, and ex-Corporal Dewhurst would rage against the fates that conspired against him: 'God knows I have tried to raise the tone of our activities. Who was it introduced you to astronomy? Right? Who was it brought you out here in the hills one night and taught you how to navigate by the stars? And who had to get a taxi back from Cleckheaton?'

'I was very pleased that Foggy became such a popular character and, I must say, I enjoyed playing him very much,' said Wilde. It showed. There was a joyousness about these episodes that communicated itself to viewers, more and more of whom were tuning in. The figures were now hitting the twelve million mark, and Wilde believed that one reason was that the humour of the trio was universal. 'You can see people like them everywhere,' he told the *Sun* in 1979. 'Perhaps they haven't been as successful as they would have wished, but they are optimists, and when they wake up each morning, they give thanks that they are alive.' He was right; there was something life-affirming about their refusal to bow to advancing years. The blend between Compo, Clegg and Foggy was much more balanced than it had been with Blamire; any combination of two could laugh at the third; any one of the three could drive the humour, even if it was Compo taking most of the falls.

The fourth series, which started in November 1977, was still going out at 9.25 p.m., and the 1978 Christmas special, which went out on Boxing Day, was even later, at 10.40 p.m. As 1979 dawned, *Summer Wine* was to receive two strokes of luck that would transform it into a national sensation.

The first was as a consequence of Kathy Staff accepting another role to fill the months when she was not playing Nora Batty. She was cast as cook Doris Luke in *Crossroads*, the ITV soap opera set in a Midlands motel that was long the butt of jokes about its shaky scenery and even shakier acting. Staff shrugged off the sniping and got on with the job, quickly becoming one of the soap's most popular characters, and that brought her to the attention of one of the country's best-loved entertainers, Terry Wogan, host of BBC Radio 2's breakfast show. Wogan had a rare gift for engaging his audience and the dialogue between them was often about what was on the box. On air one morning, he announced, 'Do you know, I think Nora Batty is Doris Luke's sister.' He had seven and a half million listeners, and the letters started to pour in. Morning after morning, the talk would be about Nora or Doris, and when it was about Nora, it would stray on to Compo. It was priceless publicity for both Staff and *Summer Wine*, driving viewers towards the 1977 episodes that were currently being repeated. Among Wogan's listeners were those who had not seen the programme before, and when they switched on to see what all the banter was about, they liked it.

An even bigger favour was done for the show by industrial trouble at ITV that summer. What started out as a local dispute between Thames TV and electricians over a pay deal quickly escalated into an almighty row with technicians across the entire network, culminating in an all-out strike that saw ITV shut down on 10 August. The screen was blank. Even Doris Luke was silenced. The strike would drag on for eleven long weeks until 24 October, costing an estimated £100m in lost advertising revenue, an astronomical sum for the time, and even when it was over ITV was crippled for months afterwards because its production of new programmes had been so badly disrupted.

BBC bosses were gleeful. Their two channels were the only ones with anything for the public to watch, and they moved quickly to capitalise on that, rescheduling programmes to take advantage of the peak slots when there would be no opposition. Mindful of the publicity it was getting from Wogan – who had a family audience – one of the shows moved was *Summer Wine*, brought forward from 9.25 p.m. to 8.30 p.m. on Tuesdays, beginning on 18 September. For the first time, the show would air in a slot where children would still be up to see it, and as the strike dragged on, six of the seven episodes would be broadcast with no opposition from the other side. The earlier scheduling involved Clarke making a minor change. He put the blue pencil through the word 'bloody'. Real swear words – however mild by the standards of what would soon be routinely heard on television – weren't right for family viewing. 'It was a bit harder in the early days,' Clarke reflected, 'but you're shaped by your audience.' From now on, any oaths would be stylised. 'It softened up,' said Jane Freeman. 'I used to charge out of the kitchen shouting, "What the bloody hell's going on in here?" and now it's, "What the blood and stomach pills?"'

Clarke was producing funnier scripts by the year. There were more visual gags than ever in the fifth series, which gave younger viewers plenty to laugh at, as well as the wry observational dialogue that their parents so loved. It got off to an outstanding start with 'Full Steam Behind', in which the trio visit a preserved steam railway and get mixed up with a runaway locomotive. It was the most ambitious episode yet, with the most location footage, shot at the Keighley and Worth Valley Railway in Yorkshire. The episode was a personal favourite of both Sallis and Wilde, brilliantly funny from first to last. Clarke had also written a pair of two-parters, 'The Flag and Its Snags' / 'The Flag and Further Snags', and 'Here We Go into the Wild Blue Yonder' / 'Here We Go Again into the Wild Blue Yonder'. The first pairing saw Foggy trying to put a flagpole up on a hill, the second him trying to launch Compo into flight on a hang-glider built by Wally Batty that resembled a giant pigeon. The four episodes were gloriously daft and the studio audiences shrieked with laughter. So did the families at home, who sent viewing figures soaring up to the twenty million mark, unexpectedly high even in the face of no opposition. What was to come next, with ITV back on the air, would prove that it was no flash in the pan.

CHAPTER 5

Mr Average

IT HAD BEEN gruelling on those hills that past summer. The upland fells of the Pennines and the cobbled alleyways of the town looked ravishing on screen, but were exhausting to film in. 'There isn't a level bit of ground anywhere,' Sydney Lotterby would complain, and the technical difficulties and exertion that caused took its toll on cast and crew alike, especially during the series just broadcast, with all its exteriors. Compo dressed as a giant pigeon charging down a hill had been a hoot for the audience, but draining for those involved. 'There comes a time when you think, I can't put anything more into this,' said Lotterby, who had invested enormous effort into his twenty-four episodes, giving the series sterling service, not only choreographing its brightest moments so far, but coping with the challenge of losing a leading actor and ushering in a new era with tremendous assurance. *Summer Wine* had blossomed into one of the BBC's best and most popular programmes on his watch, but now he was ready for a break. He would, though, still be working with Clarke, on the second series of *Open All Hours*, back after a five-year hiatus, and reuniting Lotterby with Ronnie Barker, to which he was very much looking forward.

The man who replaced him would play a unique role in the story of the world's longest-running comedy series, shaping, adapting and renewing it over the course of 28 years and 250 episodes. He would have to cope with death, conflict, jealousy, grief and even mental illness at the heart of his company; nurse the infirm and old through the twilight of their careers; argue for his show and its audience in the face of indifference from his masters; and innovate to point the way for other series. Above all, he would work tirelessly to keep it fresh while retaining all the charm and character that made it such an audience favourite. Millions at home never missed his programme, but the most devoted fan of them all was behind the camera planning his shots, spending so much time roaming the Pennine landscape in search of locations that he came to know it better than those who lived there.

Alan James William Bell was a comedy man through and through, and a BBC comedy man at that; one of a breed who had defined a golden age of sitcoms thanks to their commitment to quality, attention to detail and high production values. Bell had worked with comedy royalty, being gratified to find that Morecambe and Wise put sufficient trust in his judgement to tell them if a routine wasn't working, and would be requested by Spike Milligan. He came to *Summer Wine* not quite halfway through a career with the BBC that spanned more than fifty years, taking over when he was not yet forty, backing his own instincts about the best way to do it and severely ruffling some feathers in the process. 'I always say that I am Mr Average,' said Bell. 'If I don't like something, ten to one nobody else will. I worked on Morecambe and Wise years ago, and Eric said to Johnny Speight, the writer of *Till Death Us Do Part*, "How's the show in the studio tonight?" and he said, "I always think it's good, but they won't tell me until after the show, and if they think it's bad they say, I told you so." Eric said, "We always used to have that problem until he joined," and that's me, "And if he doesn't like it, we cut it."'

Bell had risen through the ranks of the BBC since joining in 1958, showing rushes in preview theatres before becoming a film editor. Film had fascinated him since he had made his own amateur movies as a child, and as his career progressed he got the chance to indulge his passion. It was while working as assistant director on

The Morecambe and Wise Show at the dawn of the duo's glory years as the 60s turned into the 70s that he persuaded Eric and Ernie to let him make filmed inserts. They were initially reluctant because their experience of movie-making in a couple of big-screen outings had not been happy, but went ahead and were delighted at how easy Bell made it for them. From there, it was on to directing the children's programme *Crackerjack*, for which Bell wrote and filmed more than fifty short silent comedies featuring the resident comedians Don MacLean and Peter Glaze, and then in 1979 he got the call for two episodes of the popular and critically successful Michael Palin series *Ripping Yarns*, his spoof of the stiff-upper-lip Boys' Own-style adventure. It was all on film, and the credit, 'Directed by Alan J. W. Bell', appeared on 'Whinfrey's Last Case' and 'Golden Gordon', which were among the funniest of the series. It won Bell a Bafta for best light entertainment programme, and that success led to him taking charge of *The Hitch-Hiker's Guide to the Galaxy*, Douglas Adams's own adaptation of his cult radio series, and ultimately, the call to the hills of Yorkshire.

There would be no new series during 1980 because of Clarke's commitment to his stammering shopkeeper, but the BBC kept the public's appetite for Compo, Clegg and Foggy whetted with repeats of the fourth series, with one episode, the 1978 Christmas special, 'Small Tune on a Penny Wassail', being the most-watched programme of the week. The trio would be back at Christmas 1981 with a special to kick off a series of eight. The then Head of Comedy, John Howard Davies, called Bell in and asked him to take over. Bell was delighted. 'I had always been a fan of the series, it always seemed so fresh. The comedy played outdoors, not in the living room, it got out into the countryside.' Oddly, Bell had just returned from Holmfirth, where he had been filming a segment for a Terry Wogan series called *You Must Be Joking* about the town's early film industry.

Bell felt that the dice were loaded in his favour, partially because of the mass audience that had discovered the series during the ITV strike, but especially because of the on-screen rapport between the leading men. 'Bill, Peter and Brian were the classic trio. Brian was a superb actor, underplayed everything. You knew what Brian was thinking. He didn't have to say a word, just look at him and you knew what he was thinking in response to Bill, that sufferance. And all the time he was a bigger fool than any of them, that was the great thing about the character. A man totally guided by his self-belief.' He took the three of them to lunch before they departed for Yorkshire. It was a convivial occasion, and Bell's spirits were high. They soared when the scripts started to come in from Clarke. If the 1979 series had been a corker, this was even better. From the first word to the last, it sparkled; this was the best comic writing Bell had ever seen. The omens were good, and his luck held when he arrived in Yorkshire; Owen had warned him over lunch about the travails of the weather, the lost days, the howling wind, the torrential rain, the bitter cold, but when Bell got to Holmfirth the sun was shining and kept on doing so for practically the entire shoot, which suited his eye for film-making. His was going to be a *Last of the Summer Wine* bathed in sunlight and revelling in the glorious scenery. Nine years before, Jimmy Gilbert, inspired by filming in Australia, had determined to open the comedy up by deploying the scenery. Bell would go a stage further and make the audience feel that they could almost catch the scent of the heather as his camera roved lovingly over the landscape and the trio played against ever-wider vistas.

'As far as I was concerned it was like winning the lottery. I loved *Summer Wine* and I couldn't believe it had been given to me to do. I've always had a real love of film-making, not studio, and I watched some of the programmes when I took over just to make sure I was keeping the style. It was done TV-style and there was a heck of a lot of "everybody says a line on close-up", and that always offends me because that comes from the days when televisions had nine-inch screens. I think it was good casting to put me in, I have to say. I think I was right for it, being a fan, and being filmic, because it means that beautiful scenery is put on the television.'

The sun may have been shining overhead, but there was a chill in the air, because of Wilde, whose cantankerous streak was emerging. Bell was working like a film director, laying tracks and moving the camera on them, requiring the actors to hit precisely placed marks on the ground and walk into close-up.

Wilde was scathing about the new boy, and stiff-necked in his disapproval of his working methods. 'We were told that he had done some very good work and would be good for the series. This was Alan J. W. Bell, he was much younger than Sydney and he came in with an enormous amount of enthusiasm, but not much care for the comfort of the actors. And he had a directing style that was alien to our previous way of working. Whereas we used to rehearse the scene with the director who would then shoot it to cover the way it had evolved, Alan would have very firm ideas of how the scenes would be played for his camera, and we would have to hit marks as the shots progressed. And he had the habit of using a camera dolly on tracks – all of which had to be laid over the rough hillside locations, while we stood around waiting.' Sallis and Owen – whose experience of hitting marks during film-making went all the way back to his Rank days – were much more relaxed about Bell, and growing tensions between the stars meant they were hardly likely to side with Wilde.

Despite Wilde's discomfiture, his performances were excellent, the filming sped along and Bell got on well with the rest of the cast. 'Every episode was a gem, and I really thoroughly enjoyed it, and I came back with these wonderful pictures from Yorkshire and other people couldn't believe that I'd had such good luck.'

Good fortune again favoured Bell when he needed an actor to deliver one line as a man stranded on a roof by Foggy commandeering his ladder in 'In the Service of Humanity'. Into the audition walked a part-time actor called Gordon Wharmby, from Manchester. He'd done bits and pieces on stage and television, but his real job was as a painter and decorator. Bell liked him and asked for a reading of a much more substantial part, as an oil-splattered, car-mad mechanic who builds a vehicle that Compo tries to drive to impress Nora in an episode called 'Car and Garter'.

'He read it brilliantly, it was funny. I'd seen an actor who was very good, but Gordon was one hundred per cent real,' said Bell, who decided to probe a little deeper, only to get a response that could have been scripted by Clarke:

I said, 'How good would you say you are?' and he said, 'Oh great. I can do a semi-detached, strip all the wallpaper ...' and I said, 'No, not as a decorator, as an actor,' and he said, 'Oh fine, I've done Oldham Rep and little bits in *Coronation Street*, not much, just one line.' I thought, fine, this guy's good, but how can I give a major guest part to a painter and decorator, so I went away and wrestled with it and brought him down again, just to make sure I hadn't made a mistake. He read it again, brilliant, and I said, 'How would you assess yourself, because I want someone who's not going to let me down.' 'I've never let anyone down in my life,' he says. 'Last weekend I did a flat. Took all the wallpaper off, two coats of paint ...' and I said, 'Gordon, I'm talking about this script.' I wrestled with it and eventually I thought, I'm going to cast him. And he was great on the filming, right first time, a wonderful character. And he got to the audience on the Sunday, brilliant, nothing to worry about. Spot on. And he was so good that Roy brought him back.

Wharmby would make the role of Wesley his own, and grow into one of the show's most popular characters, though at the price of undergoing a harrowing personal crisis along the way.

As the studio filming neared, Bell was taken aback to be approached by Owen and Sallis, who, despite the evidence of successively more successful series, still worried about the studio audiences. 'Peter and Bill came to me before we started filming and said, "Can you get the BBC to not have an audience?" and I asked why not and they said, "They don't really understand it, the laughter isn't as good as it should be, and it's an embarrassment." What they meant was that really funny lines weren't getting big laughs because the audience hadn't got into it, and I said, "I don't think the BBC would ever let us do anything without laughter and an audience there because it helps people at home enjoy it."' Bell was shrewd enough to realise that the ITV blackout had created a whole new viewing public for *Summer Wine*. 'When I took over the series, I inherited a new audience and every single seat in Television Centre Studio 3 was taken, there wasn't one empty seat, and the response was marvellous.' Owen and Sallis quickly cottoned on. 'When we did the first episode in the studio, they hastily withdrew their request because the audience were with every line, every word, because they understood it because of that ITV strike. We shall ever be grateful to the technicians at ITV.'

With all the episodes in the can, Bell had another stroke of luck when he bumped into the Controller of BBC1, Alan Hart, in a lift. 'We knew each other only from nodding in the corridor, and he asked what I was doing and I said, "I've just finished doing *Last of the Summer Wine*," and he told me it was his wife's favourite programme. And I said: "Would you ask your wife to ask the Controller to put the Christmas show out at seven o'clock on Christmas Day, because it'll beat everybody else, it's so good," and he laughed and said, "I'll have a word with her." And it went out at seven o'clock on Christmas night and emotionally it was the right programme, it's a family programme.'

The episode was 'Whoops' and it was something special. There was a dollop of visual humour, but it was the dialogue that mattered as the trio sought to recapture their schooldays. The air was sweet with reminiscence, as Clarke gave Clegg the chance to reflect on another aspect of his youth:

Compo: You've got to get some big excitement in your life.

Clegg: I don't think I've had any big excitement in my life.

Foggy: Come on, you must have had some big excitements.

Clegg: Yes, I tell a lie, there was that time on my honeymoon.

Compo: Well, go on.

Clegg: We met this couple from Stoke-on-Trent.

Compo: Eh! Stoke ...

Foggy: ... on Trent.

Clegg: We made a round of bridge as a foursome, the two women got on well, they used to get their heads together swapping notes, and I was left with him. He seemed to be all right except for a bit of a tendency to be over-cheerful.

Compo: So where was the big excitement?

Clegg: Well, it was him. We hadn't known him twelve hours and he started doing Al Jolson impressions. Couple of drinks down him and wallop, top of his voice, Al Jolson impressions. Now that was exciting.

Compo: Exciting?

Clegg: Well, it was to me. I didn't know where to hide, and I was on my honeymoon, remember. My nerves were all raw anyway.

Foggy: Nasty.

Clegg: I had this book in a plain cover that I'd been recommended to read, the secrets of marital harmony. I'd never seen anything like it in my life. I thought all I had to do was take her a cup of tea in the morning, and right in the middle of that, there's this herbert doing his Al Jolson impressions. To this day, I can't look at an illustrated medical book without thinking of Al Jolson.

The trio move on to a school and think back to their childhoods as they watch the children playing:

Compo: Them was the days, we knew how to enjoy ourselves in them days.

Clegg: Long-distance yo-yo.

Foggy: Freestyle spitting.

Compo: We did better than that.

Foggy: Like what?

Compo: Popping frogs down girls' blouses.

Foggy: Is there much scope, do you think, at your age for popping frogs down ladies' blouses?

Compo: Well, better than carol singing.

Clegg: I never liked handling the things.

Compo: They're all right is frogs, they won't harm thee.

Clegg: I don't mean frogs, it's the ladies.

Compo: You great pair of jessies. Oh well, all right, I suppose there is something we can do doesn't involve the ladies.

Foggy: I used to enjoy the cut and thrust of a really competitive game of marbles.

COMPO AND CLEGG GROAN

Foggy: All right then, short and shapeless, what do you suggest?

Compo: When did we last walk on our hands, shin up a drainpipe, climb up a lamppost, jump off a bus when it was still moving? We've let all that slide.

And that's exactly what they do, stand on their hands and jump off a moving bus before seeking out their old friends for a Christmas drink, only to find that the passing years have robbed them of their sense of fun. Undaunted, they press on and their pals recapture enough of their youthful spirit to climb lampposts and get stuck, while Compo, Clegg and Foggy demonstrate their refusal to grow old by jumping off a bus. It was an especially big-hearted episode, wistful without being sentimental, deliciously quirky, and hilarious. Bell closed the programme with a flourish as the Holmfirth Choral Society performed Clarke's lyrics over the closing credits, which underlined the warmth of the half-hour that had been so funny. 'Whoops' was the highlight of that Christmas Day's television, but the BBC thought its really big hit of the season would come the following day with the premiere of *Gone with the Wind*, the 1939 romantic blockbuster starring Vivien Leigh and Clark Gable. MGM had jealously guarded the film for decades, refusing to let it be shown on television and periodically re-releasing it into cinemas where it always made a massive profit. Eventually it relented and landing it was a coup for the BBC, which had been trumpeting the premiere for months as the television event of the year. The audience were bombarded with trailers of Gable frankly not *giving* a damn and Leigh suffering gorgeously in taffeta. This was going to top everything.

And then the figures came in. *Gone with the Wind* pulled in fourteen million viewers. *Last of the Summer Wine* had got seventeen million. Bell and his cast were cock-a-hoop. The actors were all old enough to appreciate what a behemoth *Gone with the Wind* was, and to beat it with a tale of old friends going to a pub and jumping off a bus astounded them, even as they were delighted. Owen would cite the figures as evidence of the series' quality and appeal for the rest of his life. More importantly, the numbers were only three million lower than 1979 when there had been no opposition from ITV's blank screens. There could now be no doubt about it: *Summer Wine* was Britain's favourite comedy programme, the inheritor of the grand tradition of shows that united huge audiences across all ages and social groups. 'Whoops' had been watched by getting on for a third of Britain's population. There would not be many more moments like this when humour with universal appeal could bring a large part of the nation together; the age of such massive viewing figures would soon pass into memories as warm as the reflections of Foggy, Clegg and Compo, as the nature of entertainment changed with the rise in home video, the advent of satellite channels and the boom in computers. This was a triumph born of years of steady growth and development as *Summer Wine* had become ever more in tune with its audience, its writer ever more assured, its cast ever more comfortable and its direction ever more inventive.

A coveted peak-time Christmas Day slot and the audience's response had been the greatest gifts of a lucky year. The show was a sensation, and the press jumped gleefully on what was a splendid bit of fun; Nora Batty was more popular than Scarlett O'Hara, and pictures of the ravishing southern belle appeared alongside those of Britain's favourite glowering battleaxe. There were acres of coverage; the adventures of Compo, Clegg and Foggy were turning into a national obsession. Newspapers started giving away car bumper stickers bearing Nora's grim features, and the show was so much a part of the public's consciousness that it was only necessary to use a picture of a wellington boot to flag up an interview with the always-willing Owen or an article about Holmfirth.

Beating off Scarlett as well as Compo with Nora's brush sealed the deal on Kathy Staff's popularity. Sailors on warships started writing in for pin-up pictures, and tongue-in-cheek odes of love began to arrive. Just as with Owen, the gulf between reality and character made for good copy. The elegantly dressed, smiling and friendly Staff, with her taste for jewellery and designer clothes, was a world away from curlers, pinnies and scowls. The public recognised Owen in the street when he was out of character, but the transformation of Staff was so profound that fans would pass her by without realising, not least because her build was so different from Nora's. To play the part, she was upped to a hefty size 24. 'I wear two lots of padding for a start,' confided Staff to the *Daily Mail* in 1982. 'The big bust is sewn to the top of a man's vest and the suspenders are sewn to the bottom. That's how my stockings get that wrinkled effect. I also have a separate piece, like a panto dame's bottom. And that's Nora.'

Compo's lust for Nora was the show's most reliable laugh, the gag that the audience talked about the following day at work or at the shops. Yet the exchanges took several years to mature into the set piece they became; valued though she was by Clarke in the wake of the pilot, her appearances were at first sporadic. It was no coincidence that the growing success of the show mirrored the growth of her role; the permanent presence of Nora was one of the elements that catapulted *Summer Wine* to the top. It was a joke that hit the bull's-eye every time, the sheer incongruity of Compo's passion for her setting the audience laughing as soon as she hove into view. Over time, her appearance would be refined, Nora stepping out in hats that resembled the worst chocolate wrappers ever committed to tinfoil and coats of headache-inducing check, all of which reinforced the image of a woman too dreadful to fancy. Clarke played up her awfulness with a sly wink at Owen's past as a film star of a bygone era by having Compo compare Nora to the most glamorous British leading lady of the 1940s, declaring without a hint of irony, 'By 'eck, she is like Margaret Lockwood.'

The formula evolved into one of the great sitcom set pieces; Compo would leap out on Nora in the street, or outrage her as she swept her steps:

Nora: I warned you, get off my steps and don't come back. Tormenting a respectable married woman!

Compo: Ugh! I see them stockings are still wrinkled.

Nora: There he goes again, talking legs. He's always talking legs. I think he's sick.

Compo: I'm sick of those stockings. That is no way to treat Margaret Lockwood's legs.

Later, it became commonplace for Compo and Nora to spar as he raised his window, bleary, yawning and clad in long johns having just dragged himself out of bed, much to the disgust of his upright neighbour.

Nora: What time do you call this?

Compo: I call it time tha came up here and carried me off to paradise.

Nora: You want carrying off somewhere, but it's not paradise.

Compo: It's midsummer, lass. Don't tha ever wake up in the morning with all tha hormones tingling?

Nora: Yours wouldn't be tingling so much if you got up at a decent time.

Compo: Oh 'eck. Don't you ever think of anything but washing and cleaning? Tha's got thaself into a rut, tha knows. Tha wants to wake up one morning and pop up here and give tha scruffy little friend a great big cuddle.

Nora: Oh, close your window and get your shirt on. I shouldn't be standing here talking to raggy underwear.

Compo: With a little encouragement I'd get myself some new underwear, provided you did the same.

For all the comic lasciviousness he expressed, Owen always went out of his way to stress the innocence of the pursuit; it was a masterstroke of Clarke's writing that however suggestive and gurning with desire he might be, Compo was the eternal yearning adolescent who never comes within kissing distance of romance. No whiff of the dirty old man who got his way ever intruded; this was as chaste as Groucho wooing the formidable Margaret Dumont. 'Any sexual exploits are all in the mind,' said Owen in the *Mail on Sunday* in 1985. 'Everyone is frightened of Nora Batty except me and I think if it came to the crunch, she would be the more willing party. Compo is the only character on television who dares goose a woman without Mary Whitehouse complaining. But then the relationship seems to be based definitely above the navel.' Staff agreed; it was what kept the joke fresh for decades. In her

1997 autobiography, *My Story: Wrinkles and All*, she wrote: 'She's an archetype of perpetual innocence. Although she's a gossip and she likes to lay down the law, she somehow never sees what Compo is up to. They always show a close-up of her face a few seconds before she is going to be set upon by Compo. It's a study of puzzlement and bewilderment.'

The relationship had reached its apogee when 1982 dawned with *Summer Wine* back in its old 9.25 p.m. slot, the figures not just holding up but unarguably supreme as fifteen million people tuned in. And what a series they saw; this was classic situation comedy, the equal of anything achieved by iconic shows like *Steptoe and Son* or *Dad's Army*. A break away to complete *Open All Hours* seemed to have invigorated Clarke. There were great visual gags – a struggle with St John Ambulance men over a stretcher in 'In the Service of Humanity', Compo trying water-skiing in 'From Wellies to Wet Suit', and a ride on a wonderfully comic contraption in 'A Bicycle Made for Three'. The dialogue was even better, Clarke creating some sublimely funny, off-the-wall humour that was startling in its originality. His love for Foggy was apparent; Wilde had the best of it, and his performance was faultless. In 'The Odd Dog Men', Foggy fantasised about becoming the Royal Family's dog walker. Sallis was bowled over by what he read: 'That marvellous stuff Roy wrote for Brian about being in charge of the Queen's corgis, that's a classic bit of television writing. You could run that just as one piece.'

> Foggy: One day – it's going to happen – the phone's going to ring and it's going to be them.
>
> Compo: Them?
>
> Foggy: The Royal corgis.
>
> Compo: On the telephone?
>
> Foggy: Not in person, no. You know what that means?
>
> Clegg: Sharp teeth in the ankles.

Foggy: It means the Royal warrant. By appointment on our letterheads and in with the chance of the OBE. (LAUGHS). I like it. W. C. Dewhurst OBE. Mr W. C. Dewhurst OBE. Sir Walter Dewhurst OBE. Of course, privately among the household, I'll still be known as Foggy. (AS QUEEN) Has Foggy come back with the corgis yet? No ma'am. Good man. They've never been so healthy, Sandringham means early morning mist and Foggy out with the corgis. Morning, Mark. (VERY POSH) Helloo. How are the dorgs? Sprightly? Very sprightly. (TO COMPO) Only for God's sake keep him out of the way. Those trousers are treasonable.

There was even better to come in Owen's favourite episode of the entire canon, 'From Wellies to Wet Suit', in which his prowess as a clown was demonstrated in a wordless sequence where he brought mayhem to a newspaper shop while wearing a frogman's outfit, but it was an exchange between Foggy and Clegg that the writer in him admired above all.

Foggy: He was weird even at school.

Clegg: Only from nine till four.

Foggy: When I remember him and Cloggy Hopwood, they must have stuffed hundreds of beetles down my trousers.

Clegg: Mainly one at a time.

Foggy: Exactly. It was a monotonous regularity. Hey up, here comes Dewhurst! Bang! Wallop! A beetle down your trousers. No, it was my mother I felt sorry for.

Clegg: Why?

Foggy: Well, she used to go around with this tight expression. I know she hated the idea, but she was striving to come to terms with it.

Clegg: What idea?

Foggy: Well, me being an only child, she had nothing else to go by, and she was beginning to suspect that it was normal for a growing lad to go about with beetles in his trousers. She used to brush my hair last thing at night and I'd be standing there all shining, you know, clean pyjamas, and I remember she used to look at me with a deeply disappointed expression every time she passed me my Horlicks. Nothing in her sheltered upbringing had prepared her for a growing lad with beetles in his trousers.

Clegg: But couldn't you remove them at school? It wasn't compulsory to bring them home.

Foggy: You couldn't always find the time or the privacy. No, it wasn't the sort of operation you could pull off casually in a public place.

Clegg: Yes, I can see that.

Foggy: And you remember what schoolteachers used to be like in the early thirties.

Clegg: Before education became optional. They nearly all had little moustaches, and I don't just mean the ladies.

Foggy: Imagine being caught by one of the old school fishing about down a pair of trousers.

Clegg: Especially your own trousers.

Foggy: Yes, try telling one of them you were merely looking for a beetle.

Only rarely had anything of this quality been heard in a sitcom; this was startlingly original in its outlook and unfolded with the logic of its own fantasy world. It was as fantastical as anything Lewis Carroll ever committed to paper and as expertly paced as anything the great comedy scriptwriters who preceded him had achieved. Clarke's gift for passages of dialogue like this was to ground it in just enough reality to make a scenario familiar and believable to his audience before edging it over into the territory of the absurd where the laughs lay. This was quintessential *Summer Wine*, striking the perfect balance between the ridiculous and the sublime, feeding not only from Clarke's vision of his characters, but the depth brought to them by three actors whose rapport had grown instinctive. Whatever Wilde's reservations about Bell, he was revelling in the best writing he ever had and giving the performance of his life.

Bell knew how good this series was: 'Everything came together at the right time, we had good weather, the scripts were marvellous and it just happened to fit perfectly. It was a good series, I don't think we've matched it.' Everybody agreed, both in the show and at the BBC; this had been real quality.

Summer Wine was matchless; no other comedy series came close to its appeal, its literacy or its ratings. Here was an undisputed winner, one of the jewels of the BBC's entire output. But then, the restless and turbulent streak in Wilde's character surfaced; his discomfiture at hitting marks and making a sitcom in the manner of a film had irked him to such a degree that he rocked the boat as hard as he could, announcing that he would not continue if Bell was in charge of the next series, presenting the BBC with the appalling prospect of having its premier comedy wrecked by the conflicts between one of its stars and the producer who had taken it to new heights. 'When it came to signing our contracts for the following series, we said we wouldn't sign if Alan J. W. Bell was in charge,' said Wilde, adopting the use of the royal 'we'. 'This didn't go down well at the BBC as Alan's first series had been a huge success.'

It was a slap in the face for Bell, but a solution presented itself. Wilde had kept in touch with Lotterby, who despite the rigours of filming was only too happy to be handed back what was now the country's top sitcom. Meanwhile, Spike Milligan came to Bell's aid with his new series, *There's a Lot of It About*. 'That solved the problem,' said Bell. 'I'd always got on well with Spike, and he said he'd like me to do his series.' Wilde said: 'I don't think that we'd have got away with our request for a change of director, but a converse problem with Spike Milligan – who said he wouldn't sign his contract if Alan didn't direct his show – saved the day and any further embarrassment.'

Lotterby took charge of a series of seven, beginning with a special for Christmas Day 1982, 'All Mod Conned', which again topped the ratings. There was plenty of visual humour as the trio went on holiday to a broken-down caravan, filmed on Spurn Point, a desolate sandbar that pokes out into the Humber Estuary on the Yorkshire coast. They also appeared in a compilation show, *The Funny Side of Christmas*, performing a sketch specially written by Clarke. In the midst of Wilde's hissy fit over Bell, Owen was quietly trying to take the series in a new direction. He had been captivated by a novelisation of *Summer Wine* written by Clarke in 1974, in which the trio helped an old pal keep an assignation with his illicit girlfriend, only to die in her arms. He went to see Bell.

Bill said to me, 'Alan, would you read this, because it would make a good film,' and I said, 'The BBC don't do films.' Syd and Bernard had tried to get it done. *Ripping Yarns* had got a Bafta award, which gives you a little bit of credibility, and there was a Royal Television Society award and things like that, and Bill said, 'With all your awards, go to them and say you want to make a film.' So OK, nothing to lose and I read the book and it was very funny. I said to John Howard Davies, 'I'd like to do a film, a TV movie of *Last of the Summer Wine*.' He said, "We don't do them," and I asked why not and he just said we don't. I said, 'But this would be fantastic, ground-breaking and new,' and he said, 'Nobody does TV movies at the BBC.' I said, 'Why don't we be the first?' So he said, 'I'll tell you what, commission Roy to write a script.' So Roy adapted the book, and it was very funny.

This *was* ground-breaking stuff. There had been feature films based on successful BBC sitcoms, including *Dad's Army* and

Steptoe and Son, but they had, at best, been mixed successes despite the quality of the writing, partly because they were taken out of the hands of the producers who had made them hits on television and given to movie directors lacking the know-how of getting the best out of companies that had developed their own ways of working together, and partly because these series were mainly done in the studio and looked out of their depth when they were expanded and the action taken outside to fill ninety minutes on a big screen. *Summer Wine* was different; it was accustomed to playing a stage much bigger than the studio, one way or another the film would be in the hands of a director familiar with his cast and subject matter, and the result would be shown not in cinemas, but on television, where it belonged and had a devoted following. A touch of professional rivalry raised its head over the film, entitled 'Getting Sam Home'. When Lotterby had first come to *Summer Wine*, he had floated the idea of doing it all on film, which had been rejected. Now that the feature-length episode had got the go-ahead, he expressed keen interest in directing.

Bell said: 'I made it quite clear that when Syd took the series back, it didn't include the script for "Getting Sam Home"; that was mine. I'd put it to John Howard Davies, I had commissioned the script from Roy, so [it was] a difficult problem for the department. Here's Syd, vastly experienced, here am I, an upstart. What the department did was say, "Both budget it," so I budgeted it at four weeks' filming, all in, including Ealing Studios, and that included night filming, and night filming notoriously takes a long time. Syd had said six weeks, and the department went for the cheaper option.'

Wilde raised his head again, and for once it was a pleasant surprise. For all his awkward streak, he was an honourable man with a strong sense of fair play and he had something to say to Bell, having seen how the 1981/82 series had turned out. 'I said that I would like to take Alan to lunch to clear the air about the stand I had taken,' recalled Wilde. 'I told Alan that at the time, I didn't like the way he worked with all the tracks etc., but that I had to admit that on the screen the results were excellent. I returned to work with Alan on the film. I think it is a classic comedy.' It would not be the last time Wilde found it necessary to swallow his pride and clear the air with his colleagues, but Bell appreciated his willingness to admit that he had been wrong. 'He could be tricky to handle, to say the least, but I liked him enormously and off camera he was fantastic, a very nice man and a gentleman. But when it came to TV, [he was] quite hard and wanted it done his way.'

Filming started in May 1983. It was a tight schedule, and the night shooting threatened to pose a problem. Bell's crew rose to the occasion; they wanted to make this film a success. 'What happened on that night shoot was the lighting gaffer said, "Can you give me the next two or three set-ups and I'll organise it," and while we were filming one, he was lighting the next one, even getting the track laid for me. We got through it in record time.' Everybody involved knew this was something special, a piece of television history.

'I thought it was brilliant,' said Jane Freeman. 'That one was my favourite, the writing was just so good.' 'Getting Sam Home' took *Summer Wine* to a new level. Clarke had written a dark farce that meditated on the mores and manners of sex and death, and cast a perceptive eye at not only what love and friendship will make people do, but the lengths to which they go to avoid causing hurt. It had all the laughs and favourite ingredients of the series, but also subtle new depths of humour and pathos. Clarke seized the potential to write a notably literate, intelligent and mature comedy that balanced the familiar and the new. There was a much more adult theme to this black comedy than anything that had gone before in the series, the basic story concerning the complications arising when Sam dies during an extra-marital liaison with the blowsy heroine, the wonderfully named Lily Bless Her, but Clarke handled the subject with an expert lightness of touch. 'I've got great enthusiasm for sitcoms because I think you can handle almost anything if you do it right,' he said. 'It's how you present these things. If you hit my audience in the face with it, they wouldn't like it, but it had Lily Bless Her, who was so decent that everybody loved her. I enjoyed that, I got a kick out of watching it.'

The only shadow over the production concerned John Comer, who had lost his voice and plainly was not well. His lines had to be dubbed by northern character actor Tony Melody. 'I knew he was poorly,' said Freeman, 'and we had a scene in bed together, and I had to boot him. I was trying to give him a great boot, but stop my foot before it actually hit him.'

The familiar company was augmented by Peter Russell as the libidinous Sam, who would rather risk everything for a night of passion than surrender to dull domesticity and his humourless wife, Sybil, played by Olive Pendleton. Lily Bless Her was Lynda Baron, an audience favourite thanks to her role as Nurse Gladys Emmanuel, the object of Ronnie Barker's desires in *Open All Hours*, and she was ideally cast as the tarty but sweet temptress of a certain age. Sam's predicament is teed up by Foggy as he and the other two sit on a hillside: 'I must say Sam's always made the best of it, preserved his marriage by a combination of Christian patience and a twice-weekly frolic with Lily Bless Her.'

Sam and Sybil's dialogue is equally sharp at sketching a marriage killed by routine as he lies in his hospital bed.

Sybil: Your Colin called. I wish he wouldn't, he smells rusty. He wanted to borrow your socket set. I told him he couldn't, he hasn't brought your tenon saw back yet. And I had the Jehovah's Witnesses at the front door. I told them, go convert somebody who lives scruffy.

Sam: (THINKS) Good skin. She always had a good skin, hoarded it like a miser, though.

Sybil: And another thing …

Sam: (THINKS) If only she'd brought to the marriage bed the same determination to get into every corner that she brings to cleaning the house.

As he leaves hospital, Sam returns to the subject:

Sam: No cream cakes, no animal fats, no fornication.

Clegg: Well, it's time you packed it in anyway. Cream cakes at your age, disgusting.

When Sam expires in a collision between sex and death, his face bearing a beatific smile for all eternity, Clarke brings out the farce in the situation:

Lily: He only wanted a cuddle. Where's the harm in that?

Clegg: A terminal cuddle. What a time to go. I saw him lying there, that familiar face, and I thought, Sam, you tactless prat.

Compo: He's dropped us right in it now. He thinks it's funny. Did tha see his face?

Lily: He wanted a bit of comfort, that's all.

Foggy: Judging by the expression on his face, I should think he found it.

Clegg: You can't trust anybody. We sneak him out once and straight away off he goes on this impulsive trip into the infinite.

And in the midst of this darkly comic tale, there is a moment where Clarke pauses the laughs for a masterfully judged and touchingly played bittersweet meditation on life that underscores the humour that frames it. Clegg, Compo and Foggy are outside their old school:

Clegg: The thing about growing up is that you get fewer scabs on your knees, but more internal injuries.

Compo: Aye, they were great days at school.

Clegg: Oh yes, they were great days. But even then, there was no real amnesty. Do you remember the day when that little yellowhammer flew straight at the window? You picked it up.

Compo: Aye, they've got lovely markings.

Clegg: It had a drop of blood on its beak. Identical colour to ours. Just one drop, like a bright bead. And then there were all those brightly plumed kids who left school, flying cheerfully and didn't get far. Ran smack into World War Two.

Foggy: That's right, look on the bright side.

Compo: Hey, cheer up.

Clegg: Little Tommy Naylor, lying in Africa somewhere. Blood on his beak. Identical colour to ours.

The story moves from Lily's house to Sybil's as the trio smuggle Sam back in, and then out again so that his girlfriend can lay him out in her spare room. Sid helps by moving the body in his chip van, in which he has to start cooking after being accosted by the police, only for Sam's arm to flop down over the counter. There are virtuoso comic sequences in which the corpse is stood up and Foggy takes its place in the coffin, terrifying a neighbour looking for his lost dog, before the funeral approaches. The trio's dilemma about ensuring the body and not a shop dummy is going to be buried is solved by the unexpected figure of Ivy. Clarke introduces a compassionate note as Sybil stops the funeral cortege and invites Lily, who is walking away from the church alone, into her car, before the three men go to scatter Sam's ashes and Foggy takes a tumble down a hill to end on a big laugh.

Wilde was right; it is a classic comedy, and in a different class to the feature adaptations of sitcoms that had gone before. Bell excelled himself in his direction. The film flies by without ever sagging and the performances of the trio shine. Owen, in particular, whose pet project this was, is magnetic throughout. After all these years, at the age of sixty-nine, he's starring in a film again, and his joy lights up his portrayal of Compo, who displays a dancing ebullience. 'Getting Sam Home' was a triumph; it broke the mould for what a sitcom could do, and pointed the way not just for future feature-length instalments of *Summer Wine*, but for extended episodes of such future BBC comedies as *Only Fools and Horses* and *One Foot in the Grave*. It went out on 27 December and was another huge hit, topping the week's ratings with 14.2 million viewers, beating *Coronation Street* into second place and the glossy American sex-and-intrigue saga *Dallas* into third.

The afterglow of 'Getting Sam Home' was blighted by sadness. Six weeks after it was broadcast, on 11 February, John Comer died aged fifty-nine. Freeman said: 'I don't think he knew it was cancer, I think he thought he'd just lost his voice.' As Sid, Comer had made a telling contribution. As the series gained increasing success, Clarke had paired him to great effect not just with Freeman, but with Joe Gladwin, and had even made him the focus of some irresistible scenes. In 'Getting on Sidney's Wire', there is a moment where Sid edges warily on to a plank between two chairs while decorating, only for it to sag gently to the floor under his weight. 'He did that divinely,' said Freeman. 'The audience were beside themselves. He was perfect, the way he delivered the lines. We became this double act and I got lots of hate mail from men. They used to defend him, and my poor husband got a lot of, "Oh my Gawd, she must be hell to live with."' Comer's loss upset the balance of the supporting cast, which had delivered laughs so reliably, and would mean a rethink for what Ivy could do without him that would see her moving beyond scenes in the café in the years that followed. The real challenge for the show, though, was containing the friction between two of its three leading men.

CHAPTER 6

❧

Loyal but Disagreeable

THERE WERE THREE separate worlds in the big, comfortable Winnebago parked high on the moors, three pockets of silence and personal space that by unspoken agreement were not encroached upon. Owen's was up at the front, near the driver, where he went through his script, counting the lines to make sure nobody was getting more laughs than him. The middle was Wilde's territory, where he stared out of the window, and the back belonged to Sallis, lost in *The Times* crossword. Apart from going over their lines together, there was little talk, and any conversation was conducted with pointed civility.

The rapport they shared on screen chilled noticeably once they returned to the mobile home that sheltered them from the elements and was the envy of the rest of the cast. Matters had improved considerably since the early days, when the cast had struggled into costume in their cars, and had to perch on the dry-stone walls between takes, with only umbrellas to protect them from the rain. By now, there was at least some cover, aboard a bus, where the supporting actors mucked in together and grumbled as they changed behind a curtain strung across the aisle. There were no such discomforts for the three stars, who enjoyed a modicum of luxury, the only drawback of which was that they had to share it. Everybody on set knew that relations between Owen and Wilde were cool, just as they knew that the quiet interventions of Sallis prevented the tensions between them boiling over into open warfare. Sometimes he could joke them out of it, at others he would need to go further and remind Owen that the success of the series was paramount and must not be jeopardised by arguments. And Sallis could have moods of his own; he had an ego too, and on occasions needled Owen. Mostly, though, he played peacemaker, mediating the wary indifference that could flare up into animosity.

There were huffy silences and sharp exchanges; barely controlled tempers and snide remarks, and the quiet of the mobile home could be more oppressive than companionable. It never got out of hand; there were no screaming tantrums or shouting matches, all three were far too professional for that, and they were scrupulous in trying not to let any antipathy show, even though it was an open secret on set. They worked together closely and valued each other's skills, knew that magic happened once the director called 'Action'; nobody was more delighted than them at the success the show had become, and so they accommodated each other and coped with the clashes by putting as much distance between themselves as they could at the end of each day, shrugging off any contact as surely as they left their costumes behind until the next morning's call.

The flashpoint for problems lay in the prickly relationship between Owen and Wilde, who shared a gift for rubbing each other up the wrong way. Owen had a high opinion of himself and made no effort to conceal his view that he was the star of *Summer Wine*, however much he spoke in public of its success being down to the chemistry of the trio. That irritated Wilde, as did aspects of Owen's performance, whether it was playing to the crowd in the studio or his sometimes approximate delivery of his lines. And then, of course, there was Owen's fondness for venting his political beliefs. As with Bates, politics was always an argument waiting to happen, because Wilde was a man of conservative outlook who had time for neither Owen's left-wing views nor his willingness to air them irrespective of whether his audience wanted to listen or not. Wilde kept his politics to himself and failed to see why Owen should not do likewise. Yet the trigger for the most serious disputes that arose between them came from Wilde, whose awkward streak manifested itself over money, contracts and even scripts. He was the one who gave Bell headaches and could always be relied upon to cause turbulence, just as he could be relied upon to go away, have second thoughts and return as if nothing had happened.

Actors do not always love each other; egos can get in the way, but for studio-based sitcoms where tension arose it was possible to escape it. After days rehearsing and evenings in the studio, home and respite beckoned. *Summer Wine* was different. Location shooting that ran from June to October meant the actors were thrown together for long periods away from loved ones and familiar comforts, and when the weather closed in and they were confined in the claustrophobic space of a caravan, the atmosphere could turn sour. It was not, of course, a constant series of rows and irritations; there was much laughter. Above all, they were scrupulously professional in never letting whatever strains there were affect their work.

'It's just that Bill and Brian were politically different,' said Freeman. 'They were totally civilised with each other. One would sit and do his crossword in one place and the other would sit and do his crossword in another, but Peter would negotiate between them. There was no incivility, but they weren't sympathetic with each other. Peter handled Bill very well. They both realised that it was in their interest to present a good face. Brian was the impossible one, the loose cannon when it came to money and other things.'

Sallis observed wryly: 'The reason that they both got on with me is that I am weak-minded and I don't have any views about anything, really, so I wasn't going to give them a hard time. I think, knowing me, having gone through my life without having an opinion of my own, I think I would be more likely to be in the corner keeping the score. It would more likely be Brian and Bill punching it out in the middle.'

They started punching it out early. It didn't take long after Wilde joined for the frictions to show themselves, and like Gilbert before him, Lotterby had to intervene. 'The two of them were having an argument and I just had to read the riot act and say, "Look, we can pack this up now, if you like, if you're going to argue, this is not the way to make a programme, we can pack up and go back and stop the programme." Once that happened, just once, but it was enough. They both wanted to do the programme, with the consequence that they bit their lips, and their tongues.'

When Lotterby took over, his budget for the programme had not allowed for the sophisticated location operation that later developed, where all the actors had their own caravans and a degree of privacy. 'We had one caravan, I couldn't afford three caravans. When you go filming, everybody's got a car, so when you change locations it's at least twenty cars flying all over Yorkshire, and they all had their special seat in the caravan, and sometimes we had a little bit of friction between Bill and Brian. They wouldn't go out of their way to be conversational with the other person. They'd talk, but it would be monosyllabic. We all separated once filming was over.'

Separation worked in keeping the relationship on an even keel. The days of the Coach and Horses, with its strippers and bleak location on the moors, were long past, headquarters having moved to nearby Huddersfield. Home-from-home for decades afterwards would be the Huddersfield Hotel, a comfortable establishment where the food was good and there were plenty of other restaurants within easy walking distance for any of the cast who wanted a change of scenery or their own company for the evening. Sallis became a fixture there, with a favourite room and a table of his own with a reading lamp in the restaurant where he would sit alone with a book or going over his lines for the next day.

Typically, Wilde wanted nothing to do with anywhere he would have to come into contact with anybody else involved in the series, and developed a social life of his own. 'He was very private and he'd stay at the Hilton Hotel a little way out of town while everyone else stayed in Huddersfield,' said Bell. 'He'd walk round to a little pub at the back and he had all his local mates there and he would chat away with them as long as they didn't talk about TV, he was just one of the boys, loved to talk about the world.'

For Owen, home on location was a rented house on the edge of Cartworth Moor, above Holmfirth, which he returned to year after year. Privacy suited him hardly less than Wilde, though he was more willing to socialise occasionally, and he told the *Yorkshire Post* of his own routines for the evening. 'After a day's filming, I can sit relaxing in my bath enjoying a glass of whisky and look through the window onto a gorgeous moorland view with perhaps just a few cattle in the background,' he said. He was strict about his rituals, and would not take a drink except in the hour between 6.30 and 7.30 p.m. 'I wait with the ice and water in the glass for the clock to chime and make the most of that hour before dinner. I can't drink after I've eaten.' And then, after his whisky and bath, he would eat, as often as not a fish pie from Marks and Spencer, which was his favourite meal at home.

The evenings offered respite, but back on set tempers were simmering, not least because of Wilde's uncompromising stance over what he was paid and a misguided decision to dispense with his agent. Bell said: 'He had an enormous potential, but never exploited it, mainly because Ronnie Barker said to Brian, "Why do you have an agent, all they do is take ten per cent of your money?" Brian got rid of his agent. If anybody rang up about Brian, they would have to speak to Brian direct, and the phone isn't going to ring from his agent because he hasn't got one. I kept saying, "Brian, you're crazy, all right you're losing ten per cent of something rather than saving ten per cent of nothing." Big mistake.' Clarke agreed: 'I think one of his big problems was that he had no agent, so he had to do his own negotiations, which is a bit off-putting because you want things like that out of the way so they're not interfering with what you're supposed to be doing.' Representing himself put Wilde under pressure by plunging him into the minutiae of contracts, and was to do him no favours in building on the popularity that *Summer Wine* brought him. Wilde was no Ronnie Barker, a major star who in tandem with Ronnie Corbett was the lynchpin of the BBC's Saturday evening entertainment, and under his own flag beloved of audiences for his two classic sitcoms. He did not have to look for work; the BBC tailored prestige productions to him. For all his talents, Wilde was simply not in the same league.

Nevertheless, Wilde persevered and drove such a hard bargain over money – backed up with threats to leave if he didn't get what he wanted – that he was paid substantially more than Owen and Sallis. The inequality between three actors who shared equal billing and expected parity of pay came to light outside the confines of *Summer Wine* when the trio were dressed in tuxedos for a cameo appearance in a song-and-dance spectacular produced by Morecambe and Wise stalwart Ernest Maxin. It emerged that Wilde was being paid twice as much as Owen and Sallis, who were furious.

There would be an even more serious clash ahead but, for now, it wasn't just being stuck in Owen's company that irritated Wilde. He became very annoyed at how he behaved in the studio.

> I can't say that I really enjoyed having to play the scenes in front of an audience, but it is the only way to get the response – and to know that we were doing it right. Bill Owen, however, loved the audience and sometimes actually played lines directly to them, which was a bit off-putting for us non-variety types. But Bill knew what he was doing and the audiences loved him. The laughter track was and is an important part of any comedy series. If someone is viewing alone the response adds to their enjoyment.... . Bill Owen had an infuriating habit; if he felt that the audience was unresponsive and missing the humour of the lines, he would suddenly mess up the scene, deliberately going wrong. The audience would erupt with an enormous laugh – this is what they came for – after all, they could watch the finished show in the comfort of their own homes. From there on, everything was received warmly by the audience.

In fairness to Wilde, he would not be the only one discomfited by Owen's behaviour over the years; once in character, he sometimes paraphrased Clarke's lines, which could be distracting for actors waiting for their cues from him.

There was another aspect of his behaviour that bothered Wilde – his assumption that he was the star of the show. 'I think he thought of the programme as his,' said Lotterby. 'It was certainly the programme he'd done most of. It made Bill famous. He got more fame from it than the other two.' Bell found the same attitude from Owen. 'Bill was always trying to say that he was the most important in the show because he was the best known, and Bill was the only one who'd had his name as the star of a film, with his name above the credits, whereas the others were TV and stage actors, but they always tried to maintain equality.'

Owen kept a distance from the others, which he felt befitted the star. 'Bill was very much a law unto himself,' said Freeman. 'I always admired him tremendously as Compo, but he was fairly remote. Peter used to deal with Bill, really. Bill and Kathy's scenes were lovely, but he was terribly self-contained, he knew what he wanted to do and he did it, and was always dead on the mark.'

Bell got on well with Owen, and found him easy to work with. As the years passed, a mutual trust and professional regard developed into a close friendship.

He would grumble to me and use four-letter words, and say, 'It's all right for you lot but I'm in front of the camera,' and you'd say, 'Bill, just do it.' I was always aware that he looked at me to see if I was laughing at what he was doing, and I would never laugh for the sake of laughing, but if it was amusing me, I could see him pick it up and do it better, because that was something he just loved to prove. I met with him for lunch once or twice before we would go up to Yorkshire, he would have a little bit of paper with things he didn't want. He didn't want to start work before nine, and he said, 'Here's one, rough ground,' and I said, 'Do you mean hills?' 'Yes,' he said, 'hills, I don't want to walk up hills,' but he'd do it. He would never not do anything if it was for the programme. He was champion of the programme, ambassador of the programme, he would do absolutely anything to make sure the image of the programme was good for both the viewers and where we filmed it. Whatever you asked him to do, he would do it. I admired Bill enormously. I never had any problems with Bill. Intonation of lines is terribly important and if I gave him a note that the emphasis was wrong, he would never say, 'No, I think you're wrong,' he would say, 'Give it me again,' and I found working with Bill very, very easy. Bill was a performer, he loved the sound of an audience.

Sallis was mostly easy-going, but still had the occasional clash with Bell. 'Peter was so good and so established as Clegg that he had his own ideas of how it should be played. Sometimes we would disagree very much over how a line should be said and once I dug my heels in and made him come to the dubbing theatre and revoice it, much to his annoyance, but when I'd watched it, it made me squirm, it was just wrong. Most of the time, Peter's very good and plays it beautifully.'

Sallis also possessed a streak of mischievousness that caused the occasional headache, as Bell recalled. 'He could be a bit troublesome, naughty's the word. We'd be filming in an alleyway, Peter would disappear, where's Peter gone? We'd search round Holmfirth, find him in the bookshop.'

Wilde, the loose cannon, then blew a gaping hole in the image of the series by revealing publicly that the affectionate bond between the three ageing dreamers on screen bore no relationship to how the actors got on. 'A journalist was interviewing me at my home for a newspaper article about the series. When it was all over, I gave him a drink and we just chatted informally. I was asked if I got on well with Bill Owen and I said, quite truthfully, that we didn't mix – we had nothing in common – I didn't like his politics and I preferred my own company. The headline in the newspaper screamed out "Trouble in Summer Wine Land" and my off-the-record remarks were freely quoted. Needless to say,

Bill Owen was furious and it took some time before we were able to put it aside. For many years, I refused to be interviewed by any journalist.'

Wilde was quoted in the newspaper as saying: 'There is friction between Bill and me. We have disagreements but they are largely over minor things. We argue over the interpretation of the scenes or the cutting of words. All is not sweetness and light. We've never walked off the set in anger – we're too professional for that – though we have a few days when we're not talking.'

Owen was understandably enraged at the remarks. The curtain had been lifted on backstage quarrels that all three actors had worked hard at keeping within the confines of their caravan. The public did not need to know that tempers sometimes frayed. What mattered were the performances on screen, which were bringing joy to millions. Owen, a consummate player of the publicity game who had always been at pains to credit the show's success to the skills of all its stars, felt Wilde had been unprofessional and naive, and he knew that the subject of how the three men got on would henceforth be an issue for any coverage of the series, and for the public.

Wilde knew he'd put his foot in it spectacularly, and became more remote than ever. Bell said: 'Brian was livid. It was said off the record. It was quite true, they didn't have anything in common, but there was no trouble at all. A man from the *Radio Times* came up and I'd forgotten all about it [the press row], so I went and told Bill and Peter and I went to say hello to him, a very nice man, and just at that moment Brian came shuffling along with a cup of coffee in his hand and I introduced him, and he said, "Well, I'm not saying anything. Two things, one I won't talk to the press and the other is they always publish *Porridge* with Ronnie Barker as the star, and I am also in it," and walked on.'

Now that the cat was out of the bag, Owen and Wilde resigned themselves to being asked about each other and put the best face they could on it. Sallis kept his own counsel and preferred to steer round the subject, at least in public. Owen confined himself to crisp comments: 'You don't have to love everyone you work with.' Wilde was a little more forthcoming, telling the *Radio Times*: 'I think you'd describe our relationship as loyal but disagreeable. We don't stay at the same hotels when we're filming – we don't really want to see too much of each other. And yes, we do argue a lot about how the characters should be played. But then there's more than one way of doing a job.'

The episode rankled with Owen, who returned to it more than a decade later, in his autobiography, acknowledging with a touch of weariness that his hunch about how Compo, Clegg and Foggy related to each other in real life fascinated the public. 'There are still busybodies who quite casually ask how we get along after all these years, hoping, of course, to see me tear my hair out and reply, "We hate the bloody sight of each other!" So they are usually abashed when I reply just as casually, "Oh, we get along."' Owen then widened the subject of personal relationships to diminish the clash with Wilde, inevitably raising the subject of politics.

But outside our shared love of classical music, about which Peter [Sallis] has enlightened me and broadened my knowledge, I think we have very little in common. Even less I feel with Brian Wilde, whom I've always found to be an extremely private person. In fact, I believe my whole concept of living is different from theirs. For instance, and I speak from experience, the subject of politics is taboo, not from any strong opposing views on their part, but simply because they appear to be apolitical ... We have a caravan the size of a self-contained flat in which we have each reserved a corner to enjoy our own privacy which is strictly observed. We rarely communicate between series, meeting the following year for the first time at a script conference prior to going on location. But, like I said, 'We get along'.

It was not just Owen whom Wilde was annoying. Fond as he was of him, Bell had much to put up with; he had not forgotten the upset caused by Wilde and his threat of resignation, and even though he had apologised and returned for 'Getting Sam Home', he was still grumbling. Bell and Clarke indulged themselves in a moment's payback. 'When he came back, he was still saying, "This is the last thing I'll do,"' said Bell. 'So I said to Roy, can you write a bit for the end where they're scattering his [Sam's] ashes, which wasn't in the original adaptation. And Foggy loses his balance and falls over a cliff, which was very funny because that was Roy's way of getting rid of Brian. I took a shot of him climbing up the hillside just so everybody knew he was all right.'

Despite his assertion that 'Getting Sam Home' would be his last outing as Foggy, Wilde signed on for the 1984 Christmas special and the eighth series that would begin a couple of months later in February, only to cause more turbulence as final preparations were being made, once again threatening to throw everything into chaos. Bell said: 'He decided he didn't like the scripts. He wanted Roy to rewrite them, and I said, "No way, it's a funny series, Brian." The scripts were good, they didn't need any help at all, so he said he's not going to do the series, and I said, "Do you mean that?" and he said yes. We're filming in a month's time, and he said, "No, I'm not going to do it." Because it's so late and there's so much money involved, I said, "You'll have to give your notice to John Howard Davies, I'm not going to get the reputation that I've frightened you off." So he came in and saw John, who said, "He means it, he's not going to do it," and he asked what we should do, so I said, "We should recast it, see what he does."'

Bell turned for his recasting to an old colleague of Wilde, Fulton Mackay, who had played opposite him in *Porridge* as the stiff-necked prison officer Mr MacKay. It had been an exquisite comic performance, lit up by Mackay's superb timing, and if there was to be a new authority figure in *Summer Wine*, he would be an excellent choice. Bell said: 'I had always thought of Fulton as a guest, so I rang his agent to check his availability, and they asked what it was for and I said *Last of the Summer Wine* and it's a big part. Well, Fulton must have rung Brian and told him, and I guess Brian must have told him it's a joke and don't do anything about it, but within twenty minutes of ringing Fulton's agent, Brian rang up as though nothing had happened, as though he'd never been in to see John Howard Davies, as if he'd never spoken to me, and said, "I've got the scripts but I haven't got a schedule," and I said, "They're not published yet, Brian." "Fine, thank you." As if nothing had happened.'

Wilde could not have been more wrong about the scripts for the series; Clarke's inspired run continued, not least in the Christmas special, 'The Loxley Lozenge', which brought back Gordon Wharmby as Wesley, who finds a rare old car. It was among the finest episodes he had written and contained some vintage dialogue, not least a fantasy for Clegg that was superbly performed by Sallis as Wesley seeks assurances that the trio will not reveal his discovery.

Clegg: I used to be an Ovaltiney. I mention this in passing.

Wesley: I'm serious!

Clegg: So were the Ovaltineys. Hitler was an Ovaltiney.

Compo: I never knew that.

Clegg: Well, it was all hushed up, naturally. They made him give his badge back. So he tried the swastika instead. They themselves had been experimenting advertising-wise with the swastika, but they decided against it on account of too many kids were liable to swallow it, so they offered it to Hitler with their blessing.

Compo: I bet he loved it. No?

Clegg: He hated it, thought it was too much like the flag of the Isle of Man.

Compo: Where he used to go for his holidays!

Clegg: You can see his dilemma.

Compo: Was it open to the public?

Clegg: There he was, raising all these mighty legions, only to have people say, who are all this lot then, oh, oh, they're from the Isle of Man. I mean, can you imagine waking Stalin at two o'clock in the morning, Eh up comrade, I think we're being invaded by the Isle of Man, so naturally he was on the point of rejecting the swastika entirely.

Compo: Well, you would, wouldn't you?

Clegg: Until the lady that he was annexing at the time decided that it might look rather dinky made up as a brooch.

Compo: Eva Braun?

Clegg: Eva brown or black, and he chose black because it matched his diseased left toenail. Little did they think when they were swearing their oaths to the Fuhrer that they were promising to die for a small bloke with a dirty toenail. Such are the mysteries of human behaviour.

Kathy Staff and Joe Gladwin were also handed a peach of an exchange, as they sat in the middle of nowhere in the motorbike and sidecar.

Nora: Well? Talk to me, say something – anything!

Wally: About what?

Nora: About anything, I don't care. Just talk to me, you never speak to me.

Wally: I spoke to you yesterday. I asked you where me elastic bandage was.

Nora: That was Monday. It doesn't matter where we go, you don't talk. You just sit there. You used to like my company once.

Wally: Oh aye, once. But I've got it all week now.

Writer Roy Clarke, 1976. 'It has its own world, a nonsense world. That's why it's survived fashion changes.' *Author's personal collection*

Original producer James Gilbert. 'When I read it, I was bowled over.' *Don Smith*

Holmfirth, the Yorkshire mill town that was to be transformed by the series. *Alamy*

'Excuse me, weren't you Samuel Pepys?' Sallis had been a familiar figure on television since starring in the BBC's adaptation of Pepys's diaries in 1958. *Getty Images*

The original trio, from left, Compo (Bill Owen), Clegg, (Peter Sallis) and Blamire (Michael Bates). *Don Smith*

'By 'eck, she is like Margaret Lockwood.' Kathy Staff as Nora Batty is disgusted by the thing in Compo's matchbox. *Malcolm Howarth*

The Richard Burton and Elizabeth Taylor of Huddersfield – John Comer and Jane Freeman as Sid and Ivy. *BBC Photo Library*

Loyal but disagreeable – the definitive trio of Clegg (Peter Sallis), Foggy (Brian Wilde) and Compo (Bill Owen) on location in Holmfirth, early 1980s. *Author's personal collection*

'Don't you ever think of me as a woman?' Joe Gladwin and Kathy Staff as Wally and Nora Batty. *Malcolm Howarth*

The third trio – Owen and Sallis with Michael Aldridge as Seymour in motorised wheelbarrow. *Malcolm Howarth*

On location for Owen's favourite episode, 'From Wellies to Wet Suit', 1981 – Peter Sallis, John Comer, Bill Owen, Brian Wilde and producer Alan J. W. Bell.

'Wes-lay?' Gordon Wharmby and Thora Hird as Wesley and Edie. *Malcolm Howarth*

'Oh, Barry!' Sarah Thomas and Mike Grady as Glenda and Barry. *Malcolm Howarth*

Still loyal, but rather less disagreeable – the classic trio reunited, early 1990s. *Malcolm Howarth*

'I think we've really cracked it this time.' Robert Fyfe and Jean Fergusson as Howard and Marina. *Malcolm Howarth*

'You've got ideas bigger than your natural capacity.' Robert Fyfe and Juliette Kaplan as Howard and Pearl. *Malcolm Howarth*

Up-two-three, drink-two-three, down-two-three – the ladies take coffee. From left, Pearl (Juliette Kaplan), Ivy (Jane Freeman), Nora (Kathy Staff), Edie (Thora Hird) and Glenda (Sarah Thomas). *Malcolm Howarth*

'The easiest script I've ever had to learn.' Jean Alexander as Auntie Wainwright. *Alamy*

The fourth trio – Frank Thornton as Truly with Owen and Sallis. *Malcolm Howarth*

The last post for Bill Owen and Compo – Owen's final day of filming, with Frank Thornton and Peter Sallis. *Malcolm Howarth*

The final trio –Russ Abbot, Brian Murphy and Burt Kwouk.

In the studios at Shepperton. *Malcolm Howarth*

On location high in the Pennines – Owen, Sallis and Wilde with Alan J. W. Bell.

The crew prepare to film the trio close to Hade Edge, above Holmfirth. Stand-ins for Owen and Sallis are visible at the top left. *Malcolm Howarth*

The writer and producers, who brought it all to life, at a gathering in the early 1990s. From left, Roy Clarke, James Gilbert, Bill Owen, Bernard Thompson, Peter Sallis, Sydney Lotterby, Michael Aldridge and Alan J. W. Bell.

'There comes a time when we all have to think of a place where we end up.' Bill Owen's grave, overlooking Holmfirth. *Author's personal collection*

Nora: Don't you ever think of me as a woman? A person? Am I always just a wife?

Wally: You've never been just a wife. You're about as much wife as anybody could handle. There's nobody had more wife than I have.

Nora: You just sit there. I wonder sometimes if you'd ever miss me if I left.

Wally: We could give it a try.

In addition to dialogue of such quality, there was a healthy dollop of physical humour that the audience loved, especially a climactic scene of a sofa falling off the carcase of the car and rolling away down a hill with the three men seated on it. The episode was another winner in the ratings and the perfect curtain-raiser for the new series, which began with a bang with 'The Mysterious Feet of Nora Batty', a glorious romp in which an argument develops over whether the eponymous heroine has big feet. Once again, Clarke's dialogue was at its quirkiest, as the the trio quizzes Wally about his wife.

Foggy: We shall, of course, treat any information you might give us on this subject in the strictest confidence. (SHAKES HIS HAND)

Compo: Not a whisper. (SHAKES HIS HAND) You ain't got much of a grip there, Wal.

Wally: It's as much as I need for anything that's available for a person of my age.

Clegg: Good grief, is it really as slack as all that?

Compo: It is.

Clegg: (SHAKES HIS HAND) My God, it is, yes.

Compo: It's like half a pound of liver.

Foggy: Look, never mind his grip.

Compo: Never mind his grip? How's he going to protect Nora with a grip like that? Suppose some bloke who was frustrated and lonely suddenly leapt out on our Nora?

Clegg: My goodness, how frustrated and lonely can you get?

Foggy: The mind boggles, doesn't it? I mean, let's be rational about this, I mean who the heck is going to leap out on the woman, she's terrible. Oh, begging your pardon, Wally.

Wally: Point taken.

Compo: Listen, blokes leap out on women all the time – there's me for a start!

Wally: Well, let's face it, I'm in no condition to go punching people about.

Clegg: Wally, you're in no condition to go screaming for help.

Wally: It's true. If she was attacked right in front of me eyes, I'd have to stand there helpless. Helpless! She could have the bloke mauled to death before I could drag her off.

The episode drew an audience of 18.8 million, and set a new benchmark for Clarke, who found that he was competing with himself for the top comedy show of the year. When the figures for 1985 were compiled, *Open All Hours* was the most watched with 18.95 million, with *Last of the Summer Wine* running it a close second. The remaining five episodes of the series – 'Keeping Britain Tidy', 'Enter the Phantom', 'Catching Digby's Donkey', 'The Woollen Mills of Your Mind' and 'Who's Looking After the Café, Then' – were all wonderful half-hours. Each had memorable dialogue, as in 'Enter the Phantom', where Foggy is dragging a breathless Compo and Clegg up a steep hill.

Compo: Oh dear, I am glad we came. Aren't you glad we came, Norm?

Clegg: Me? Oh, I'm just looking back nostalgically at the old days when there used to be such a thing as oxygen.

Foggy: Come on, you men, we're nearly there.

Compo: Nearly where? There's nowt up here.

Clegg: Oh, oh, don't tell me that we've come all this way and God's not in.

Not a trace of the off-screen tensions is visible in the performances; Owen, Sallis and Wilde are more believable than ever as the three old friends. There was something else, too – a deepening comic relationship between Ivy and Nora, who were getting more scenes together and delivering some wonderful laughs. The closeness of their on-screen rapport was mirrored off-set. Kathy Staff and Jane Freeman had grown into the best of friends, and regarded the shenanigans involving Owen, Sallis and Wilde with resigned amusement that could occasionally be tinged with resentment at how they were cosseted and indulged. There were three dressers available to the cast, and the men had the services of two of them. Staff was well aware of what a crucial role she played in the show's success, and how popular she was with the public, and came to feel she was not given her due – or anything like the pay that the stars received. Nora Batty was a comedy icon, the ultimate battleaxe, as recognisable as any other character in the show, and one which the force of her own personality had brought to life; she accepted that the men carried the show, but even when caravans and shelter from the elements were available to all the cast, the gulf between the trio and the rest was still galling. Staff wrote in her autobiography: 'The three men are there all the time, so they do deserve the "number one" dressing room, but it's become a bit of a social thing – everyone else is second class compared with the three men.' Bell knew how she felt, and sympathised, saying: 'I think Kathy felt a little hurt inwardly that she'd been in the programme as long as Bill and Peter, yet she didn't get the fees they were getting or the billing, and over the years I gave her a caravan.'

Freeman said:

> Kathy and I became great friends. It was wonderful. At one time, I did more studio and she did all outside, and we grew to each other slowly, and then after about two series, we were trolling off to the Ritz for tea and doing things after rehearsals, because we rehearsed in London for so long. We rehearsed all week and then shot it on the Sunday, so we would go out shopping and all sorts of things. If there was one character in that programme that was popular, it was Nora Batty, and she spent her entire time opening shows, doing benefits, doing programmes, *Sunday Half Hours* and goodness knows what else, and she really was one of the stars. I don't know that she was always given her due. It's a classic performance. I had a wonderful experience. I was on an escalator in a big store and there was a husband saying to his wife, 'Oh, pull your tights up, you look like Nora Batty,' and as he said that they looked across and saw me. But there they were, completely in their own world, talking about *Last of the Summer Wine*.

Staff was not only concerned about herself. She wanted more recognition for the other supporting actors, not least Joe Gladwin, of whom she was very fond. Freeman agreed with her, but was more stoical about the realities of a hit show. 'The men all liked their own little hole, really, and in the early days I took my car and Kathy and I sat in it and had our lunch there to get away from everybody. As we got older and more decrepit, Kathy and I had a little caravan and Peter and Bill had a very big caravan with separate rooms. They had their rituals, and they were spoilt, but the bulk of the programme rested on them, so there you are.'

Like Owen, Sallis and Wilde, Staff and Freeman got away from the rest of the cast at the end of every day, not because of tensions, but simply for the sake of home comforts. Staff lived in Cheshire, a twenty-minute drive away across the moors, and Freeman stayed with her and her husband, John, during location filming. Theirs was a happy, mutually supportive friendship that would endure for the rest of Staff's life. 'If you say she was a good Christian, that conjures up all sorts of things,' said Freeman. 'She was a good Christian, and that to her meant to be warm to human nature, be kind to people. She could give you a few broadsides, she wasn't a pushover, but she was my good friend and I miss her dreadfully.'

Back in the Winnebago, the atmosphere was neither happy nor supportive. The tensions and disagreements were, if anything, worse since Wilde had inadvertently gone public, and he was growing weary of them. He was also restless, saying, 'Being an actor, life should be varied.' There had been nine exceptionally successful years for him, and for the show, his arrival coinciding with the full flowering of Clarke's talents as a comedy writer, and the series catching the public's imagination as never before; Foggy had developed into *Summer Wine's* definitive third man, a character which had helped elevate the show to classic status. Wilde had finally had enough, and a new occupant would have to be found for his corner of the caravan; change was in the air once again, and with it would come a new, expanded cast.

CHAPTER 7

~~~~~~

Extending the Family

FOR MILLIONS, IT was as comfortable as a favourite pair of slippers, the most reliable pleasure on television. Around it, the entertainment landscape was changing. The first shots had been fired in the 'alternative comedy' revolution; eleven days before Compo, Clegg and Foggy had found themselves marooned in a broken-down caravan for the 1982 Christmas special, the first series of *The Young Ones*, starring Rik Mayall and Adrian Edmondson, was finishing its run on BBC2; as Wilde was departing for pastures new two years later, the new wave of in-your-face stand-ups who had made their mark in the burgeoning number of comedy clubs in London were being showcased in Channel 4's *Saturday Live*. Old certainties about what made people laugh were being challenged and the audience was fragmenting. The alternative comics' protestations about what they perceived as sexism would soon kill Benny Hill's career at Thames Television, and other much-loved entertainers were bowing out; Morecambe and Wise's peak years had ended with their departure from the BBC in the late 70s, and their ITV work showed a marked decline. Even so, Eric Morecambe's death in May 1984, only six weeks after the loss of another beloved comic, Tommy Cooper, seemed to mark the end of a golden era in television entertainment. Christmas 1985 would see the start of the final series of *The Two Ronnies*, and the classic comedy series that had held sway when *Last of the*

Summer Wine began were years past. There were new pretenders to the crown as the BBC's most popular sitcom too. *The Black Adder*, starring Rowan Atkinson, had launched in 1983, and another prolific solo writer of sitcoms, John Sullivan, was attracting millions of viewers with two fine series, *Only Fools and Horses* and *Just Good Friends*.

Yet none of the new directions or shows had quite the same grip on the public's affections as *Summer Wine*, which remained a bedrock of the BBC's schedules. A measure of its immense popularity was the number of outside invitations from producers keen for its magic to rub off on their projects. Everybody wanted a piece of it: a national newspaper, the *Daily Star*, used it as the basis of a strip cartoon, Owen and Staff appeared on Terry Wogan's chat show – typically, Wilde turned down two invitations – as well as the frantic outdoors game show *It's A Knockout*, and the trio appeared in the 1984 Royal Variety Performance in a specially written sketch by Clarke, as well as singing 'Tiptoe Through the Tulips', which brought the house down. A little later, a revamped trio would even be hired for a short film promoting the British Rail pension scheme, again with a script by Clarke. Professionals knew how good it was too, voting it the best BBC programme in the 1984 Television and Radio Industries Club Awards.

The stars capitalised in their own way on the fame the show had brought them: Owen, still revelling in the publicity, was always willing to take part in a tabloid stunt like going for lunch at the Savoy in his Compo costume, and moved seamlessly into pantomime, where he could indulge his fondness for hearing the laughter of an audience. For several years, he paired with Staff, a dream team for theatres that guaranteed 'house full' signs. They even released a record, 'Nora Batty's Stockings', in April 1983, a cheerful ditty over a Dixieland-ish background from Hazlehurst, but it went nowhere, achieving the less-than-dizzying heights of number 97 in the charts for a single week before vanishing, not helped by a B-side that featured Owen solemnly intoning his lyrics to the *Summer Wine* theme. Panto was a safer bet, and Staff developed a healthy career of her own, generally playing a variation on Dame Nora, though she also appeared as Mother Goose and the Empress of China.

Owen also took on more challenging projects, returning to the National Theatre for a production of Eugene O'Neill's *The Long Voyage Home*, and later ending the 1980s on a high note, when Lindsay Anderson turned back the clock twenty years to invite him once again to star in a new David Storey play, *The March on Russia*, as a husband looking back on sixty years of marriage. It was a demanding role for an actor of seventy-five, but Owen carried it off superbly and deserved the rave reviews he received, noting with satisfaction: 'I was being offered the prize of a lifetime when it's normally too late to look for prizes.' Sallis too returned to the theatre, gratified to find himself more in demand than ever, and able to take his pick of productions, even returning to the Old Vic, where he had been a lowly supporting actor early in his career, to occupy the star dressing room and play the lead in *Pride and Prejudice*.

Not all the outside projects ran smoothly, as the BBC found to its cost when it played fast and loose with the characters for a Christmas special starring singer Val Doonican, whose cosy crooning was a mainstay of the festive schedules. The trio was co-opted to go Christmas carolling with Doonican, and the scene required fake snow to be spread around a Buckinghamshire village not once, but twice, because of a technicians' strike. It was an expensive interlude in a showcase production. Bell said:

> There was a Christmas party at the BBC, which they always had for the stars and the directors and the writers, and someone went up to Roy and said, 'Really enjoyed the bit with the three *Summer Wine* men in the Val Doonican show,' and he said, 'What bit with the three men?' They hadn't asked him. All the words had been written by another writer, and Roy said, 'You've seen it, but no one else will,' and this chap who had broached it went over to the Head of Entertainment and said, 'I think I've put my foot in it,' and the Head of Entertainment

went to see Roy, who said, 'I know nothing about it, but no bugger's going to write words for my characters.' So it never went out. He wouldn't agree terms or anything, so it's been put on a shelf and never seen.

One spin-off, though, was a huge success, and would bring lasting benefits to the series. Clarke had written a stage treatment of *Summer Wine*, and offered it to the three principals in the early 1980s. Owen and Sallis accepted, but Wilde refused, not, he claimed, because of tensions within the trio, but because he didn't like the play. Freeman agreed to appear, and there would be five new characters: Howard and Pearl, a married couple; Marina, a widow; Crusher, a hulking youth; and his girlfriend. Foggy's absence would be explained by having him in bed with a bad back, allowing Compo and Clegg to periodically shout upstairs to him. It was an undemanding romp about Howard, Clegg's neighbour, being the pen friend of Marina, who throws him into a panic when she announces that she is coming to see him, prompting Howard to plead with Clegg to switch places with him. When the predatory woman arrives, the mistaken identity was the cue for a lot of Clegg being chased round the stage. The atmosphere was quite different to the television series, but in the hands of producer Jan Butlin it worked, and opened at the Bob Hope Theatre in Hanwell, Middlesex, in the summer of 1983 before moving on to Devonshire Park, Eastbourne, where it proved ideal seaside entertainment for packed houses.

'It was terrible, but the audiences loved it,' said Freeman. 'Take away Holmfirth, and our programme's only half there. The wandering, lingering quality which is such an attraction of the show, you can't do that on stage. We were having to resort to beds shutting with people inside them, and ladders and all sorts of things.' Sallis noted that it helped when things went awry on stage: 'The very first play, which we did in north London, in one of the early scenes there was Bill and me and another man – because Brian never wanted to do it at all – and we were sitting at this table and it started to give way. It finished with us tearing the table to pieces and throwing it off into the wings. It wasn't exactly Shakespearean, but it got a big laugh and a round of applause, so we used to pray that something would go wrong, and more often than not our prayers were answered.'

The man-eating Marina – all blonde wig, false eyelashes and skirt fifteen years too short for her – was Jean Fergusson, a Yorkshire-born actress who had come up through rep and also done some television work in *Crossroads*. Chance played its part in her landing the role after she sent a get-well card to a former director who had fallen ill.

The next day I got a phone call saying, 'We want somebody to play a blowsy blonde in this stage version of *Last of the Summer Wine*, could you go for an interview tomorrow?' And I thought, that's bizarre, and I went for the interview and as I walked into this rehearsal room, they were already rehearsing. There were Bill, Peter and Jane, all rehearsing. Anyway, I talked to the director and read a piece of the script and he said, 'Right, ring your agent, you've got the job, you start now, this very minute.' I found out some weeks later that this director friend of mine that I'd sent the card to, he'd just opened my card when the phone rang and they said, 'Can you think of anybody who can play a blowsy blonde?' A long time later, he admitted to me, 'If I hadn't got your card in front of me, because I hadn't seen you for five years, I would not have automatically thought of you.'

Marina drove the action throughout the second half of the show, to the audience's delight, even if it was a long way distant from lying in the heather ruminating on the world, as Clegg, dressed as a French onion seller, fended off the love-struck Marina. One incident stuck in Sallis's mind: 'On the first night, this butterfly came down and landed on Bill's head and everybody saw it, the audience saw it, that was curtain time. But the butterfly came back, on the last night. How could it know that it was the last night? But it came down and settled on his head again. Things like that you really don't forget.'

Reviews of the show were generally kind, and it proved such a commercial success that it was booked into Bournemouth for the following summer. Fergusson remained, but Howard and Pearl had to be re-cast since the actors who had appeared in Eastbourne were not available. For Howard, Jan Butlin turned to a busy jobbing actor she had worked with previously, Robert Fyfe, who had extensive stage experience – including a couple of plays with Freeman, who he knew – and a television career that had ranged from *Dr Finlay's Casebook* to *Coronation Street*. Fyfe said: 'It was end-of-the-pier entertainment, and if anything went wrong it was capitalised on, and people had a lot of fun, it went over wonderfully with the audience. I can remember when the thing went wrong, Bill would step down to the front of the stage and say, "Talk amongst yourselves".'

For Pearl, Butlin called Juliette Kaplan for audition. Kaplan had a long career in rep behind her, but was at a low point, having recently been widowed. She admitted being sharp with Butlin at the interview: 'She said to me, "Can you do a Yorkshire accent," and I said, "Well, I am an actress," in a very sort of snide way. So I did this little reading, and the next day I got a call back, and I went up to London again and said, "Look, I really cannot be going up and down the motorway, either they make up their minds or they find somebody else," and by the time I'd got home, they'd phoned and offered me the part. Now, Bournemouth is my home town and Pearl was my mother's name, and I got a bit of a shiver at the time, and I thought, this is a bit strange, going back to Bournemouth and doing a part that was my own mother's name. I thought, something's going on here.'

Something was. Clarke and Bell both saw the show. Bell didn't like it, but loved the performances of the newcomers. 'It was awful. Peter felt uncomfortable. Peter's agent said, "You must get out of this, it's terribly bad for your career." They came out of the script now and then and just talked to the audience. Really, Peter would talk to the audience and say, "There's only another twenty minutes to go." It wasn't good, but just to show how important casting is, they did the stage show the previous year and the actor playing Howard was OK, and the woman that played Pearl was OK, but here's Robert Fyfe and Juliette Kaplan. Same words, same play, suddenly they were hysterically funny, brilliantly played and I said to Roy, "We've got to try and use them," and he said, "I've seen it, I agree with you, which ones do you think," and I said, "I'll go down and see them," and we took four from the cast.'

The two stars were co-opted to make the approach. Fyfe said: 'One Saturday night, Bill Owen came to my dressing room and said, "I've been asked to ferret around." He'd been primed to find out if I was interested in becoming a regular member of the cast, and he said to me, "Look, I don't believe in all this pussyfooting about, would you like to do it or would you not?" He was quite a direct gentleman, so I said yes, naturally.' It was Sallis who spoke to Kaplan. She and Fyfe had discussed the possibility of a transfer to television with Fergusson, who was not getting her hopes up: 'We all said, "I shouldn't think that's likely, this is just for the stage." *Summer Wine* is what it is, and it won't have all these extra characters in it.' The fourth character to make the transition from stage to screen would be Crusher, played by Jonathan Linsey, who would be deployed as a foil for Ivy in the café, going some way towards filling the gap left by the loss of John Comer.

Clarke was expanding his palette. What had started out as a comedy series about three men was evolving into stories about an extended family of characters who peopled the town, the café and the hills, interacting with each other. The trio would remain at the heart of everything, but the background of their world was becoming more detailed, thanks to increasingly familiar peripheral figures. The impending loss of Foggy would mark a watershed in the structure of the series, and Clarke was treating it as an opportunity to move in a new direction. Whatever the merits or drawbacks of the stage show, he would ever afterwards give an affectionate nod towards it in his scripts; an encounter between Clegg and Marina would be a guaranteed laugh as her face lit up and she advanced on him with all the purpose of an armoured division, always with the greeting, 'Norman Clegg that was,' as he drew back in horror. The first came in 'Catching Digby's Donkey':

Marina: Norman Clegg that was, who once dallied with my affections.

Clegg: I never dallied, I never even dillied. Tell her I never dillied.

Viewers who never saw the stage show laughed at the exchanges, but could be slightly mystified by them. Fergusson said: 'People often ask me, and sometimes even write to me to ask me, what does Marina mean when she says in the series, "Norman Clegg that was"? Well, of course, the "was" is that one time in the play, he was somebody that I thought was my suitor, and of course it was all lies.' The play would be revived again but, with Sallis declining to appear and Owen the only member of the trio on stage, it was retitled *Compo Plays Cupid*.

Howard, Pearl and Marina opened up new comic possibilities for Clarke. The spectacle of the downtrodden little moustachioed man in pursuit of the glamour girl who had seen better days, while in turn being forever caught by his glowering, thin-lipped wife, was inherently funny and the three newcomers played it to the hilt. The furtive liaisons between Howard and Marina offered great potential for the three stars, who would stumble upon them in the most unlikely places, and the exchanges between Clegg and Howard, the pensionable flat-capped Romeo dreaming of excitement and escape from the drudgery of cleaning the windows while wearing an apron, gave Sallis some enviable lines.

Clegg: Morning, Howard.

Howard: Is it, Cleggy? Is this it? A good morning? What are the bad ones like then?

Clegg: You've been reading glossy male magazines, Howard, exposing your soul to discontent.

Howard: There has to be more than this. Where's the glossiness in our lives?

Clegg: Well, there's a lot to be said at our age, Howard, for a plain matt finish.

Howard: You're too young, Howard, they used to tell me when I wanted to elope with that showgirl.

Clegg: You were only sixteen.

Howard: Well, I was on holiday.

Clegg: She was thirty if she was a day.

Howard: At sixteen I loved thirty, I was keen, idealistic, ready to devote my life to thirty-year-old showgirls ...

Clegg: She was horrible!

Howard: ... Even horrible thirty-year-old showgirls.

Clegg: She had big feet.

Howard: She had fishnet tights.

Clegg: She had stockings with holes in them.

Sallis and Fyfe played off each other with polish and precision from the start, and their dialogue would often provide a curtain-raiser to the main plot of the half-hour that followed. As Bell had noted when he saw them on stage, Fyfe, Kaplan and Fergusson were all ideally cast. In Howard, Marina and Pearl, Clarke created quintessential *Summer Wine* characters that mirrored his trio; the would-be lovers were eccentrics and eternal optimists, and the love triangle has just a touch of melancholia about it. He had experimented with infidelity at the very start with Wainwright and Mrs Partridge in the library; this was a more accomplished and much funnier take on extra-marital shenanigans.

The status of Marina as a widow in the stage show was dropped, leaving her simply an unmarried woman of a certain age, desperate for romance, but finding only the semblance of it, and then with the most unglamorous of suitors who introduced lunatic ideas and locations for their liaisons with the words, 'I think we've really cracked it this time,' before his plans invariably came a cropper as Clarke put them in canals, up trees, on the roof of a barn and hidden in undergrowth. Fergusson took to the cartoonish aspects of the role with aplomb, tottering across moorland in perilously high heels, and bringing a skewed dignity to her embarrassments and frustrations that set the audience laughing before she had spoken a word. Fyfe also exploited the physical aspects of Howard, with his bicycle and tracksuit, looking anything but love's young dream as he scuttled between wife and illicit girlfriend with all the timidity of a frightened mouse. Wisely, Clarke kept the relationship as chaste as that between Compo and Nora; the laughs lay in the couple's thwarted passions as they hid behind dry-stone walls and in the woods. They were as innocent as little boys and girls holding hands on the way to nursery school, and as irrepressible; however many disappointments they suffered, they were never unhappy for long. As the years passed, Fyfe and Fergusson would be astonished to receive fan letters from very young children who found Howard and Marina hilarious because they recognised their childlike natures.

In Pearl, Clarke created a new model battleaxe, whom Kaplan gave the sourest face yet seen in the series, pursing her lips, folding her arms, biding her time and never terrifying Howard more than when she smiled. This was a different sort of fearsome woman; while Nora and Ivy bawled, bridled and berated, Pearl dripped acid.

Pearl: You've got ideas, it's always been your trouble. You've got ideas bigger than your natural capacity.

Howard: I've never had any complaints about my natural capacity.

Pearl: Well, you're getting one now.

MARINA PASSES BY

Marina: Good evening, Pearl. Howard.

Howard: Oh, good evening, er ... er ... er ...

Pearl: Her name slipped your memory has it? A likely story.

Howard: I told you, practically a stranger to me.

Pearl: You should have no problem remembering the name Marina. Just think of it as a place frequented by sailors.

There would be other new arrivals to people Clarke's comic world but, for now, the one thing occupying his mind was how to replace Foggy when Wilde hung up the field jacket, cap and walking stick. Inevitably, as with the loss of Bates, an air of uncertainty hung over the show; Foggy had been hugely popular and finding a character and actor to fill his shoes would not be easy. 'It's emergency time again,' said Clarke. 'We're recovering after Foggy so it's game on, you're looking for another extreme character. I came up with Seymour. Some people liked him, some people didn't, but he was good enough to keep us going. He wasn't as easy to write as Foggy, strangely enough, he wasn't as believable. There was a kind of believable unbelievability about Foggy, those daft stories he used to tell.'

Seymour Utterthwaite would be Clarke's third loopy authority figure. This time, he set the off-kilter military background of Blamire and Foggy aside, along with the old school association with Compo and Clegg. Seymour would be new to them but, like Blamire, he would consider himself several cuts above. He was a gentleman, albeit one frayed at the edges, the retired headmaster of a very minor and very broken-down public school for boys, in his own mind one of nature's aristocrats who wondered at the vagaries of fate that brought him into the company of a pair of aimless ageing layabouts. Seymour was a man convinced that the world's recognition of his genius was just around the next corner and his inventions would put him on top – his rightful place, naturally. It was a much broader character than Foggy, not as nuanced, a combination of nutty professor and Will Hay-ish form master, and the trigger for *Summer Wine* to move into broader comic territory as well, into stunts involving madcap machines dreamed up by Seymour, though the premise of the leader of men whose self-confidence was only matched by his total lack of competence remained. He would be introduced with a bang – literally, in the case of an exploding motorised wheelbarrow, and metaphorically with the second feature-length episode that would, in comparison to what had gone before, feel as if it had a cast of thousands. There would be a new emphasis on visual comedy, as the show became more family-friendly than ever. Reaction to Seymour would be mixed, but then Foggy was the hardest of acts to follow; this had to be different if comparisons were to be avoided.

Clarke tailored his writing to the delivery of the man Bell approached to play Seymour – Michael Aldridge. He was a far from obvious choice, nothing like as familiar to television audiences as Bates or Wilde had been, but an actor with a more distinguished stage career than either of them. They had been supporting players, but Michael William ffolliott Aldridge was accustomed to top billing, one of the most widely admired and versatile leading men of his generation, the very model of tall, dark and handsome, and blessed with a rich, mellifluous voice. He moved with ease between the classics, farce and musical comedy, and was much in demand for all of them. He had been born at Glastonbury, Somerset, on 9 September 1920, the son of a doctor, and had a passion for acting even at school, getting himself into every production and pestering one of the governors, playwright Ben Travers, for advice. Aldridge made his professional debut in 1939 in Terence Rattigan's *French Without Tears*, but his career was interrupted by the war, during which he served as an RAF air gunner, observer and navigator in Africa, the US, the Middle East and the Mediterranean. On being demobbed in 1946, he went into rep in the Midlands before joining the Old Vic company and playing Horatio to Michael Redgrave's Hamlet. Great classical roles were starting to come his way, including Othello and Macbeth, but Aldridge embarked on a new direction, joining the musical comedy *Salad Days* for three years, and then leading in its successor, *Free as Air*. Much of his finest stage work came at the Chichester Festival Theatre in productions of works by Anouilh, Eliot and Shaw, where his commanding presence was highly praised. Back in the West End, he played a leading role in Alan Ayckbourn's *Absurd Person Singular* before joining the Royal Shakespeare Company for an acclaimed portrayal of Prospero in *The Tempest*. The West End called again for him to star in the musical *Jeeves*, as well as plays by Alan Bennett, his old acquaintance Ben Travers, and hit runs of *Noises Off* and *Bedroom Farce*.

His was a glittering record, and Aldridge was among the British theatre's best-known figures, even though the wider film and television audience knew less about him because roles in both had been sporadic. That began to change in his mid-fifties as producers woke up to his talents and offered some choice parts, notably the supercilious and disgraced spy chief Percy Alleline opposite Alec Guinness in the BBC adaptation of John Le Carré's *Tinker, Tailor, Soldier, Spy* and the crumbling waster Rollo Aspen in ITV's adaptation of H. E. Bates's *Love for Lydia*. The part that would take him towards his most notable television achievement came in early 1985, in the BBC comedy drama series *Charters and Caldicott*, scripted by Keith Waterhouse. It paired Aldridge with another fine actor, Robin Bailey, as a pair of archetypal cricket-mad English duffers investigating a murder. The characters had originated in Hitchcock's 1939 thriller *The Lady Vanishes* and, as played by Basil Radford and Naunton Wayne, proved so popular that they developed a life of their own in films and radio for more than a decade afterwards. Waterhouse's revival of them was witty and popular with audiences, and Aldridge played a splendid innings as Caldicott, all bumbling pomposity, old-world courtesy and unworldly innocence, with tea being taken on the dot at the same time every day, and the batting averages treated as holy writ.

His performance caught Bell's eye: 'I'd been a fan of the *Charters and Caldicott* series, even in the films I thought they were wonderful characters, and I thought Michael was such a funny player and would be different enough from Foggy not to be compared. Of course, inevitably he was compared. He hadn't really done much film or television, he was much more of a stage actor, he was a wonderful bluff character, a buffoon in *Charters and Caldicott*. I invited him for lunch and we talked, and he was very pleased, delighted. He was a very confident man, and it was very clear that he wouldn't be playing Foggy. And because he had more of an educated voice, Roy wrote him to be an ex-headmaster, which was entirely different from Foggy. Roy wrote it for him.'

Aldridge looked the part as a retired headmaster. At sixty-four, he was a heavy-set bear of a man with a mane of thick grey hair, whose dark good looks of his youth had weathered appealingly into a craggy warmth. More than once over the years, reviewers of his stage work had noted a touch of nobility about Aldridge's manner and bearing, and this exceptionally fine actor gave that quality the subtlest of tweaks to invest his portrayal of Seymour with an air of faded grandeur. Blamire and Foggy both fell from their pretensions and aspirations; Seymour would seem to fall farther because of the loftier outlook Aldridge implied. He brought a lifetime's experience to bear on his new character, and the comic timing he had honed in front of West End audiences was impeccable. Clarke had some breathing space to tailor his script to Aldridge, because a ninety-minute special was being produced rather than a full series. Aldridge took full advantage of what had been written for him; the dark expressiveness of his voice and the gravitas of his delivery highlighting the lunacy of what Seymour had to say. Oddly, for such an expert actor, he admitted some difficulty with his northern accent, which would come and go as unpredictably as the clouds over the Pennines, telling the *Radio Times* in 1985: 'I tried to do a Yorkshire accent, but it didn't really work, so I think I more or less use my own voice.' It didn't really matter; Seymour considered himself superior to Compo and Clegg so there was no reason why he should not sound somewhat posher.

His debut special would be 'Uncle of the Bride', which revolved around the marriage of Seymour's niece, Glenda, to fiancé Barry. The jewel in its crown would be a guest appearance by one of the most beloved figures in British show business – Thora Hird, as Edie, Seymour's sister, Glenda's mother and Wesley's wife. Bell had his own wife, Constance, to thank for landing her. 'Edie wasn't a big part, but it was a good one,' he said.

> The big problem was, who could I get to play her who would make the character funny and be different from the tough Yorkshire women – like Nora Batty, Ivy and Pearl – who were already firmly established in the series. My wife immediately suggested Thora Hird. I treated this suggestion with my usual respect and told her not to be silly and mind her own business. There was no way that Thora Hird would join us to play such a relatively small part in a long-running series. But my wife was insistent. She had seen Thora being interviewed on television – having just finished *In Loving Memory* – and had picked up that she admired the Yorkshire countryside and had fond memories of working there. With nothing to lose, I tentatively rang Felix de Wolfe, Thora's agent, and asked him if she would be interested in being a guest star in our TV movie. He immediately said that he was certain that she would and would ask her. He called back straight away and said that she would be delighted to be with us. From that moment on, the production rose in stature and we were making a really special 'special'.

Clarke was ecstatic. 'It knocked me out. I was thirty-five before I sold anything, so I've got half a life gone before I get in the business and so I've seen all these people up to then as any member of the audience sees them, and so when somebody says to me, "We've got Thora Hird," that's tremendous to me, because it's somebody I watch on screen and love, and suddenly to find they're in something you've written is a hell of a kick. Even though I've been in the business all this time, writing and writing, I'm still as star-struck as I used to be to get someone like that.'

Clarke's reaction chimed with that of the wider audience. It was a measure of Hird's extraordinary place in the public's affections that she became one of those very few actors and entertainers universally and unselfconsciously known by her first name. Part of the love for her had its roots in admiration of the extraordinary longevity of her career – her first appearance on stage came when she was eight weeks old in 1911, and she was still performing nearly ninety years later – so she seemed to have been part of the landscape forever, playing charwomen, nags, vituperative mothers-in-law and, latterly, the grandmother everybody wished they had. More than that, audiences embraced her because they felt she was just like they were – honest, open-hearted and down-to-earth. She was all of those things, and on her part held a genuine regard for the people who came to see her or watched the box at home, always happy to talk to fans, and deriving great pleasure from the warmth they invariably showed her.

She was also a hard-headed and highly skilled professional who worked hard for her success, had been astute in what she accepted and canny enough to carve out a unique niche in star character parts as she aged; producers and writers came to her because nobody but Thora would do for certain roles. Both Thora and *Summer Wine* benefited when she said yes to Edie; she brought an audience of her own to the show, and it gave her one of the signature roles of the glorious Indian summer of her career, a part which would last almost to the end of her life, and from which she derived immense satisfaction.

That career had taken her from a babe in arms on the stage of the Royalty Theatre, run by her father in her native Morecambe, via films and television to such a degree of pre-eminence in the public's regard by the mid-1980s that readers of a national newspaper voted her the second most popular person in Britain, behind the Queen Mother, who had, of course, been around even longer than Thora. Thanks to her father, the theatre was second nature to her and, after a brief spell working as a Co-op shop assistant, she was in rep by her teens, reaching the West End in 1940 and moving into films a year later. Like Bill Owen, she was signed by Rank, and worked steadily in character parts. On stage, though, she was winning starring roles, notably in R. F. Delderfield's *The Queen Came By*, twice on stage and twice in television adaptations. She worked opposite Olivier in the film of John Osborne's *The Entertainer* in 1960, and three years later hit the jackpot on television with *Meet the Wife*, a funny and popular BBC sitcom written by Ronald Wolfe and Ronald Chesney, which paired Thora with another northern comedy favourite, Freddie Frinton, and ran to five series.

Offers came pouring in, and Thora embarked on a punishing schedule of work, which she took in her stride. She rehearsed *Meet the Wife* in the morning, then appeared twice nightly at the Palladium alongside Harry Secombe and Jimmy Tarbuck in *London Laughs*, as well as recording the radio show *One Born Every Minute*. Guest spots in *The Good Old Days*, *Call My Bluff* and dramas including *Dixon of Dock Green* took up any spare time. More successful series followed: *The First Lady*, written especially for her, in which she was a steely county councillor with a heart of gold; *In Loving Memory*, where she was the wife of an undertaker; and *Hallelujah*, in which she was a Salvation Army captain. All were quality work; she was too smart to accept anything less. It made no difference whether she was Ivy or Emily or, for that matter, Edie; they were all Thora, all tailored to a personality bigger than any character. Thora's public adored her whatever she played, and some heavyweight writing talent adored her too, notably Alan Bennett, who gave her a signature role in his play *Intensive Care*, and would later, in two of his *Talking Heads* monologues, 'A Cream Cracker Under the Settee' and 'Waiting for the Telegram', provide her with scripts that drew out the greatest screen performances of her life, winning her Baftas for both. It was not just the consummate acting skill that endeared

Thora to millions; what cemented her status as a national treasure was her seventeen years presenting *Praise Be!*, starting in 1977, which invited viewers to select their favourite hymns. The show was a Sunday evening staple for the BBC, and a labour of love for Thora, a devout Christian, whose enjoyment of the programme was plain. It was the apotheosis of Thora; the moment when she and her audience achieved a divine rapport, and they followed her into *Summer Wine*.

Clarke's script ticked all her boxes. Edie was funny, feisty and formidable; the heart of gold beneath was a given. It was a role that fitted to the T of Thora, and illuminated her star comic persona better than any sitcom ever had. If Bennett created her definitive dramatic roles, Clarke provided her most memorable comic character. She knew what a gift it was and, at the age of seventy-four, Thora embarked on a journey that was to last seventeen years in a series of which she was a devoted fan: 'It's so refreshing to see a programme where there are no nude people in bed, isn't it?' she would ask rhetorically of both interviewers and the public who approached during location filming.

Bell's expanded cast was completed by the nearest thing Clarke ever wrote to juvenile leads. For Glenda and Barry, Bell picked Sarah Thomas and Mike Grady, both with extensive stage experience and both with a good track record on television. Grady was recommended to him, and had played a key supporting role in John Sullivan's first series, *Citizen Smith*, as Ken, best friend of the suburban Che Guevara, Wolfie Smith, a part that had propelled Robert Lindsay to success. Thomas had appeared in the hit ITV children's series *Worzel Gummidge* with Jon Pertwee. She had been knocking on doors at the BBC for some time. Bell answered, coincidentally while she was performing in a play with a northern setting, J. B. Priestley's *When We Are Married*.

I used to write letters to particular comedy and light entertainment people at the BBC, and one of my letters happened to come on to Alan Bell's desk when I was doing a play at Leatherhead, and it happened to be a comedy and it was a Yorkshire play. Alan lived just down the road, and in our last week he brought the family to see the play and so I did an audition on stage without knowing he was there, and on the last night I had a phone call in between the matinee and the evening performance to say if I wasn't working between June and July that year, would I like to give Alan Bell a ring and go and see him the following week because he might have a part. So I went, and he said he wasn't a hundred per cent sure that Thora Hird would be playing Edie, and if she did agree to play the part, then he could probably offer me the part of Glenda. He didn't say, 'I want you to do it,' so I left the BBC thinking, oh yeah, and I got back to my flat and the phone was ringing and it was Alan to say, 'I came after you, but you'd gone, and I'd like to offer you the part.'

Bell explained that he cast her because there was a slight resemblance to Thora: 'That annoys me, seeing somebody who could not possibly be a son or a daughter of the actor playing a parent, but there was a semblance there, you could say Sarah could be her daughter, and Thora loved working with her.'

Bell had his new third man, his supporting cast, and a guest star he'd been lucky to land. All was set for his 'really special "special"'. Another new era was about to get under way, though not without its heartaches.

PART THREE

Stunts and Stories

CHAPTER 8

The Lady and the Gentleman

BELL'S PHONE RANG. It was Gordon Wharmby, asking if what he had heard was true. 'He rang me up to say, "I've just heard that playing Edie, my wife, is Thora Hird," and I said, "Yes, brilliant, isn't it," and he said, "Yes, but Thora Hird," and I said, "Yes. Good isn't it," and he said, 'But Alan, *Thora Hird!*"' Wharmby was overwhelmed at the prospect of working with her; he was nervous, and becoming ever more so as the filming, due to begin in May, approached.

Wharmby had repaid Bell's faith in him. He'd carried off his second appearance, in 'The Loxley Lozenge', with such assurance that Clarke brought him back for the finale of the series that followed, 'Who's Minding The Café, Then?', in March 1985. Again, he had been funny, affecting and warm. Clarke liked Wesley and the way Wharmby had brought him to life and, as was his preferred method, began tailoring the dialogue to suit the actor's characteristics. Wesley was useful to Clarke; he offered scope to do more with the trio, getting them out and about in his battered old Land Rover and setting up sight gags as he tinkered with all things mechanical. The old corrugated tin garage at the end of a lane where he clattered and revved and had his cap set afire as engines blew up in clouds of smoke that billowed out of the doors was a great set piece. But at fifty-one, Wharmby was neither a confident, nor even full-time, actor. His day job was still as a painter and decorator, and when he'd finished his first two episodes of *Summer Wine*, that was what he went back to. Now, Wesley's role was being expanded. He would introduce Seymour to Compo and Clegg, have to be the doting dad who walked Glenda up the aisle, have to convince as Barry's father-in-law. Most of all, he would have to embody the henpecked husband to Thora in full flow as the archetypal domineering northern wife. This was more, much more, than he had ever been called on to do before, a world away from the bit parts such as a milkman in *Coronation Street*; it required more range, more flexibility, more assurance, and he was terrified. There was for him, more than for any other member of the cast, a strong element of reality in his portrayal of Wesley; like his character, he was a working-class man who had for years got his hands dirty to earn a living, and that had been key to his landing the role. Bell had recognised that and cast him for the honesty he brought to it; Clarke had recognised it too and wrote accordingly. Wharmby could act and do it well, and knew that the lucky break that had come his way was the stuff of show-business fairytale. But luck came at a price, and the looming challenge spooked him to the extent that he started drinking to steady his nerves.

He had progressed way beyond his expectations of being cast as just an interesting face with a few lines; now he was a recognisable actor from the telly, and having trouble coming to terms with it. 'On the Sunday, he walked round Holmfirth and he was astonished by the number of people coming up and asking for his autograph,' said Bell. 'A painter decorator. And what it turned out to be, he was terrified of working with Thora, this grand lady of the theatre, him a painter decorator from Manchester. He was so in awe of Thora, how could he possibly be working with this icon of theatre and television?'

His worries shook him to pieces. Wharmby became erratic and agitated to the point where he was marching up and down, pretending to be Bell, shouting 'Action'. He threw a plant pot through the window of the White Horse at Jackson Bridge and had to be restrained. A nervous breakdown had overtaken this gentle man who was giving his utmost, and he was admitted to hospital for psychiatric treatment. Bell was deeply concerned, both for Wharmby's health and the production; Thora was about to arrive in Yorkshire, and had to be told. This was going to be difficult; the only way to get the filming done would be to use a stand-in as Wesley, hardly the scenario that a guest star expected, and hardly the way to bring out her best performance. Thora, though, was a brick; the compassion that implied the heart of gold in even her most hard-boiled characterisations was no act, and Bell was touched and relieved at her reaction.

> I decided that the only way to break the bad news to Thora was over dinner. So for support, I invited Bill Owen and Peter Sallis and my assistant, Mike Cager, who had already done some emergency doubling as Wesley. I told Thora of my predicament and that I would, for instance, have to have her talking to Wesley out of sight under the sink unit in order to get any of her scenes with him on film. I said that if she chose to withdraw from the film, she could, and we would all understand. Thora's response was immediate – 'The poor love, he must be feeling terrible having had to let you down like that. Of course I'll carry on, I'll do anything you want to help you get the film finished.' Thora's concerns were more for poor old Gordon, and at the end of the evening she announced she would be praying for him.

He tweaked both scenes and schedule. Meanwhile, the rest of the filming was going well. After a frustrating and fruitless search for a home for Seymour, a derelict cottage belonging to an iron company on the edge of a bleak stretch of moorland had been found, prettied up and even given a pond. The garden was filled with eccentric machines that span and spilled water, and a suitably eccentric backdrop for the almost-a-gentleman inventor was created. Aldridge took to the part as naturally as the ducks to the new pond, with wild hair, brown overall coat and motorised wheelbarrow that brought him charging into *Summer Wine* round a corner of the cottage as his latest invention ran away with him. He cut a magnificently barmy figure of threadbare dignity and the dialogue fitted him like a glove as he recalled his school:

Seymour: All it wanted was the old pigsties pulling down, new roof and a few trenches filling in that the army had left. All the rest was all cosmetic.

Compo: Where was this place then?

Seymour: High on the North Yorkshire Moors amidst superb natural scenery. God, it was cold. Of course, it was splendid for all our outdoor activities. I used to run adventure courses in roof repairs, window replacements, digging drains; we were a practical school. I had this vision of the Utterthwaiteonian as a good all-rounder. Naturally, all the little swine really wanted to do was play rugby. Have you ever played rugby? Ye gods, it's frightening.

Aldridge was a pleasure to work with and, as the new boy, at pains to get involved with everybody, as Sarah Thomas recalled: 'Michael was absolutely lovely. On the first day, he'd learned all the names of the crew and he'd go up to them and introduce himself and chat. He'd just made the effort to learn people's names, and that's a lot to put to memory, but it shows a very caring side.' Not only that, Aldridge was proving to be an admirably flexible and enthusiastic colleague. Mike Grady said: 'He was fabulous to work with. He had that quality of being able to go with it if you decided to do something slightly different during a rehearsal, he was quite intuitive, considering that he wasn't a particularly young man.'

The atmosphere on set was different, lighter, more upbeat than it had been when Wilde was the third man, and that was down to Aldridge. 'When Michael came into the show, it changed, radically, because I believe it hadn't been the happiest show to work on, but he was a party animal,' said Grady. 'He was ebullient, he was full of stories, galvanised people, he attracted good cheer, he was a tremendously decent character and he and I got on immediately, and he was just one of those people where everything changed around him and he just made everything happier to work with. Peter became happier, Bill became marginally less grumpy than he had been before, a bit more malleable, and it was just a great bit of casting on Alan's part. Michael brought all his *joie de vivre* to it, and wouldn't brook bad moods, it just didn't happen around him, and there was plenty of opportunity for bad moods on a show like this, where there were a variety of personalities and egos, and he just cut right through it.'

It was the same when filming was over. Owen still went his own way to the rented cottage, the strictly timed whisky and the fish pie, but back at the Huddersfield Hotel Aldridge was the catalyst for a much more convivial atmosphere and a great deal of laughter that engendered a new closeness among the cast. Outgoing and gregarious, he was temperamentally the exact opposite of Wilde's reserve and privacy. Jean Fergusson said: 'There was a little sitting area near the bar and Michael would say, before we all went upstairs after we'd finished work, "Come on, we're going to have a nice little drink and a little chat, and chew over the day," and I remember that with great fondness because it was the company getting together and sitting down because maybe during the day we hadn't had the opportunity, so it was really nice, and I respected him for that and loved him. He was a really, really nice man.'

It was not just the supporting cast that Aldridge drew out. He and Sallis clicked immediately, and a previously solitary dinner table quickly became home to animated conversation. 'Before Michael came, Peter was always on his own,' said Fergusson. 'So Peter didn't really have a mate. He'd join us, and we'd often join him, but he'd still have his table. There was a time when he'd have a table on his own with a reading light, so he could have his food and read his book, and then he'd come and sit down with us for half an hour on his way to bed. But when Michael came, they were like two little kids, because they had an immediate bond, and they laughed at each other and really had such fun. They didn't always eat in the hotel, they went out, and Michael would often say, "Come on, why don't you come," and we'd go out for meals with the two of them and that was really nice.'

Aldridge was an old enough hand to realise that Sallis and Owen had to be handled tactfully, and acknowledged that the quirks of life in the star caravan that had become ironbound during Wilde's tenure needed to be observed. 'It's rather like joining a new common room if you're a teacher,' he observed wryly in the *Radio Times*. 'You have to learn the social conventions. Peter Sallis and Bill Owen were wonderful hosts, introducing me to the local people and so forth. And there were social conventions in our own caravan. Bill always sat at the end next to the driver and Peter sat at the other end. You have to watch out for these things. They are very important.' There were none of the disagreements of the Wilde years, not least because Aldridge was infinitely more tolerant of Owen, whose attitude towards the show and his part in it was immediately apparent to the newcomers. 'He did behave like he was the star,' said Grady. 'He was very approachable, but he just knew his status within the company, which was probably a little larger in his mind than it was in reality. What do you say? He was Compo. He was very much a law unto himself. It wasn't that he didn't suffer fools gladly – he didn't suffer anybody. Never knew his lines, more or less whatever came into his head, something akin to what Roy had written, and Peter and Michael worked around it, and he delivered that performance which the audience adored, so nobody really minds what he does.' Thomas found the same thing: 'He used to count the number of lines to make sure he had plenty, and then didn't know them. He used to paraphrase them, which is never easy for the other actors because you don't get the right cue.'

She and Grady hit it off immediately and they were both funny and appealing as the young couple surrounded by grizzled eccentrics. Going on location to Yorkshire for the first time was a steep learning curve for Thomas. 'It was very exciting, quite scary, and I remember wearing a pair of white leather shoes that I'd bought new for the first day on location and when we got there I got out of the car into a muddy puddle. They were ruined, and I learned that location means muddy puddles. In the early days, we didn't have many caravans. There was a coach, but we used to have to wander around. That film, I remember wearing a wedding dress and wellingtons with my hair in rollers, just sort of wandering around the countryside.'

The weather was being mostly kind as the shoot progressed, and the only cloud on the horizon was Wharmby's health. Bell was approaching the point where a double simply would not do, and went to hospital to see if there was any possibility of him being well enough for a couple of scenes. He was distressed by what he found, but the prospect of getting back to work on the film brightened Wharmby.

'I needed him for two shots, the one where he looked at the bride and said, "Ee, lass, you look wonderful," and one in the church. I couldn't do those with a double, and I went to see the psychiatrist, and Gordon was fine apart from his eyes were red-rimmed. The thing for me was going in to see him in this place, and the way they locked the doors behind us. I broached the subject and said, "Maybe if you could get back to filming, they might let you do a couple of bits," and he leaped out of the chair and went and saw the charge nurse.'

Wharmby was discharged under Bell's supervision and returned to work. He was fragile, but determined. What set him on the road to recovery was the very person over whom he had worried himself into illness, who unwittingly demonstrated that she wasn't some sort of demi-god, but just another human being, as prone to failings and fluffs as anyone else.

Bell said:

There was a scene where Thora had to brush him down and said to him, 'You're going to wear a suit,' and Thora's next line was, 'It's a decent social occasion and you're wearing a suit.'

And Thora couldn't remember the line, about six or seven takes. In the end I said, 'Thora, say, "You're wearing a suit" and brush him and I'll say off camera, "It's a decent social occasion".' Nobody noticed, I'd take my voice off. That was the turning point, because Gordon suddenly realised that this grand lady of the theatre wasn't perfect, and he completely changed and was magnificent thereafter, and he wasn't frightened of Thora. You can imagine, a painter decorator thinking, my God, I'm going to be mixing with someone who really knows how to act, but when Thora couldn't remember the line, that was it.

Wharmby came through, and gave a performance of notable warmth. He would still have his jitters over working with Thora for some time yet, but his crisis was over and he began to come to terms with a new, different life as a popular character in a hit series. Mike Grady said: 'Once he was through that, he accepted that he had this status, and we all liked him enormously and thought he did a great job. He was very, very hard working, well ahead of his lines and a damned nice bloke. You didn't want to play cards with him though –a right scally when it came to playing cards – but he knew what a lucky break he'd had, getting fan mail and having a few bob, and he took it with good grace, God bless him.'

'Uncle of the Bride' made no attempt to replicate the knowing tone of 'Getting Sam Home'. This was a romp that set out to introduce Seymour and gloried in the presence of its guest star and the possibilities of its extended cast. It was much more physical, as *Summer Wine* adapted to life without Wilde. 'They brought five of us in to replace Foggy,' said Grady. 'He was the most popular character. To this day, people still ask about him and say, "I never liked it after Foggy left."'

To explain Foggy's absence, Clarke turned once again to Clegg receiving a letter, as he had from Blamire, this time from Bridlington on the Yorkshire coast, where the former corporal signwriter had been bequeathed a suitably offbeat business.

Clegg: His uncle left him this decorating egg business in Bridlington. He has got a stall on the harbour selling decorated eggs to visitors.

Howard: No wonder the place is crowded.

Clegg: You can't take enough precautions, can you? They warn you in general terms to be careful, but how can you avoid some uncle who's careless enough to die and leave you decorating eggs?

Clegg and Compo decide to use the decorated eggs sent by Foggy as wedding presents for Barry and Glenda, and hook up with Wesley, who is delivering Seymour's laundry, lovingly done by Edie. The new trio join Barry for his stag night, where Seymour unveils a gadget that switches all the pub lights off before the groom decides on a run across the moors, only to fall down a hole, spraining his ankle. He is rescued, but Clegg manages to reverse the car taking him to church into Seymour's pond, so naturally the groom has to be taken there in the motorised wheelbarrow.

It was broadcast on New Year's Day 1986, and the audience held firm, with 18.1 million tuning in. The critics, though, were unimpressed; for the first time in its thirteen-year history, the reviews were lukewarm, lamenting both the absence of Foggy and the increased emphasis on physical humour. Mark Lawson in *The Times* wrote, 'at first taste, the 1986 vintage is an indifferent one and the series shows frightening signs of the long-haul palsy likely to afflict every veteran television runner', adding: 'A unique series has been cheapened. A victim of its brilliance, *Last of the Summer Wine* has been made into a ratings chaser and the director and writer have pitched the show lower, aiming at those extra millions you get for skimping on originality and difficulty. And those who loved it as it was get a swap they never wanted; cheap beer for fine wine.'

Criticism notwithstanding, Clarke, Bell and the BBC were all happy with 'Uncle of the Bride' and pressed on in the new direction.

The show remained one of the BBC's bankers, running neck-and-neck with *Only Fools and Horses* and *Just Good Friends* as the top comedy. Seymour had made a good start and needed to be firmly established with the audience. Bell recalled: 'I said to Roy, "What we should do is a double series next year so that people forget about the previous characters," and it worked well, when we did the double series, he was embraced as the third man.'

Clarke undertook more *Summer Wine* writing for a season than he had ever attempted – thirteen episodes, which would begin with a Christmas special on 28 December 1986 and run all the way to late March. The trio would be more vigorous than ever – there would be stunts, and gadgets that might have sprung from the batty imagination of a Heath Robinson Q equipping a geriatric James Bond for a licence to pratfall in the Pennines. A bike with an oil-drilling attachment, an ejector seat on top of a car, a waste-disposal unit that splatters a kitchen, a sailboard on roller skates. Compo would fall through the bottom of a canoe, tumble from a roof and career downhill on an improvised ice-cream wagon. Seymour would get locked out thanks to his revolutionary electronic security system that failed to respond to the password 'Codfanglers' and tumble into the river as he tries to rescue Wally from the tyrannies of Nora. This would not only be the longest series yet, it would be by some way the most energetic.

One or two of the older hands in the cast regretted the new emphasis on visual humour, but recognised its popularity with the audience, as well as acknowledging that the show had to change to accommodate the expanded cast. Freeman said: 'We got all the visual gags, sofas running downhill, people falling over walls, and all that became very popular. We got a lot of new people and you had to adjust to the new personalities, and we went off on a different tangent, because you can't write for Thora and Gordon what had been written before, and so we had explosions in the shed. It was for a different audience really, but I'd loved it when it was speech-based.'

Visual humour sat naturally with Clarke, who harked back to

an early idol, Buster Keaton. 'My comic hero in physical movement is Buster Keaton, that man had such remarkable neatness and economy of movement, and Bill Owen had this, and that was a huge bonus for me because it was Bill's capacity as a physical clown that shifted the programme from talking heads, as it began, into things that were much more physical.' The reaction from the audience to the stunts and outlandish inventions that came out of Seymour's workshop or Wesley's shed encouraged him further. 'The stunts were a huge success. I was drawn into it because of the feedback from the people. It started very talky and then when you'd do an odd bit physically, the reaction was such that you realised there was room for these. Alan had this special effects department who would lean over backwards to come up with these weird machines and you do all these daft things. Physical humour, if it's right, knocks dialogue for six – and I'm a dialogue writer. It was a big part, became half the script, what the stunt was going to be, or what weird machine, it was great to have people who were not only willing to have a go, but keen to have a go.'

Bell's designers consistently came up with the goods, and the principal cast embraced the physicality, not least Owen, who even though he was now in his seventies remained game for some arduous tasks in often trying circumstances. 'Bill would do a lot of stuff,' said Grady. 'Climb up on a roof, run across a field. There were a lot more stunts in those days, we had a couple of stuntmen who did a lot of work for us. Never for me, I did all my own driving and it was scary, really scary at times because you had other people in the car and it was their lives. They would say, "Drive faster down the hill," even though Bill, or a stuntman looking like Bill, was sitting on top of the car in a chair. It's incredibly dangerous, because you go round a corner at forty miles per hour, the whole thing will tip over. We were going into rivers where there were rats and Weil's Disease, people were falling off considerable heights. It was, in its own little way, quite a dangerous show.'

Bell made increasing use of the stuntmen as the quota of visual gags increased. He also made more use of doubles for his principal cast, partly as a way of saving time because it was easier to get them to the top of a hill for a long shot on which the dialogue would be dubbed in later, and partly to conserve the energies of three ageing actors for the scenes in close-up. Artful editing disguised the use of doubles, and for years afterwards the audience would be unaware of them until Bell revealed their existence in the mid-1990s. The larger cast also eased pressure on the stars, as it freed the trio from carrying all the action for the duration of each thirty-minute episode, and gave Clarke more options. 'It's been useful for me because I've always got something to fall back on,' he said. 'When I'm writing, I can hear them saying, "Where's my bit," and I've got to get a piece in and it helps in a way. Having that wealth there, that range to choose from, is a good get-out from scenes that you've had enough of. It's nice to know there's somewhere to go.'

The expanded cast gradually eased into becoming regulars; the *Summer Wine* way was to introduce a character, see how it worked and then consider where to take it. 'There was no indication that the character would continue,' said Grady. 'Alan said, "Maybe, maybe not," they didn't really invite you to stay, they just sent scripts and the scripts would arrive randomly, and I'd say, "OK, am I free that week? Yes, I'm free, I'll do that," and bit by bit you become a regular and people start writing letters to you saying, "I like your character in our series," and suddenly you find you're part of it.'

Best of all, Thora had agreed to return for a couple of episodes. Her billing would still be as a guest star, as it would remain throughout her tenure, but she fitted comfortably into the ensemble, not least because of a couple of superb bits of comic business that became as familiar and indispensable parts of the show as Compo's matchbox. One was the ritual placing of newspapers on the floor of her immaculate kitchen for the filthy Wesley to stand on. This was to develop into such a finely honed routine between Thora and Wharmby that with split-second timing she could raise a newspaper flat against a doorframe to protect her paintwork as his oily hand reached out, to roars of laughter from the audience. Her other great gift to the series was her patented mock-posh voice, in which 'Wesley' would become '*Wes-lay*', 'nice' was transformed into '*naice*' and 'here' into '*he-ah*'. It never failed to reduce the audience to hysterics, and was performed matchlessly by Thora, who gave Edie the most gracious of smiles and a tinklingly refined – even '*refained*' – laugh to go with it. Like all the best gags, it was rooted in reality. Edie's determination to be a cut above – at least when she poked her head out of the back door to summon her grubby husband from his shed – tickled the audience because the putting on of airs and graces was so familiar to them from everyday life. The plummy tone had been part of Thora's comic armoury for more than twenty years. She had first used it on television in *Meet the Wife* in 1964, and then only at the urging of a producer who overheard her reducing co-star Freddie Frinton to helpless laughter during breaks in rehearsals. Sharp observer of human behaviour that she was, Thora had drawn the voice from reality, in this case from an aunt who ran a shop. 'Auntie Nellie's voice was a piece of childhood observation that slumbered volcano-like into middle age,' Thora told the *Yorkshire Evening Post* in 1985. 'Nellie had a shop and when I was eating my tea in the back room, she would speak to me quite plainly. Then the shop bell would ring and Nellie would sally forth through the curtain, trilling at the customer in a really cultured voice.' The voice was entirely in keeping with Edie's pride in her brother, the intellectual of the family, and Thora underlined the air of desperate striving for social superiority with a microscopic facial twitch of discomfiture at moments when Wesley or Glenda would simply be too common. She developed another bit of physical business too, bumping her rump against the front door to check if it was locked.

There would be another addition to the cast during that ninth series, Danny O'Dea, a 75-year-old music-hall veteran and expert panto dame, who was brought in for one episode, 'Jaws', as a Mr Magoo-like figure, Eli Duckett, a friend of Wally Batty. This would – literally – be a sight gag as Eli, in bottle-bottom glasses, wreaked havoc in a pub as he tried to play darts. The scene was hilarious on screen, but O'Dea was hard work for Bell. 'It was a struggle getting anything out of him. I managed to cut it all together, but never again did I want to work with that man. Lovely man, but couldn't play mime comedy. Ronnie wrote the music for him, rat-a-tat music-hall stuff, and Peter Sallis said, "You've got to have him as a regular," and I said, "No, never," and Roy said, "I want to use him again, he's great," and it was a struggle. I had to talk him through it. He just couldn't do anything, honestly. Twenty takes. He was a lovely old man, but his forte was pantomime.' O'Dea stayed, and his cameos as he walked across roofs of cars into a skip, mistook a hearse for an ice-cream van and Marina on all-fours for a dog, became, thanks to Bell's patience, a bright spot in every episode in which Eli appeared.

Ronnie Hazlehurst was not only underlining Eli's antics musically. Bell was making increasing use of the masterful composer's talent for framing the action. Hazlehurst had a genius for bending his wistful little theme tune into shapes that would add laughs. One of his larger-scale achievements had been to adapt it for a brass band to play as a runaway steam locomotive sped past a bemused civic party in 'Full Steam Behind' in 1979, and now he went a step further, using an augmented orchestra and imaginative scoring to create pastiches of familiar film and television themes, so that in 'Set the People Free', as the trio tried to liberate Wally from Nora's chores, the music evoked Elmer Bernstein's jauntily defiant tune from *The Great Escape*, beloved of the audience from its frequent Christmas screenings on television. Current shows also had the mickey taken out of them with sly wit, and Hazlehurst aped their music with such precision that a blistering call came from the makers of *Dallas*, the glitzy oil-and-sex US series that topped the ratings for the BBC and announced itself with a declamatory theme for each week's episode featuring the villainous machinations of J. R. Ewing. The episode was 'Why Does Norman Clegg Buy Ladies' Elastic Stockings?', a wonderfully offbeat comic take on the national obsession with the miseries of the millionaire Ewing clan on their Southfork ranch. In Clarke's vision, the stockings were needed to run Seymour's oil-drilling machine, attached to an old bike, naturally.

'I said, "This is like *Dallas*, play it in the *Dallas* style",' said Bell, and Hazlehurst produced a wickedly accurate parody. 'The *Dallas* people rang up and said they were very angry and they were taking legal action against us for using their theme without permission. Seriously. I said we hadn't done that, and they said we had, they'd got recordings of the programme, and it's definitely the *Dallas* theme, and I said, "It's nothing of the sort, it's in the style of, and there's nothing you can do about that." The argument went on for about a fortnight, and then they accepted it. It was the *Summer Wine* theme, and Ronnie did it with *ET*, and in another one it became a tango theme, and in another it was a military march. He was a master of music, and miracle worker of music.'

He was a master of mischief as well, and kept a straight face while getting a laugh at Bell's expense, coaxing him into outlining what he wanted by *dah-dee, dah-dum*-ing what he had in mind.

I would ask for something a bit more sombre and do the instrument noises, so he said, 'Come in and tell the orchestra,' and he would have a great deal of fun at me doing all the instrument voices. 'Got that, boys?' he'd say. When we did 'Getting Sam Home', he said, 'You've got such a clear idea of what you want, get a video recorder and a tape recorder and record the music you want throughout the whole film.' So I said, 'Really?' and he said, 'Yeah, I'll be able to play it and know exactly what you want.' So I did, and he used to play it to friends at parties, because it was so silly. He did what I wanted, though.

Hazlehurst was always happy to oblige, and gave Bell a helping hand when he became frustrated at BBC continuity announcers talking over the closing credits, breaking and extending the theme tune. 'The only way to stop it was to carry the action on until the very end, so I would have some dialogue, and the music didn't ever sound like vamping, he managed to make it sound complete. Very clever.' Hazlehurst put tremendous time and effort into his scores; a single episode could take ten hours or more, and his work was more than ever a factor in the show's continuing success.

So was the dialogue. As that long series designed to establish Aldridge progressed, it became clear that for all the visual gags, Clarke had written some top-drawer material, not least for Seymour, as when he reflected on the curiosity of Compo's ferrets: 'As a former headmaster, I can tell you small boys are like that – into everything. The number of times I had to replace matron's hearing aid. Well, I suppose curiosity is natural at their age, but it meant I never dared employ anyone with an artificial limb. They'd have had it unscrewed in a trice.'

Aldridge's grave delivery and expression of wonderment made such lines all the funnier. Clegg's observations on humankind's foibles remained as sharp as ever; if once they had been about religion or politics, now Clarke let himself take a gentle dig at modern life.

Clegg: I've got this cousin in Barnsley with a grandson who's got ten O-levels, well how's that for bits of paper, and all he wants to do is wear a ring through his nose and dye his hair purple.

Compo: Does he want to be a parrot?

Clegg: Mind you, they did christen him Wayne, they set him off to the worst possible start. When they used to call people things like Herbert, it helped enormously to keep them steady in the face of the world's growing tendency to be ridiculous.

Clarke was also making the most of Thora's talents. Wharmby was over his nerves, and Thora's rapport with him and Thomas was delicious, as in 'Edie and the Automobile', in which Wesley tries to teach his wife to drive, before enlisting the help of Barry and Wally Batty.

Glenda: You're the wrong age.

Edie: Will you shut up about age?

Glenda: You failed your test seven times.

Edie: Only because that damn car did something stupid every time.

Wesley: Here we go again then.

Edie: Now don't you start moaning. All you have to do is sit there and be bossy. Is everything working properly?

Wesley: She's running sweet as a nut.

Edie: Yes, but what kind of a mood is she in?

Wesley: They don't have moods, Edie.

Edie: Don't tell me they don't have moods. She behaved like a lunatic last time.

Glenda: You ought to let somebody younger go with her.

Wesley: I was younger when we started.

The audience loved Thora as Edie, and the viewing figures were holding up, but the show would have to continue without one of its favourite characters. On 11 March 1987, three days after 'Edie and the Automobile' was aired, Joe Gladwin died at the age of eighty-one. He had been frail for some time, but his spirit was indomitable, and his portrayal of the hangdog, downtrodden Wally remained a strength of the show. Clarke had long before latched on to the chemistry between him and Kathy Staff, and the scenes he wrote for them were among his funniest; Gladwin's selfless support had done much to make Nora the icon she had become. Even when ill,

Gladwin was a born entertainer who would set out to cheer those around him, Staff recalling in her autobiography: 'Right up to the last he used to tap dance and sing for us. He'd started on the piers at Blackpool as a tap dancer and he had been a "feed" for Dave Morris, a comedian.'

Gladwin had been a trouper, turning up to entertain the studio audiences even when his health was failing. Bell said: 'He would stand at the side of the stage and be not well at all. And I would say to the audience, "Let's meet Wally Batty – Joe Gladwin," and he would throw the old man robes aside and he would bound out and say, "Eh up, everybody," and then back to the side, where he was a little old man again.' Staff was deeply saddened by Gladwin's loss. He had been an ideal foil, and their working relationship went back beyond *Summer Wine* to shows with Harry Worth and Hylda Baker. A warm friendship had developed between them, not least because of their shared faith. Like Staff, Gladwin was a devout Christian, devoting so much time and effort to good works for the Roman Catholic Church that he had been knighted by the Pope. Staff was the last visitor Gladwin talked to before he slipped into unconsciousness, and ever afterwards she believed divine intervention had given her the opportunity to say goodbye to her old friend.

Gladwin's death meant Clarke had to rethink Nora's circumstances; the love-hate relationship with Compo would remain, but increasingly she would be thrust together with the show's other on-screen widow, Ivy. Gradually, they would be brought together with Edie, Glenda and Pearl to form The Ladies, a gossiping group that would become emblematic of *Summer Wine*, and one of its most popular features.

For now, though, Clarke had something else on his mind – a new show based on the old, and it fired him with enthusiasm. 'Why didn't I think of doing it ages ago?' he said at the time. *First of the Summer Wine* would take the characters back to 1939, and the prospect of writing adventures for a youthful Compo, Clegg, Foggy and Seymour brought ideas tumbling out. Clarke said: 'It sort of arose slowly and naturally from thinking, you've got these characters, they're all that age, what were they like? What would Foggy be like at eighteen?' According to Bell, the seed of the idea came when Clarke was working on the script of 'Getting Sam Home'. 'I said to Roy, "What I'd really like to do is a prologue showing the three of them in school playing together as twelve, fourteen-year-olds, just as a little montage, which would help anyone who hadn't seen the series and was seeing it as a one-off," and he said, "I'd like to keep that as an idea," and the next thing he's written a pilot for it, very funny, and we start to cast for the series, and we're going to have auditions up north.'

There would be a firm handhold for fans of *Last of the Summer Wine*. Sallis agreed to play Norman Clegg's father in the new series. Bell was enthusiastic, but never got his hands on the show. The then Head of Comedy, Gareth Gwenlan, decided to take the project over and make the pilot before handing it to producer/director Mike Stephens. The casting was a gift for getting publicity; everybody wanted to know who was going to play younger versions of some of television's most popular comedy characters, and there were acres of coverage for Helen Patrick, the very attractive young actress chosen for Nora Batty. Four fine actors were cast as Compo, Clegg, Foggy and Seymour – Paul Wyett, David Fenwick, Richard Lumsden and Paul McLain, and the production was handsomely mounted to recreate pre-war Yorkshire, complete with period vehicles. Clarke's dialogue for his characters in the first flush of youth was as sparkling as anything he had written for the adventures of their dotage. The principals faced a difficult task; they had to make the parts their own while at the same time evoking Owen, Sallis, Wilde and Aldridge, and all coped well. Everybody was hopeful, and the 45-minute pilot broadcast on 3 January 1988 was well received by critics and audience alike. A series of six was commissioned, which began its run on 4 September. The antics were comfortably familiar to the audience; Wally was dangled off a cinema balcony, Foggy was busy turning himself into a ruthless fighting machine, Seymour's car goes into a ditch. It was funny and redolent of the characteristic *Summer Wine* spirit, yet somehow it wasn't working. A second series was commissioned, which ran from 3 September 1989, but it failed to settle and develop like *Last of the Summer Wine* had done in its infancy. The heart of the problem was that the central jokes were missing; old men refusing to act their age had been proven to be hilarious, but young men chasing girls and getting into scrapes was entirely predictable. The idea of the decrepit Compo lusting after the dreadful Nora was inherently funny, but there was no reason in the world why the presentable Paul Wyett should not wish to dally with the delectable Helen Patrick. There was none of the wistful nostalgia that gave the original its characteristic flavour, because young people do not have the perspective to be nostalgic. And good though they were, the cast had an uphill struggle; there could only ever be one Compo loved by the audience, and it was Bill Owen, just as there could only be one Foggy who could be simultaneously bombastic and vulnerable, and that was Brian Wilde. There would be no more *First of the Summer Wine*.

Clarke felt let down:

> That was the major disappointment of my career, no question about it. I'd got so many ideas and plans, and there were so many opportunities there to show the two series at the same time, not necessarily back to back, but even in the same week, and the cross references and the cross currents between the two would have been really interesting telly, I think. I would have loved to have taken the *First of the Summer Wine* young people through the Second World War at the same time as the oldies were looking back, and you could have drawn from one to the other, and I think the BBC missed a trick there. At least it would have been original, nobody else had done it, and I was sorry that that didn't happen. Why it didn't happen was not because the kids who were cast were wrong, but because they spent too much: they went and spent so much on buses and things that it was too expensive, and I think that scared the

BBC. It could have been done a lot cheaper and still worked, but didn't get the chance. I was sorry about what happened, I really thought it could have gone in all sorts of directions.

Bell felt the absence of Hazlehurst's music hobbled the show: 'Ronnie Hazlehurst's music set the mood for *Summer Wine*. Gareth went for the old thing of using records of the day, which didn't give you the spirit of Clegg, Foggy and Compo, it just didn't work.'

And Sallis believed the key lay not with any faults in the new series, but the unique appeal of the old: 'I think it was a good try, but looking back on it, you make a great success out of *Last of the Summer Wine*, but then you take it back a generation, it's never going to be the same thing. It was worth trying, but to see me playing my own father isn't really guaranteed to make you laugh. If a thing has got that popular, you feel that anything goes, which isn't always the case.'

No matter. The original was as popular as ever, one reason being that, unlike *First of the Summer Wine*, it was not tied to a particular era. It made its own time – and its own place.

CHAPTER 9

❧

Summer Wine Land

PETER SALLIS COINED the name, and it represented as much an attitude of mind as a place; a parallel universe, a fantasy world summoned up from Clarke's imagination and brought to life so beguilingly by the show's producers that large sections of the audience thought they recognised in it an evocation of a gentler, kinder age when the pace of living was slower and its problems less troublesome. Time stood still here, and modern trends rarely intruded, whether they concerned clothing or technology. Norman Clegg's cap, cardigan and mac were no more fashionable in 1973 than they were thirty-seven years later, and the only inventions that mattered were those that came out of Wesley's shed or Seymour's workshop. Only the cars on the streets of Summer Wine Land betrayed the passing years as the clunky designs of the 1970s gave way to the sleeker models of the decades that followed. Beyond those glimpses of one era passing into another, there was little to pin *Summer Wine* to any year. It would be well into the 1990s before Clarke admitted references to the trappings of real life, like electronic pagers or the internet, into his comic world, and the new millennium would pass before mobile phones appeared.

Early on, he had flirted with reality; the scenario of redundant middle-aged men pondering their place in the world and musing on politics struck a chord with the Britain of the early 1970s, a time of industrial strife and social changes that left many wondering where their country was going. The cast was alive to that sub-text, even if it was played for laughs. Jane Freeman said: 'It was started at a time when you got things like middle management being made redundant for the very first time. Before then, working men got laid off, but this was the first time managers were losing their jobs, so three men walking about with nothing to do was very much on the pulse. They were people who for the first time didn't know what to do with their time, and that was happening in the country.' Clarke soon moved away from that, even though he always kept Clegg as a trenchant voice to comment on reality; a world of his own making was a better place for his trio to live, a setting not so much frozen in time as creating a time of its own that was so comfortable and seemed so familiar that viewers felt they had once known it.

'It's in a time warp,' said Bill Owen. 'Nobody gets old, people don't die, people are always there.' The cast became used to fans telling them in person and by letter that they enjoyed the show because it reminded them of how life used to be. 'It's timeless,' said Jean Fergusson. 'People say to me, "What era is it?" and I say, "Any time," because if you look at Peter's costumes, it was what he was wearing thirty-odd years ago, and I'm wearing the same things I was wearing twenty-five years ago, so it's all sort of now, but it's magical. It's another world, but it has to be as real as possible.' Veteran actor Burt Kwouk, who would enter the series in 2002, also found the audience convinced the show was a nostalgic look at a better age: 'People say it's an England that's gone. It isn't. It's an England that never existed, it was never like this. It's fairyland, it makes everything look very pretty.'

Even though Summer Wine Land was no more real than Captain Mainwaring's Walmington-on-Sea, Hancock's East Cheam or Del Boy Trotter's Peckham, it was given a substance that none of the other classic, studio-based sitcoms ever achieved thanks to its setting on the Pennines, and that was a factor in bringing in sackfuls of fan mail from the late 1970s onwards. As he had with *The Misfit*, which had earlier attracted a huge postbag, Clarke's characters and the world they occupied had touched something in the audience. Amid the usual requests for signed photographs of the actors, and the lunatic fringe – such as the man from Cumbria who sent Brian Wilde information about a patented boot-drier with the request that it be passed on to Compo, who would undoubtedly need it because he ended up soaking wet so often – there were earnest letters asking for advice on what to do in retirement, and admiring letters heartened by a show that firmly turned its back on the familiar comedy cliché of stereotyping older people as doddery liabilities in favour of portraying them as still vigorous and full of life. 'We ploughed a new furrow,' Owen insisted in the *Sunday Mirror* in 1989, 'And I think we played a part in a minor social revolution by changing people's attitudes towards old age.' Bell said: 'I used to get letters from people who were retired, and they used to get up in the morning, and have coffee with their wife, and they watched *Summer Wine* and now they go places, they get on the bus and go into the country and walk around, and they don't do the daft things they do on the programme, but it gets them out, which is important in life and that in itself is a good thing.'

There were also letters from young people who loved the show, and it would be them who played a vital role in turning *Summer Wine* into the success it became. One of the BBC's most popular shows was *Multi-Coloured Swap Shop*, a Saturday morning extravaganza hosted by disc jockey Noel Edmonds. It was quality children's television, lively and generous of spirit, that engaged its audience by getting viewers to ring in and exchange unwanted toys and games, in between appearances by pop groups and stars of the day. A devoted following never missed it, and in the early 1980s the show introduced awards for its young viewers' favourite programmes and personalities, which were voted on using a coupon printed in the *Radio Times*. Thousands were sent in, and on 11 April 1982, Edmonds announced that they had declared the funniest television programme to be *Last of the Summer Wine*. It was further confirmation of the programme's family appeal after the ratings triumph at Christmas 1981. Owen was the obvious choice to collect the award, given his status as the show's most recognisable figure as well as his affinity with young people, and there he was, twinkling, charming, cheeky, looking every inch a benevolent grandfather figure to the children in the studio and enjoying himself in their company. As ever, he was the ultimate cheerleader for the show he so cherished. This was not an occasion for one of his well-cut suits, so he wore a T-shirt emblazoned with the legend '*Holmfirth – the Summer Wine Town*', which he talked about.

The town's name was already familiar. Virtually everything written about the show since 1973 had mentioned Holmfirth, and Owen's affection for it had made him a tireless proselytiser for its charm and the warmth of its people. There had been a steadily growing tourist trade from viewers curious to see where their favourite comedy was made, but the *Multi-Coloured Swap Shop* award, coming as the audience peaked, turned that stream of visitors into a tide. Not that Holmfirth was ever referred to in the programme – the name could be seen on the destination boards of buses and on signposts, but it was never uttered in dialogue. Yorkshire as a whole and nearby Huddersfield in particular were name-checked on a regular basis, but the trio customarily referred to their town and the countryside as 'round here', because Summer Wine Land was much more than Holmfirth – it was a composite drawn together from differing landscapes, towns and villages edited together into what appeared to be a seamless whole. A couple of key locations – Nora Batty's house, and Sid and Ivy's café in Towngate – belonged to Holmfirth, as did another that became familiar by the late 1980s, the row of houses where Clegg was neighbour to Howard and Pearl, which stood on the hill behind the parish church. Other permanent settings, though, were some way away, not least the White Horse pub, which was a couple of miles distant in Jackson Bridge. As a location, Holmfirth had its limitations, not least its narrow streets that were all too easily brought to a standstill by filming, and all four *Summer Wine* producers found it necessary to cast their net wider to find what they needed.

Nevertheless, Holmfirth was emblematic of the series, and the interest it attracted was something of a culture shock. This was a town which, if not unknown beyond the Pennines, had worked hard but quietly throughout its history, not attracting much attention except when disaster had befallen it with the Holmfirth Flood of 1852 when eighty-one people died after the Bilberry Reservoir burst its banks and sent a torrent of water crashing through the streets, a calamity that horrified the entire country. By then, the town had almost 600 years of history to look back on, growing from a settlement around a corn mill and bridge established in the thirteenth century. It was a hardy community – it had to be, the bleakness of the Pennines was uncompromising – and gradually grew into one of the heartlands of the textile manufacturing that characterised the old West Riding of Yorkshire for a century or more, fanning out from the great industrial centres of Leeds, Bradford and Huddersfield into the Holme Valley. The cities, the towns, the valleys of this rugged north country would stamp their hallmark on the worldwide trade in cloth. Its origin was its calling card, the stamp 'Made in Yorkshire' a guarantee of quality, and Holmfirth was proud of its place in that great tradition. The flood could not break the spirit of this community as robustly woven as the cloths it produced, and within ten years it had grown into one of the great wool towns of the north, its mills and dye houses enjoying an enviable reputation for the material they turned out. Over the hill to the west, in Marsden, which would also claim a key place in Summer Wine Land, the gigantic Titanic Mill turned out mass-produced cloth, but that was not the Holmfirth way. Its valley was home to fifty-odd smaller mills, supplying only the best, the finest worsteds and cashmeres, to the tailors and cutters of the most exclusive establishments well into the 1960s. The chances are that the sharp suits Owen was ordering to fit the image of a Rank leading man were being cut from cloth woven in the place that would become his second home, but by the time he and the other actors arrived to film the pilot, Holmfirth was in trouble. The textile industry that had sustained so many jobs, and created considerable wealth in the Holme Valley, was collapsing, unable to compete with cheap imports from the Far East and the Indian subcontinent. The town's other main industry, the Bamforth postcard factory, was not the force it had been either. Visitors came, but only to walk the hills that looked down on the town, which was descending into scruffiness.

It took a while, but *Summer Wine* changed all that. It created a whole new industry for Holmfirth, and sustained it thanks to the series' longevity. Television makes stars, and it made a star of this unassuming northern mill town, giving it a career that outlasted that of most actors. This, for the visitors, was *Summer Wine* brought to life, and once its residents had grown used to the annual invasion by the film crew, they mostly embraced the fame and set about making a living out of it. The show was one of a select handful of television programmes that lent lustre to an area: farther north in Yorkshire, the success of the BBC series based on the best-selling stories of country vet James Herriot, *All Creatures Great And Small*, created a new tourist trade around the market town of Thirsk, which started to bill itself as Herriot Country. In Wales, the quirky model village of Portmeirion made a living out of its location for the gnomic Patrick McGoohan thriller series *The Prisoner*, and on the Pennines, once the Yorkshire tourist authorities woke up to the success of Clarke's creation, Holmfirth and its surrounding area were dubbed Summer Wine Country.

As the series gathered viewers and worked its way towards being the country's favourite comedy show, the numbers of tourists packing into Holmfirth's narrow streets increased relentlessly. The 60,000 who arrived annually was more than treble the town's population, and they came in cars that jammed the streets and competed with residents for parking spaces, and aboard sixty coaches a day at weekends and during the summer. This benevolent invasion could annoy the locals, who grew weary of hordes of people traipsing past their homes and gawping through their windows in search of places they had seen on the telly, but mostly the town was tolerant and appreciated the benefits that the series brought, as derelict buildings were brought back into use and existing businesses were smartened up. The malodorous former fish and chip shop and paint store that served as the exterior of Sid and Ivy's café took its lead from the series and became a real café, complete with effigy of Compo outside, and was a magnet for the visitors.

So was Nora Batty's house, which was regularly besieged by sightseers. They and the series were fortunate that its occupants, Sonia Lee and her family, put up with the attention with good humour, even when curiosity drove the tourists to become intrusive. 'There were droves and droves of visitors,' said Lee. 'I had two small children and if they came in with their mates, because the tourists saw them walking into the house, they all walked in with them. We could be sat down in the kitchen for our tea, and people would walk in. Easter was the big attraction, and if I looked out of my daughter's bedroom window, you couldn't see anything for people. Once or twice, we did have people knocking on the door asking if Nora was in. One Christmas Day morning, I had some friends over, and they said, "It's lightning outside," and I said, "No, it's only the tourists taking pictures."' Lee, who moved into the house shortly after the pilot was filmed in 1972 and stayed until 2004, greeted cast and crew with a warmth that was reciprocated. Kathy Staff, who was irrevocably associated with the house, would drive over from Cheshire to visit the family, and sent a present when Lee remarried; Owen would keep an eye on the children between takes if their mother had to go out. 'They were a great crowd,' said Lee. 'When they were filming it felt like family had come to stay.' Number 28 Huddersfield Road became one of the most familiar settings in all television comedy, and great care was paid to preserving its look. When a new front door was needed, Bell had one fitted and kept the old blue-painted one, which went back on for filming. The house eventually became a holiday let, and developed a brisk trade from fans of the series who rented it as a base to explore Holmfirth and the hills.

There was a similarly warm welcome at the White Horse, where landlord and landlady Ron and Ruth Backhouse became so much a part of Summer Wine Land that they appeared on screen and he was given the occasional line. The pub became a key setting in more ways than one from 1978 onwards. In that pre-mobile phone era, pubs around the area became like staging posts on the Pony Express, places where messages could be left for the crew as it moved from location to location. The White Horse became the principal base for mail, a refuge from the rain, the venue for end-of-shoot parties and a home-from-home for crew members who were so fond of the Backhouses that they insisted on staying at the pub even when the guest rooms were being redecorated. In summer, the Backhouses were playing host to coachloads of visitors who arrived every twenty minutes, some stopping for a drink, others lingering to look at the photographs from the series that covered the walls, all posing for their own pictures outside. The White Horse had been bankrupt when the couple took over; *Summer Wine* would turn it into a thriving business.

Elsewhere, technicians who returned year in, year out for increasingly lengthy shoots found billets that they liked, and became comfortable and friendly with the people of the locations where they filmed, one even developing such affection for the locals that he established a second family that lived in blissful ignorance of the one he had in the south.

Holmfirth cashed in enthusiastically. There were Compo mugs and Nora tea-towels and Foggy key-rings for sale, table mats, figurines and postcards; coach tours of the locations that departed from outside the café, a Wrinkled Stocking Tea Room, and a *Last of the Summer Wine* exhibition featuring props and costumes that had Owen's personal seal of approval, and which he officially opened in 1996. From the beginning, the producers were acutely aware that they needed to keep the goodwill of the town, and were at pains to minimise disruption, and that meant a trade-off with the people who were making money on the back of the series. Bell said: 'The head of licensing came up and couldn't believe all the Compo things and I said, "Look the other way, because that's our passport to filming." If we get heavy with them, they'll turn round and say, "Don't come, don't block our streets, don't make our lives a misery."'

Not that the BBC was always savvy when it did receive requests from businesses that wanted their slice of the tourist trade. Bell recalled:

> There was a fish and chip shop in Holmfirth that went big time, they rebuilt it and they wanted to call it Compo's Café. So they rang me up, and I said, 'I can't give you permission, but I'll find out,' so I rang BBC Worldwide and told them, and they said, 'Oh yes, we'll ring you back,' so about a week later I got a call from BBC Worldwide and this voice said, 'Oh, hello, now there's a fish and chip shop in Holmfirth that wants to call itself Compo's Café. Have you any objection?' And I said no. And a few days later, I get a call from this girl in BBC Worldwide, who says, 'We've checked it out with the producer, and he says it's OK.'

There was, though, an undercurrent of ambivalence in Holmfirth at the intrusion. It had shown itself early, as Jimmy Gilbert discovered as he put the finishing touches to location filming for the pilot. 'I sometimes think the people of Holmfirth have no cause to thank us for choosing the town. I remember the end of the first week's filming, and we were just about to wrap, and an old lady came up, she was taking her dog for a walk. She stood beside me by the camera and she couldn't have been sweeter or nicer, and she said, "Have you enjoyed yourself here?" and I said, "Yes, we've had a very good time and been very successful, and we're very sorry we're going back home this afternoon." She just said, "Good", turned on her heel and went off with the dog.'

Sydney Lotterby found the town welcoming but wary as the series began to gather an ever larger audience. 'At times I felt we were intruding on them. I got on really well. They'd see you walking around – I had to go and find locations and things – and they got to know me, and they'd say, "Is there going to be another series?" and I'd say yes, and they'd say, "That's good, that's good," but they didn't welcome me with open arms as they did later. They go through a process: "We're famous, our town is being shown on telly", and they go through that phase and they get to a point, "Oh no, not again", because we hold up traffic, get in the way of people's way of living.'

Co-operation came at a price, and there were those who, living up to the Yorkshire stereotype of being canny with money, pushed it up. The demands began in the mid 1980s when the show was flying high, and an attitude developed in some quarters that it could pay for the privilege. The first battleground came on the terrace where Clegg, Howard and Pearl lived, a charming location overlooking the centre of Holmfirth, but not easy for actors or crew; a narrow pavement with very little room for manoeuvre above a steep drop made it difficult to film, and Bell needed all his ingenuity to make it work. What he didn't need was an awkward resident. 'There was a girl at one end, a single mother, and a pensioner down the other end, and they liked the money. What we paid wasn't huge, a hundred pounds or something like that, but for three days, it's lot of money for somebody who's out of work, and we never abused our stay there, or took advantage. So this woman in the middle turned up and said she wanted three hundred pounds and we said no, and she got very cross and said, "Well, you can't film," so I said, "If we can't film, we'll go somewhere else," and that's what we did, and she wrote to the Director General complaining at the way she'd been so shabbily treated.'

The beauty of Summer Wine Land was that it could be created anywhere that fitted the look and feel of the programme, so the on-screen neighbours were moved to a private road close to the White Horse, where a row of cottages felt exactly right, not least because the houses looked out on to the hills. It was a vast improvement over the original location; actors and crew had elbow room, and there was plenty of space in front of the cottages to play out scenes impossible to stage on the cramped pavement in Holmfirth. Clarke covered the transition with two crisp sentences of dialogue between Clegg and Howard about being rehoused, and the new setting settled into a permanent part of the show.

A more serious spat would arise over the most iconic location, the spot that every visitor to Holmfirth wanted to see and photograph. Close by Nora Batty's house, building works were taking place and the noise would make it impossible to film. Talks went ahead. 'He said he'd stop them, so there wasn't any noise for the day, five hundred pounds, please,' said Bell. 'First time, he got us. The first year, we paid five hundred pounds, and then the next year we made sure there wasn't going to be a problem, and then suddenly it's another five hundred pounds or there's going to be noise, and I said no, and that was war.' Bell did the unthinkable – he moved Nora out of the setting she had occupied since the opening moments of the pilot episode, away from the steps and the front door that had become almost as familiar to viewers as their own homes. 'I filmed a little bit with Kathy coming down the steps and stopping and looking back, and there was a "For Sale" sign on the house because she'd had to move. That would have gone in during the titles to explain her living somewhere else. Nobody was going to twist my arm into paying. It was blackmail, really, saying you come along and film and we'll make a noise.'

It was never seen, and the dispute was settled. Even those who had no time for the presence of *Summer Wine* in Holmfirth recognised the benefits it brought, and with the same Yorkshire pragmatism that had helped it over flood and decline, the town got on with making a living. Mediation was sometimes needed between the programme and locals with ruffled feathers, and more than once it was carried out by Andrew Bray, a greengrocer and leading light of the Holme Valley Business Association, who went back a long way with the series, to when he was a child and a car had pulled up alongside him and a stranger asked for directions to a hotel. 'I was only eleven,' said Bray, 'And a couple of days later I was fishing at a local dam, and all of a sudden all these BBC people turned up, and this guy who'd asked me the way walked up to me and recognised me and asked if he could borrow my fishing rod, so I said, "Aye, fine," and somebody said to me, "Do you know who that is, it's Bill Owen," and I said, "Who's Bill Owen?" I hadn't a clue who he was.' Owen took to the youngster, and a friendship sprang up. When Bray took over his greengrocer's shop aged just fifteen, Owen offered encouragement, visiting and eventually arranging for him to supply the location caterers. It was a characteristically generous gesture towards a young person making his way in the world, and as Bray matured into a fixture in the Holmfirth business community, his closeness to the series made him a natural choice to help smooth out any difficulties.

'*Summer Wine* transformed the centre of Holmfirth,' he said. 'At that time, there wasn't a tea shop or restaurant, you couldn't even get a bar meal. The valley's always been very tolerant. There have been inconveniences from time to time, but people have appreciated that they've got a job to do. Over the course of thirty-seven years there's only been about five serious problems, where I've been asked to mediate, but we've always managed to sort things out. There have been people over the years who have virtually tried to extort money out of them, but not many.'

Ron Backhouse also found himself batting off criticism from time to time. 'I used to get it more than most from some of the regulars. "You think more of *Summer Wine* than the locals," they'd say, but I'd say, "Excuse me, *Summer Wine* was here before you, they came here when the pub was bankrupt." It's never done any harm to Holmfirth, it does it good.'

One person, more than anybody else, did it good. Owen's restless, questing spirit had always pushed him into new challenges and settings; the ups and downs of his personal life had seen him play the gracious host at a country pile he could ill afford and then become the man who threw the parties everyone simply had to attend at an elegant pad in Brighton before ending up living modestly in London. But in this unglamorous mill town, he found something that touched him deeply. There was no artifice in his oft-professed affection for Holmfirth; he did love it and its people loved him in return. There was something almost spiritual in his reaction to the town, a sense of personal homecoming.

Even in 1982 he was telling the *Yorkshire Post*: 'Yorkshire for me, as an actor before *Last of the Summer Wine*, was Hull, Bradford, Leeds, and it was between the stage door and your digs and the most comfortable pub, and that was it, and suddenly there I was, all those years ago, dumped at the Elephant and Castle at Holmfirth, and for me it was as though I had been there before. I identified immediately with that place.' The town appealed to Owen's sometimes romanticised socialist outlook, its people getting their hands dirty doing honest jobs, unpretentious, resolutely working class. This was the image of his mind's eye made real, and with the added bonus of not being an austere industrial landscape that might have been just a little too working class if Gilbert and Clarke had plumped for the steel town of Rotherham instead of choosing the picturesque backdrop of the Pennines. Owen's Summer Wine Land, for all its unpredictable weather during filming, never suffered through the bleakness of winter. By then, he was back home in London, the summer and early autumn months of filming over, the idealised vision of the best days when the sun warmed the stone buildings and lit up the heather on the hills fixed in his memory until the next spring came around and he returned to be chauffeured from home-from-home to location.

The town gave him something else – the adulation he had craved since first signing for Rank. Thanks to Holmfirth, he had found real, enduring stardom late in the day, and it gratified him as well as offering a degree of financial security he had never before enjoyed. 'At my time of life to have gone round the clock and to have this kind of popularity again is wonderful. I'm not going to bite the hand that feeds me,' he said. While he was there, he was part of it. 'Probably for the first time in my life I have wanted to belong,' he wrote in his autobiography, and belong he did. Saturday was his day off, and unlike other cast members who went their own way, he pitched in to the life of the town and the surrounding area. He opened fetes and even public lavatories to cater for the visitors; led a torch-lit parade and had a hand-carved bench made for the riverside; roped in fellow actors to sign autographs to raise money for the scouts; spoke at churches to raise money for roof repairs; recorded with schoolchildren and the Holme Valley Silver Band to raise funds for good causes; went farther afield to appear at miners' galas and rallies of pensioners demanding a better deal. He was visible, accessible, and mostly loveable. 'If you talked to people around Yorkshire, they loved him,' said Mike Grady. 'He'd always fetch up, and he was great at that. He had a lot of energy.'

Once in a rare while, his streak of irascibility surfaced, and he could be short with an autograph hunter. Bell said:

If Bill was doing something, he couldn't be bothered with the fan side of the business. We had a situation at Jackson Bridge once, and it was raining and the three men got into their car and started going through their lines together, and a little boy came and tapped on the glass and they gestured for him to go away, but the little boy, about nine or ten, tapped on the glass again, and they wound the window down and Bill told him very unceremoniously, 'Get out, we're working,' and the little boy went away and cried his eyes out to his mother, who then wrote to me saying he was a fan of the series and loved Compo, and his hero did that to him, and he couldn't believe it. So on the schedule for the next block of filming, I put something to the effect that the public are our viewers and it's because of them that we are still making the programme, and they must be treated with enormous respect, because anything that's done that upsets the public will spread out because people will say, 'They're not as nice as they seem,' and I put this on the top of the schedule. I was always insistent that they should never treat the public badly, because they are important and they don't know that you're working, you've got to say, 'I'm terribly sorry, do you mind waiting a minute.' I've always regarded the relationship with the public as absolutely vital.

Mostly, though, Owen was charming and put in much time and effort. In his 1994 autobiography, *Summer Wine and Vintage Years*, he wrote: 'I went out of my way to be a part of that community of Holmfirth, by mixing and offering to do anything and everything. After all these years, I still go out on my day off and open something or close it or whatever.' Owen was conscious of what the series had done for the town and had no time for the grumblers, adding, 'There is a body of opinion, of course, that would wish us elsewhere and their feelings have been expressed to me personally and to our director in no uncertain terms. Do they really wish to return to those days when we first arrived, when the river was a mess and changed colour according to what material was being dyed up at the mill at the end of Hollowgate?'

'Bill was an ambassador for Holmfirth to the rest of the world, and loved the glory he got from being Holmfirth's number-one guest citizen,' said Bell. It was not just being an ambassador for Holmfirth – as *Summer Wine* gathered a huge national, and later international, audience, the boy from Acton whom everybody except Gilbert considered too Cockney to be Compo came to be seen as the embodiment of a Yorkshireman – at least outside the county. Even within it, his portrayal was acknowledged, the Yorkshire Society, a charitable body that acted as a cheerleader for all things Tyke, making him an honorary Yorkshireman.

Owen's identification with Holmfirth ran so deep that from the early 1980s onwards, he declared his wish to be buried there. 'It's all arranged,' he told the *Daily Express* in 1994. 'It's in my will. There comes a time when we all have to think of a place, or a casket, where we want to end up. I know the churchyard well because we've filmed there many times and we've used the church where I'd like the burial ceremony to be.' The church was St John's, Upperthong, a mile or so above the centre of Holmfirth, overlooking the valley, which had appeared in several episodes ever since the early days, including 'The Inventor of the Forty-Foot Ferret', 'The Three Astaires', 'Flower Power Cut' and 'Small Tune On A Penny Wassail'.

Even though the series was inextricably linked with Holmfirth, Summer Wine Land was extending itself over an ever-widening area as Clarke and Bell broadened their horizons. The increasingly filmic nature of the show, as well as the growing importance of stunts, demanded space and wide-open vistas, and Holmfirth was becoming a victim of its own success as the tourists flocked in. 'When I took over the series, we could film along the main road,' said Bell.

> That would be on a Sunday. Now on a Sunday, you can't film after nine o'clock in the morning, because it's practically bumper-to-bumper with coaches coming in with visitors. It's an enormous industry. The town was shabby, and once you turn a spotlight on a town, it makes them think, we'd better do it up a bit, and it's a very respectable town now. It's a bit overcrowded, and because of that we've had to go farther over and we find ourselves filming in Marsden a lot more, but even that's coming up. When I went to Marsden, it was almost a ghost town, with a lot of shops boarded up, now it's a very beautiful place. We find ourselves filming all over the Holme Valley. Roads are blocked off that were once open to us, fields with a beautiful view now have rows of houses in them, pubs that were there have closed down, the whole thing's changed.

Bell ranged far and wide over the Pennines and beyond in search of locations, especially those that were remote enough not to be either thronged with tourists or so heavily populated that closing roads would cause major disruption. One of the gems that he found, and returned to with increasing regularity, was a slender trace on an Ordnance Survey map high above Jackson Bridge. According to the map, Intake Lane meandered along the top of a hill and then petered out. It was isolated, not on the way to anywhere, and had the loveliest of backdrops, with the hills and valleys stretching away for miles. It was the ideal setting for both stunts, where a bicycle made for three was towed along on a low-loader before apparently tipping the trio over the handlebars, and for passages of dialogue in which the men could lie in the heather and muse on the world. Other settings would also become familiar – the villages of Marsden, Meltham, Slaithwaite and Hepworth were all co-opted into the fantasy world, as was the canal a few miles east of Holmfirth, at Brighouse. Hade Edge, close to Holmfirth, with its wooded hillsides, became a favourite setting, as did the Digley and Holme Styes reservoirs in the hills above the town.

Bell said: 'I reckon I know this part of Yorkshire better than anybody else, certainly Holmfirth. They always come up to me, the locals, and say, "Where was that, never been there." I used to get the scripts about three months beforehand and come up and think, where can I film that? And I usually know exactly where to go. There was a storm blew up, and we could hardly stand up. I said, "Just hold fire for twenty minutes," and I went down into the valley and found a different location which was sheltered, and moved everybody down there. You can't do that unless you've got an idea of the area. It was completely sheltered and if you watched the programme you'd have no idea that further up the hill trees were being blown over.'

Summer Wine Land could be an uncomfortable place to be. Countless episodes featured actors apparently bathed in sunshine as they chatted in idyllic settings, the only clue to reality being the furious flapping of their clothing as they were lashed by an icy breeze. 'I was introduced to thermal knickers up there,' said Juliette Kaplan. 'I have never known the wind get so bad. Oh God, it can be deadly.' Some suffered more than others. Jean Fergusson, in Marina's skimpy outfits, became accustomed to being chilled to the bone, and sometimes soaked, as Clarke's scripts called for her assignations with Howard to take place in increasingly bizarre settings and Bell chased consistency of light for the scenes. She recalled: 'We were disguised as divers in the river, in wet suits. Because we were in the river and they'd got us all ready under the bridge, they decided that they were going to go and film another shot somewhere, and left us standing in the water. We just had to stand there and wait because it wasn't practical to get us out and put us back in again, and my suit sprang a leak. It soaked all the clothes underneath, like long johns, and I was frozen, it was terrible.'

Worse was to come when Marina and Howard had to fall out of a boat into the canal at Marsden, a less than appealing prospect as there were oil slicks on the water and, as it later emerged, rats carrying Weil's Disease. Robert Fyfe had neglected to tell anybody he couldn't swim. 'The next minute, I saw the water going past my eyes because Robert had put his hand on top of my head,' said Fergusson. 'I went under this foul, foul water. There's still a pair of earrings somewhere in the Marsden Canal, and somehow we got to the shore, and I don't know how Bob did it, and I was completely soaked, the wig was soaked.' The shot did not look right, and Bell decided to do it again at the end of the day, when the weather was even colder. Fergusson and Fyfe were given a helping hand into the water by a crew member who tipped the boat over to make it look funnier. 'That was almost more frightening, and Bob still hadn't told me that he couldn't swim. There was a washing line strung up at base, and there were all our clothes hung up to dry, and my wig was hanging up to dry as well. It looked like a gipsy encampment. Anyway, at the end of the day it got quite a bit colder, so it wasn't as jolly, and it was quite worrying because the visual-effects guy was ducked down behind the boat, and on cue he just had to tip it up, so we went in again. I thought, we'll be fine, but what does Robert do? He gets hold of the lapels of my jacket and pulls me under again. If he'd told somebody he couldn't swim, they might have put a double in for a long shot.'

There was not always time for doubles, as Bell had to be fast on his feet to take advantage of the changeable conditions on the Pennines. 'There was one night when we did "The Loxley Lozenge" when the sun was going down and there were about eight different shades of pink going to crimson across these old slag heaps from a disused pit. I said, "Quick, get the actors to go across the top." Absolute pandemonium getting them across, grumble, grumble, and I cued them and it's one of the finest shots because you see the three men walking off into eternity. It's a wonderful end shot – a slag heap in silhouette.'

It was all part of the illusion, just another magical moment in the fantasy world that so enchanted the audience; in Summer Wine Land, even a slag heap could be made to look lovely.

CHAPTER 10

❧

Thora's Table

THE ATMOSPHERE WAS relaxed and happy. The long ninth series had achieved what it set out to do; Seymour was firmly established as part of the landscape, and 1987 would close with a feature-length Christmas special, to be broadcast on 27 December. The new trio clicked on screen and enjoyed an amiable relationship off it, and the rest of the cast were equally comfortable with each other, to the extent that Gordon Wharmby began making suggestions to the grand lady who had terrified him on how she should play her lines. This was not a good idea, as Sarah Thomas recalled: 'He became stronger and stronger and more confident, and I remember one or two occasions where he actually suggested an emphasis on a line to Thora and got a very sharp rebuff. They were magic moments! I think it was perhaps his slight lack of experience that made him think, oh, it might be better if she played the line like that. No. Not at all. She made it very clear he'd made a big faux pas there.'

There could still be moments of friction. Bell had a few tense exchanges with the guest star of the special, 'Big Day At Dream Acres', hell-raising Irish actor Ray McAnally, who did not always take kindly to direction. He played the central character, a wily tramp, in what would be a romp set against the backdrop of a garden party at a country house. Nora is dressed as a waitress, much to Compo's excitement, and the plot centres on the tramp's efforts to make money out of betting on a donkey derby by switching the favourite for another runner. Despite bright moments and a ripe performance from McAnally, it was the weakest special so far, the plot feeling just a little too convoluted and the film seeming over-long. The series that followed, though, was much better, five of the six episodes, which began on 16 October 1988, featuring Thora. It was to be an especially warm-hearted and collaborative series, in which the ensemble played a bigger part than ever, and saw Clarke once again extending his cast of characters. Glenda and Barry were becoming ever more central to the plots, she as the unworldly participant in a developing scenario involving the ladies mulling over the oddities and annoyances of menfolk, he as the hapless helpmate of Wesley and bewildered witness to the trio's adventures. Clarke's writing for Barry and Glenda's scenes together was not only funny; it had an undertone of sweetness entirely in keeping with his creation of a young couple embarking on married life, even when it was tempered with a touch of tartness, as in an exchange in 'That Certain Smile', when Seymour calls in search of a sedative for a dog.

> Barry: I can hardly believe it happened really. I find myself stopping in front of mirrors. I look at this bloke in the mirror, and I think, that's you, you fool. You're married. And do you know what's, what's really weird? I haven't got the first idea how it actually happened.
>
> Glenda: It happened because I have to make all the decisions for him. (TO SEYMOUR) We've got these travel sick pills. They make you feel dozy.
>
> Seymour: Oh, they'll be fine, dear, just the job.
>
> Glenda: At least, they made me feel dozy. Barry went to sleep.
>
> Barry: What's so terrible about going to sleep?
>
> Glenda: We were on honeymoon!

The dog in question belonged to a new character who proved to have legs – long, gangly, comic legs at that. Clem 'Smiler' Hemingway would, to an extent, take the place of Wally Batty as the resident lugubrious presence, and Bell delved back into the audience's collective memory for the man to play him. Stephen Lewis had become a national favourite in the early 1970s in the bawdy ITV sitcom *On The Buses*, in which his turn as Blakey, the humourless inspector with the Hitler-esque toothbrush moustache, contributed much to the immense popularity of a series which asked a lot in the way of suspension of disbelief on the part of its viewers – notably to accept that the tubby, middle-aged Reg Varney as driver Stan Butler would be irresistible to a procession of mini-skirted females half his age. It was Lewis's definitive comedy role, and as Blakey he gave the country a new catchphrase: 'I 'ate you Butler'. The gloomy newcomer looked as if smiling hurt as he meandered from disappointment to disappointment in flat cap and gabardine overcoat.

There would be two other additions from the former PC Clarke – a pair of comic policemen, whose officiousness and certainty of their authority were matched only by their ineptitude and cowardice, a theme that nodded to one of his earlier series, *Rosie*. A Yorkshire character actor familiar from roles in both television drama and comedy, Ken Kitson, played one, and Louis Emerick, soon to depart for a lengthy hiatus as a central character in the Channel 4 sitcom *Brookside*, was the other, being replaced by a lubricious comedian and folk singer, Tony Capstick. For years, the characters would be known as PC1 and PC2, until Clarke finally equipped them with the names Cooper and Walsh when Kitson and Emerick, who returned after Capstick's untimely death at only fifty-nine in 2003, developed a stage show around them. Unlike Smiler, the policemen would only gradually develop into regulars, but their cameos became so exquisitely judged and played that the audience began laughing as soon as they appeared. Another character, though, would be quietly dropped. Crusher departed the café never to return, because Jonathan Linsey had lost so much weight on a crash diet that he no longer bore any resemblance to the hulking figure Clarke had written. Bell felt he had no option but to axe him.

The two main female characters were being well served by Clarke. Nora and Ivy had been thrown together by widowhood, and their exchanges had a delicious touch of waspishness, not least when Clarke reached back to the very beginnings of *Summer Wine* for a sly dig in the ribs at the mores of religion as they left church:

> Nora: I don't think it's necessary to sing loud. Personally, I've never been one for singing loud. I think what matters more is how seriously Christian you can make your face look.
>
> Ivy: I think you've cracked it.

The series balanced itself between dialogue and sight gags: 'The Experiment' saw Seymour hoisted upside down from a rope, 'The Treasure of the Deep' pitched Howard and Marina into the rat-infested canal, 'Downhill Racer' had the men skiing on tin trays, and 'The Day of the Welsh Ferret' saw Compo chasing the animal into a pool table. It was in the best way formulaic; the audience knew what to expect and revelled in it. Mike Grady said: 'The audience loved the writing, they thought the scenery was beautiful, but when you add into that the chaos that would occur at the end of every episode, that's what clinched it for the audience. You knew it was all going to go wrong, and it did, and that was fine, but you also knew it was safe. Nobody swore, nobody waved anything about, it was basically the *Beano* on screen.'

Familiarity worked for *Summer Wine*; it had already been around long enough to feel like an old friend to an audience that was still hovering around the seventeen million mark, and if new members of the extended family in the Pennines felt like old friends too, so much the better. A very old friend of viewers arrived to close 1988 in style, cast as Auntie Wainwright, the grasping, conniving proprietor of a junk shop. Clarke deftly tied her in to his world, making her the aunt of Howard, and a character the trio were as wary of as earlier incarnations had feared another Wainwright, the librarian. This Wainwright, though, inspired terror by her unwavering ability to sell utterly useless objects to anybody who passed through the door of her shop.

To play her, Bell secured the services of an actress who could give Owen and Thora a run for their money in the 'national treasure' stakes. Jean Alexander had become a much-loved part of the television landscape thanks to her twenty-three years as the shrewish, head-scarved and hair-rollered Hilda Ogden in the daddy of all soap operas, *Coronation Street*. She brought the expertise of extensive experience in rep to that role, and though often enough used for comic relief in tandem with her on-screen husband Stan, played by Bernard Youens, she reduced a massive audience to tears with a riveting performance when Youens died. Alexander was such an affectionately regarded presence in Britain's living rooms that it became front-page news when she decided to call it a day as Hilda; there were campaigns to keep her in the Street, but it was her decision to move on, and she stuck to it. Offers came in, and she turned them all down – except for the show that, like Thora, she already admired.

'I was offered several things, and I read the scripts and didn't like them. And then I was offered Auntie, and as soon as I read the script I thought, this is it, this is what I've been waiting for. It's the sort of character I love to play. I loved it to bits, I thought, I've got to do this,' said Alexander. The offer would take her from one hit series into another, and Clarke's writing whetted her appetite. 'I like comedy that has got wit in it, and Roy is witty. It's the easiest script I've ever had to learn. You don't need to read it more than twice and you know it, because it flows so well. Every sentence follows the other and you can link it all up. It's perfect. Transposing a sentence would make it wrong. You can't alter it, because it is exactly right. They were wonderful scripts, those, incredibly good. They were beautifully written.'

Like Thora, and to a lesser extent Lewis, Alexander brought with her a fund of audience goodwill, and her presence enlivened the Christmas special, 'Crums', an hour-long episode in which the three men, all dressed as Santa, tour the town collecting money for charity. Auntie Wainwright, beady-eyed, querulous of voice and all in black, scuttled around her shop like a money spider, hands clasped firmly in front of her, insisting that she was the most harmless of old ladies until she winkled cash out of the customers, upon which she grasped it with the ferocity of a steel trap. She was the most colourful of the new arrivals, and this was a vintage *Summer Wine* special, the ensemble given full rein in a sub-plot about Barry buying Glenda a water bed, Howard and Marina finally kissing below the canopy of the shop, Compo singing and playing the banjo, and the episode closing with a feel-good party scene. There was something else; a touching, bittersweet scene that tipped a hat – or perhaps a flat cap – to the two loveable comic talents who had been lost, which gratified Kathy Staff and Jane Freeman, who felt that Joe Gladwin and John Comer deserved acknowledgement for everything they had done to make the series the success that it had become.

Nora: Funny, isn't it? All this time, and still sometimes when I hear that door open I keep expecting him to walk in like he always used to, daft as a brush, semi-plastered.

Ivy: Oh, I know. It's having all that bed to yourself that gets me.

Nora: I'll say this for my Wally, he never did take up much room. It was like having a bed to yourself anyway.

Ivy: Oh, mine used to spread himself all over the place. Every night it used to be like being trapped in the January sales. You never realise how much you're going to miss things.

Nora: I know. I just hope wherever he is, he's being careful about airing his vest.

'We were both quite distressed that we couldn't talk about our husbands who had died,' said Freeman. 'It was absolutely lovely when we were able to do it, and Kathy and I had scenes talking about the old days, and we did feel much better then. We hated the fact that Joe and John had disappeared somehow. I was fond of John and Kathy was fond of Joe.'

The audience was fond of all of them. 'Crums' had been one of the best of all episodes, and the most popular BBC comedy of the year, scoring 17.1 million viewers and coming in at number seven in the corporation's top ten programmes across all genres. Auntie Wainwright was another strength and her shop – the exterior of which was bolted on to a house at Marsden to create another landmark in the fantasy that was Summer Wine Land – would become another comfortable setting for viewers, who were now not just in Britain. The BBC was selling the series abroad too, and it was gaining fans in the United States, Australia and New Zealand. There were even some tentative negotiations involving Clarke and Bell about producing an American version of the show, possibly featuring the veteran film star Mickey Rooney – who was a fan – as Compo, but they came to nothing.

The cast was no less comfortable with the series than the audience. A convivial social scene had developed at the Huddersfield Hotel, primarily because of Aldridge's bonhomie, which was so infectious that he even winkled Owen away from his cottage and whisky-and-fish-pie routine. 'When Michael Aldridge joined, he insisted on socialising,' said Bell. 'He says, "Now, Bill, you're coming to join Peter and I tonight, we're going to a restaurant," and Bill said, "No, no, I'm quite happy with my Marks and Spencers fish pie." "No, no," says Michael, "You're meeting us at seven o'clock tonight, get yourself a taxi and come along to the Huddersfield Hotel," and Bill very reluctantly went along and then enjoyed it, because Michael was much more a team player, and they were happy years for everybody.'

Happy though they were, uncomfortable incidents could blow up around Owen when his temper flared suddenly, unpredictably and unaccountably. 'You just got the feeling that you didn't want to mess with him,' said Grady.

> He was an angry man, I don't know why. Some people are
> angry. He didn't display it, he didn't go around shouting all the
> time, screaming at people or demanding stuff, but he was
> brittle. Sometimes you'd be on the end of conversations with
> him and think, I don't need to be around this. He could be very
> spiky and suddenly get very defensive about things, and you'd
> think, well, nobody's attacked you, why are you being
> defensive? We came back to filming after lunch and I think
> they'd been to a hostelry somewhere, and I said, 'Did you have
> a good lunch, Bill?' It was as innocuous as that, he and I had a
> scene together, and somehow I said I didn't go to the pub, I
> actually don't drink, and he turned on me and said, 'Are you
> one of these TT people?' and went off on a quite cross fantasy
> on what I was like and what people who don't drink are like. It
> lasted like fifteen or twenty seconds, and I thought, I'm not
> even going to go into this conversation, there's nothing to
> defend. Then it was fine, and we filmed. It was very rare, but
> there were those moments with him.

They tended not to happen around Aldridge, whose gift for
jollying everybody into good humour could even overcome
Owen's curmudgeonly moods. Even Aldridge's fondness for
socialising, however, paled beside the grand lady of the company
who held court in the dining room of the Huddersfield Hotel.
Gracious, funny, sometimes using language that would have had
her *Praise Be!* audience reaching for the smelling salts, and drawing
on a seemingly bottomless well of reminiscences from her long
career, Thora loved to hold forth and talk. And talk, and talk, and
talk until her companions gave up the unequal struggle to get a
word in. The habit of performance was so ingrained that dinner
became another show as Thora twinkled and acted out the parts in
stories that reached all the way back to her childhood in Morecambe.
'My God, she could talk,' said Jean Fergusson. 'We had what we

called Thora's Table, and we still call it Thora's Corner, and it was a big round table and it sat about eight people. She did like to have an audience, and one member of the cast – and I won't say who it was – one day said, "I never ask Thora how she is, because I know she'll tell me and it goes on forever." Once she got on a roll, that was it, and when she used to have a little caravan to herself we used to crawl round it, we wouldn't let her see us, because she'd hammer on the window and ask you to come in.'

The relentlessness of her conversation – and its repetitiveness – could be wearing. 'She told long stories about the past, which we all revelled in, but we heard them about three or four times,' said Bell. 'The men eventually refused to go out to dinner with her, because Thora would like to be the centre of attention. Michael would say, "I did a film once with Orson Welles ..." and she would immediately say, "Don't talk about Orson Welles ..." and then it was back to her. Peter would say, "But you can't do that for long, because if the film's short ..." "I did a short film ..." [she'd say] and that was it, she had the floor again, and in the end you saw the three men just sitting round the table looking across a candle or whatever.'

Her ego and tendency to steamroller all conversation except her own particularly irritated Sallis. Grady said: 'Peter once stopped me while on location somewhere and said, "Mike, Mike, is it my imagination or did I see you, last night, in the hotel, chatting to that ghastly Thora Hird?" He had no time for her. You're talking about people's egos coming into people's territory. To work together was fine, they would do that, but they would no more consider meeting up for a drink or a chat or visit each other's caravan than fly. It was curious to watch because you had a certain sort of unwritten animosity, but it never would explode into anything truly awful.' Sallis's disdain for Thora was an open secret, according to Sarah Thomas. 'I think Peter came from a classically trained side, and I don't know why it was but he didn't care for her and made no bones about it. Everybody knew his feelings, and it didn't really matter. Whether she knew it or not, I don't know.

Sometimes Thora would take the floor, and I think Peter found her a little bit boastful, she could be holding the fort and that was something he couldn't be bothered with.'

Exasperating though she could be when in full flow, Thora nevertheless inspired tremendous affection among the rest of the cast, especially the younger members, who respected her experience and expertise in playing comedy; and when there was not an audience to entertain, she was less overpowering. Grady said: 'I used to drive her occasionally, and the first time I rather dreaded it, because she could anecdote for England, but she stopped doing that when you were alone with her, and she would just chat and listen and talk and ask, and she was lovely company on those occasions when she wasn't performing. Very egotistical, very driven, could start a fight in a room on her own, but usually didn't, and if you knew her, you were never offended. Sarah was closer to her than anybody, and because she played her daughter, she was expected to assume the position of daughter, and was treated as such and was beckoned and phoned up in the night. The edges got a bit blurred.'

Thomas grew very fond of Thora, and the warmth was reciprocated. 'She said on a couple of occasions, "I've got a lovely daughter in real life, and if I could have another one, I'd adopt Sarah," which she said on national television, which I never quite knew whether Jan [her daughter] appreciated or not.'

Thomas often had to cope alone with the full onslaught of the anecdotage, not least when Thora was reluctant to be alone.

Thora hated her own company. When we were at the Huddersfield, I used to have the bedroom next door to her and she would regale everyone with these wonderful stories at supper, and then we'd go up and she'd say, 'Just pop into my room and we'll run lines,' and it wasn't to run lines, it was to have company. And I used to sometimes pin up her hair, or help her with something or other, and then she'd start telling the same stories she'd been telling downstairs and I'd be saying, 'It's half past ten, it's eleven o'clock, I really must go,' and I'd be ready to stand up and go to bed, and she'd say something like, 'Well, that was the end of my last day at the Co-op, and the next day …' and I'd sit down again, and eventually you had to be tough and say, 'I must go to bed.' Yes, she liked company.

She also liked the company of her public, and would make a point of being seen. 'She knew who she was, she knew her status,' said Grady. 'One of the great things was in Huddersfield when Thora would be taken out by her carer in her wheelchair, and be pushed through the market and along the streets and through various shops. And on market day – she would make sure it was a busy day – the crowd would part like the Red Sea in front of her, and would stand and watch her go by, and she would do this rather regal wave she used to do, nodding to the right and to the left. That's true, that's how it was. She was well aware that they enjoyed seeing her, and she enjoyed being seen.'

Thomas also took Thora out, and witnessed her rapport with the public:

We'd go and have coffee somewhere, and people used to come up to her and say, 'Is it Thora?' which was the title of her second autobiography, and she loved talking to them. Just going out and about with her, it was incredible to see how loved and popular she was. They couldn't believe she was there, and long conversations would emerge and she would always introduce me as her television daughter. In the early days we would travel on the train together, and she would have a first-class ticket, but she went in second class, and I'd meet her at Kings Cross, and she was always there half an hour early and I would always arrive at the last minute with my case flying open, and she would be at the front of the queue with all these fans, chatting away, perfectly at ease.

One of the qualities that endeared Thora to those around her was her sympathy for others, which had helped the show get over the problem of Wharmby's breakdown. In 1994, her husband, manager and confidant since 1937, James Scott, died and Thora telephoned Juliette Kaplan. 'She said, "You've lost your husband as well, haven't you?" and I said yes, and she said, "I just wanted to let you know I feel for you because I know what it's like now." It was so simple and touched with humanity.'

Thora not only fostered a social scene at the hotel; she also engendered closeness between the female cast members on set. Kathy Staff and Jane Freeman – exempt from the evening shift of anecdotes in the hotel – along with Thomas and Kaplan would join her in her caravan when time allowed. Here there was none of the studied quiet and separation of the men's Winnebago. Here all was laughter, chatter and the occasional card game to pass the time when the weather turned foul.

Staff was an equally beloved figure to her colleagues. 'Kathy was very, very good to me, personally,' said Kaplan.

> She was a real Christian, not that she preached religion, she just behaved it. She actually got me my first panto. She said to me, 'Do you do panto?' and I said no, and this was back in 1990, and she said, 'Phone these people, because they like your work, and I think they'll offer you panto.' Well, I phoned them up and they gave me a job, and I did panto for twenty years after that, and that was Kathy. A few years ago, she said, 'I've received a script which is appalling and I wouldn't dream of doing it, but I think you might be right for it, would you like to read it?' It was the story of three old-age-pensioner office workers who get made redundant because of their age, so they take over one of the offices and set up a telephone sex line. You can't imagine Kathy doing that, but she passed it on to me and I did two tours of that. That was all through Kathy helping out another artist.

The women's exterior scenes together often revolved around Edie's appalling driving of a red Triumph Herald convertible, into which all five were crammed. It was a terrific sight gag: Glenda in the front, brow furrowed with worry, Nora, Ivy and Pearl jammed so tightly in the back that they were almost on each others' laps, faces like stone as Edie fought a running battle with the gearbox. The open-top car had been chosen to make filming dialogue scenes easier. Since Thora did not have a licence, all the driving was done by a stand-in, Amy Shaw. It could sometimes be hairy. 'I hated that car,' said Thomas. 'It never felt safe. I remember being on a hill at New Mill and Thora's stand-in was driving it and the wretched car started slipping backwards because the handbrake wasn't working properly and I remember somebody leaping in the car, and it was quite a nasty moment. And even when Thora and Kathy and Jane were in the car things happened, I remember Juliette saying, "I'm getting out now," because the brakes never felt very safe and the doors didn't open properly. We've got numerous out-takes of people saying, "I'm going to do so-and-so," and then couldn't get out of the car, or the handle came off.'

The car and the ladies would feature prominently in the seven episodes of the eleventh series, to be shown as the 1980s drew to a close. And as the decade ended, so did Aldridge's tenure in the show, due to a personal crisis that seemed to those around him all the crueller for striking such a good-natured, kindly man. He had been struggling with a bad hip that made walking painful, but bore that stoically. His real heartache was that his wife since 1947, Kirsten, was sinking into dementia. Bell said: 'She had Alzheimer's and he got letters from neighbours saying, "How can you be so cruel to leave your wife, and we find her down the town?" I got back to the Huddersfield Hotel, and Peter said, "Alan, Michael's very upset, would you go and see him in his room," and I said, "Yes, what's wrong," and he said, "He'd rather tell you himself." Michael was in tears, really crying, and he said, "Alan, playing Seymour is the best job I've ever had, and I've loved it more than anything, but as you know Kirsten isn't well and I'm getting letters from neighbours saying I'm being cruel. Kirsten worked hard to support me as a young actor and I owe it to her to look after her." I said, "I fully understand, Michael," and that was it. It was very honourable.'

Grady admired Aldridge not only for his sense of where his duty lay, but also for the spirit he displayed. 'He found it incredibly wearing to deal with and he dealt with it with great humour, and I'm not at all surprised that he retired basically to look after her. His family were all very supportive, but only Michael really could look after her. It was a great shame, but he dealt with it as well as he could.'

The air of sadness surrounding Aldridge's impending departure was only deepened by the quality of his performance in the new series, notably in three episodes which ranked with the show's finest, 'Come Back Jack Harry Teesdale', 'Happy Anniversary Gough And Jessie' and 'Three Men and a Mangle'. The first of these was enlivened by a splendid comic turn from Bert Parnaby as the hapless Jack Harry Teesdale, whose inability to reverse a caravan into the driveway of his house drove his wife to despair. It was a beautifully crafted episode with a central visual joke as Seymour directs him in that was as ingenious as anything Clarke had yet come up with. Another epic sight gag involving Nora Batty's unwanted mangle lay at the heart of the final episode of the series, as it was dropped from a viaduct through the roof of a police car. 'Happy Anniversary Gough And Jessie' was a different proposition, a talking show with a charming guest spot from the toothy veteran comic Cardew Robinson as the fifty-years-married Gough who is inveigled away from his anniversary party and gets drunk. In all three, Aldridge hit the heights as Seymour, all bemused authority and misguided pomposity. His troubles, though, were there to be seen in his face; the lines had become etched a little deeper and he seemed suddenly to look old. There would be a Christmas special to close the year, 'What's Santa Brought For Nora, Then?', the closing shot of which gave the audience a clue as to what was about to happen as Nora and Ivy open a present to find a decorated egg and a letter, their mouths falling open in astonishment.

He was on his way back. The definitive batty authority figure would return as the 1990s dawned, if not a changed man, then one who was certainly mellower; the years since Brian Wilde had left *Summer Wine* had not been especially successful. His refusal to pay an agent to find work hampered him more than ever, not least because he had, to an extent, dropped out of sight after his initial stint as Foggy. 'A lot of people thought he'd died,' said Bell. 'I think he was disappointed. What happened when he was working on *Summer Wine* in '84, he was being used for commercials and voice-overs a lot, and that's because he was around. Once you go off the screen, people forget.' Wilde's big hope for success on his own terms had come in 1988 when the BBC built a sitcom around him, *Wyatt's Watchdogs*, in which he starred as a sort of supercharged Foggy, a retired major running a neighbourhood watch scheme. The omens were good – the scripts by Miles Tredinnick were funny, Wilde would be reunited with Bell as producer/director, and there was expert support from the vastly experienced sitcom hand Trevor Bannister. 'I thought it was a good series,' said Bell. 'In those days, if you didn't get ten million straight away you were a failure, but looking back they were quite fun. It wasn't a milestone in television, but it was a reasonable comedy series.' The public, though, was underwhelmed, possibly because Wilde had become a victim of his own success in bringing Barrowclough and Foggy so brilliantly to life from scripts of the highest quality. For all his skills, he could not make Major Wyatt anything like as memorable, and the series was cancelled after its initial six episodes.

For all his admiration of Aldridge, Bell knew that there could never be a third man to rival Foggy, and when he met Wilde at Joe Gladwin's funeral, he raised the idea of a guest appearance. 'I said, "I've been thinking about you, would you come back and be a guest star for an episode or two?" and he said, "Oh, I don't think so, I'm thinking of going to Australia." I said, "I think that's a bit extreme." I don't think he meant it, but that's what he said. Anyway, the next night he rang up and said, "Did you mean that?" and I said, "Yes, we would love to have you back."'

The initial draft of 'Crums' was designed to reintroduce Foggy from his sojourn decorating eggs in Bridlington, returning to look after Auntie Wainwright's shop. Bell said: 'The script was very good, but with great respect to Roy the characters of Foggy and Seymour weren't separate enough and one more or less echoed what the other had said, and it wasn't a good reintroduction of Foggy. Brian rang up and said, "I'm a bit disappointed," and I said, "I know what you mean," so I went through the script and changed it to Howard, Brian's lines, but it showed that he was interested.' When Aldridge announced his departure, Bell had no doubt where to turn, even if, typically, Wilde needed a little coaxing. '"Can I come and see you?" I said, and he said, "Well, I'm considering doing a tour." He hadn't done anything. I went back to see him and he wasn't sure he should come back, but after a few drinks he agreed to come back and play Foggy. It was great, he was marvellous again.'

For the first time, there would be an episode in which two third men would appear. Gentleman that he was, Michael Aldridge agreed to set his personal problems aside and make a brief appearance in the opening episode of the 1990 series, 'Return of the Warrior', as Seymour departs to take up a post as a relief headmaster. He is given a proper goodbye from the series from Compo and Clegg as they help him on to the bus, and a last flourish from Clarke for his superannuated head boy as he looks forward to – literally – getting back into the swing of school life, only to be astonished to find he has been left behind by the times.

Seymour: It's a very important teaching post. I shall be acting for the headmaster when he is absent. Did I pack my cane?

Compo: It feels like tha's packed an electric chair.

Clegg: It's no use packing your cane anyway, you're not allowed to use it any more.

Seymour: Not allowed to use it any more?

Clegg: Somebody who probably has two nannies for their kids has decided that it's illegal.

Seymour: You mean somebody's removed my freedom to hit back?

Compo: Tha's not allowed to beat kids any more.

Seymour: Not even here and there?

Clegg: Especially there.

And that was that. This episode within an episode, Aldridge's thirty-first, was not only his farewell to a show he had loved and enlivened, it was effectively his curtain call on a distinguished career. At sixty-nine, he retired and returned home to care for his wife.

As Seymour's bus pulls away, the episode virtually begins afresh as a second bus passes by with Foggy glimpsed on the upper deck by Clegg. In 'The Man from Oswestry', it had been Compo bemoaning not being bossed about any more by Blamire. This time, it was Clegg's turn to rue the lack of purpose in their lives now that Seymour had gone. 'Suddenly life is like first-class mail. There doesn't seem to be any urgency any more.'

There were other echoes of that first episode to feature Foggy in 'Return of the Warrior'. Once again, he struggles to get his luggage off the bus, managing to wallop two men between the legs with his cane in the process, and once again it would close with him careering away down a hill with his bags. In the interim, though, he misses Compo and Clegg by moments as he visits Nora's and the café in search of them, and it is there that Clarke serves notice that all is well in Summer Wine Land now that his favourite authority figure is back, with an exquisitely crafted exchange between Foggy and Ivy that Wilde plays with subtlety and just the right hint of poignancy as he struggles to conceal his disappointment that his friends have spared little thought for him while he has been away.

Foggy: Did they ever mention missing me?

Ivy: Not to my knowledge.

Foggy: Not that I care, of course. But I mean – not once?

Ivy: Not a peep.

Foggy: That would be the military training I gave them, you see, I taught them how to keep their emotions under iron control.

Ivy: Yes, well, you did a good job.

Foggy: Yes, well, that's the Dewhurst legacy, you know, I leave a trail of stiff upper lips behind me. Yes, well, it's nice to know all your efforts haven't been wasted. Yes, I shaped them in my own hard image, did I? What, they never said they missed me once? I think that's overdoing it.

Wilde, who seemed lankier and more angular than ever, slipped back into character with an ease and skill that brought the dialogue to life with a sparkle that announced another classic era was under way. 'Return of the Warrior' was a very bright start for a superb series of ten episodes and a Christmas special. It would also herald the arrival of another great sight gag that became as beloved of audiences as Compo's matchbox – the synchronised coffee-drinking of the ladies as they raised their cups in unison at the close of their deliberations on the best way to keep men in their place. The scenes had grown increasingly popular and developed into one of the most reliable pleasures of the show, not only for the dialogue but for the genteel but determined competition between the ladies for the cream éclair on the plate of cakes being passed around. 'I think some of Roy's best writing has been in those scenes,' said Thomas. 'They were very memorable and wonderful to play, and I used to wonder where he got all his lines from, because they stretched all over the British Isles often, and they were all the characters' memories too, the older women remembering trips to Scarborough, and they gave early life to the characters too, the fact that Kathy's and Jane's characters had been young once.' Young they may have been, but growing older had made them stern with their menfolk, as Clarke's comic take on the sort of women he had met as a young PC demonstrated.

Nora: Well, personally I think the trouble these days is they just seem to let them roam loose without any thought of punishment.

Ivy: Oh, it's true. It's no good just confining them. They should be made to do useful work.

Pearl: But are they capable of useful work?

Edie: Under the right supervision.

Nora: It has to be careful supervision. There's nobody trickier to manage than the average husband.

Ivy: It's a full-time job.

Glenda: You're talking about husbands. I thought you were talking about criminals.

Pearl: It's easy to see how you might get them confused.

Glenda: It's as if you think husbands should be punished.

Edie: Well, everybody must be house-trained, I mean you can't just let them do what they want because they're cuddly and wag their tails occasionally.

Nora: What's the use of them being married if they don't know they're married?

Ivy: You have to keep the pressure on.

Glenda: What do you think it is that makes men so unreliable?

Pearl: Practice.

Nora: Well, I blame a lot of it these days on diet. Food these days just isn't stodgy enough. In my day, you fed your man right and he couldn't move fast enough to get into mischief.

Pearl: I feed mine, and he cycles it off. Every time he comes home, he's got lipstick on his bicycle clips.

Ivy: How is your Barry?

Glenda: Oh, he's half asleep most of the time.

Nora: Oh, that's a good sign. You must be feeding him right.

Edie: Well, I don't see why not. She's been raised in the finest culinary tradition.

Glenda: I've started him jogging.

Pearl: Does he like jogging?

Glenda: He hates jogging.

Nora/Edie/Ivy/Pearl: Aaah!

The scenes were gems, and the final polish that made them gleam was born of necessity, with Bell acting as coffee-morning drill sergeant, according to Kaplan.

The drinking of the tea came about because Alan said to us on the set, 'We've got to fill in twenty seconds, and what I suggest is that on the signal from me, you all raise your cups at the same time, drink at the same time, and put them down at the same time.' And Jane Freeman said, 'Alan, that's got no bearing on reality,' and he said to her, 'Jane, the whole show hasn't.' So what we would do is sit there with our coffee cups, and he'd say, 'Up-two-three, drink-two-three, down-two-three,' and apparently after that scene was shown, the switchboard was flooded. The audience loved it that we were all drinking simultaneously, choreographed, they went wild for it.

There was much for the audience to enthuse over now that Foggy was back in the fold. Clarke was writing some of his most imaginative dialogue, as well as dreaming up visual comedy that Bell brought to life, and each episode featured an hilarious set piece – the trio on bicycles playing polo in 'Walking Stiff Can Make You Famous', out on the water in a boat in 'Das Welly Boot', running headlong down a hill in padded barrels in 'Roll On', Compo being fired out of a cannon in 'That's Not Captain Zero'. There was also room for Owen to reach back to the variety of his juvenile years, singing 'You Must Have Been a Beautiful Baby' to a picture of Nora in 'The Last Surviving Maurice Chevalier Impression', an episode which pointed to the future by featuring a star guest spot from Gorden Kaye, popular as the lead in the knockabout French resistance wartime comedy 'Allo, 'Allo.

Summer Wine's third decade as a fixture of the television landscape was under way in style. These would be adventurous, expansive, settled years that would see the show enter another vintage period.

CHAPTER 11

❦

Late Vintage

A**S HE PASSED** his sixtieth birthday, Roy Clarke had never been busier. From now on, he would write more episodes than ever, typically in series of ten instead of the more usual six or eight; 1995 would even see twenty broadcast, including two specials, the series scheduled for autumn 1994 having been held back until the start of the new year.

This was the sort of comedy-writing work rate that only the teams responsible for US sitcoms could rival, and all the more remarkable for coming against a backdrop of other projects that demonstrated his versatility and assurance in moving between genres: a detective drama for ITV, *The World of Eddie Weary*; a film, *A Foreign Field*, starring Alec Guinness as a Second World War veteran returning to the battlefields to pay his respects to the fallen; and a comedy series with the very adult theme of adultery, *Ain't Misbehavin'*, which reunited him with Jimmy Gilbert, who returned from retirement to act as executive producer. Not for the first time, Clarke found that he was competing with himself. The year Foggy returned also saw the arrival of Hyacinth Bucket on the BBC in *Keeping Up Appearances*, another huge hit that would eventually outstrip *Summer Wine* in the ratings.

These were professionally successful, gratifying years; they were blighted, however, by personal sadness with the death of his wife, Enid, in 1993. Clarke was lauded by his home town with the

Freedom of Doncaster, by universities with a series of honorary degrees, and by his peers with the presentation by Bafta of the 1996 Dennis Potter Award for outstanding writing, a prize that not only put him in the company of such other great comedy writers as Spike Milligan, Ray Galton and Alan Simpson, and Dick Clement and Ian La Frenais, who had all received it, but also outstanding dramatists including Harold Pinter and Alan Bennett. A trip to Buckingham Palace to receive the OBE would follow a few years later, in 2002, and by then it had emerged that the show had a friend in a very high place indeed. During the Queen's seventieth-birthday celebrations in 1996, the royal household allowed a few details of the monarch's home life to emerge, among them that her favourite television programme was *Last of the Summer Wine*, and woe betide anybody who interrupted her enjoyment of Compo, Clegg and Foggy in the drawing room at Sandringham.

The quality of Clarke's writing was not compromised by his prodigious output. The return of Wilde seemed to galvanise him once again and it became a familiar pattern for Foggy to have a starring scene towards the start of an episode in which he either bored or alarmed a bystander with tall stories about his wartime exploits, complete with falsetto evocation of the diminutive tribesmen who had worshipped him as a god out east, or a bloodcurdling mania for the black arts of combat. Wilde shone in these magnificently absurd solo excursions, his superb underplaying of lines which were surreal to the point of utter lunacy rendering them somehow plausible, such as when he approached a wary librarian:

Foggy: Have you anything on silent killing?

Librarian: If there is anything, you'll find it under sports and pastimes.

Foggy: How about unarmed combat for the over-sixties? You see, I've had a look round and all I can find for the over-sixties is old-time dancing. Well, I mean, it's all very well in its way, but if you're mugged in the street you can hardly valeta him to death, can you? Haven't you anything on strangulation? It isn't as though I haven't been trained in all this, you know, but I'd like to check on the literature, see if anything's been updated. It might be done by remote control these days.

Librarian: I'm afraid we've nothing of that nature.

Foggy: Oh, it's typical isn't it, typical. You've got shelves full of doctor and nurse romances, just hard luck if you're interested in strangulation. Oh well, just have to remain faithful to the old techniques.

Clarke, too, was remaining faithful to his old techniques, rarely venturing near studio or location, finding all the inspiration he needed in the view from his home, jokingly referring to himself as The Yorkshire Hermit. When he did put in one of his very occasional appearances, his extraordinarily fertile talent impressed everybody anew. For all the millions who watched at home, his most ardent admirers were those in front of and behind the camera, who stood in awe at his facility and ear for what fell so naturally for his cast. Bell said:

We were under-running by about forty-five to fifty seconds on an episode called 'Passing the Earring', and Roy was visiting. I said, 'Roy it's under-running, could you write a very short scene for Jane and Kathy in the café, a stand-alone scene that doesn't affect the plot?' 'Fair enough,' he said, 'when do you need it?' I told him, now. He pulled a pencil from his pocket and a piece of paper, and he sat down and wrote this scene, and it's a classic little exchange. Without any pause he wrote it, and it was done in the length of time it takes to write it down. I don't know anybody else who could do that.

Clarke was equally unfazed by requests for special material, such as when Juliette Kaplan asked if he would be willing to write a show for her. 'I phoned him and I said, "Would you like to write me a one-woman show?" and there was a long pause and a sharp intake of breath, and he said, "Why not?" And he actually wrote Pearl a full-length play called *Just Pearl*, where Pearl talks about her previous life and Howard is presumably off stage, and we got that on the road and I did forty dates throughout the country with it, and it was the most marvellous experience.'

Instinct guided him, and it usually led him in the right direction. 'I think you've got to feel there's a standard kept,' said Clarke. 'I don't particularly think in terms of audience figures, but I've got to enjoy what I'm doing, and if I do I tend to think it's all right. It's not always. When I see it sometimes, I hate it and I see everywhere where it's gone wrong, but at the time I would think that script would be as good as any other I've put in. I don't put anything in that I don't think is right, but you can be awfully wrong sometimes about what is right.'

A couple of other considerations also guided him – the visual nature of the show and the advancing ages of the three principals, especially Owen, who had turned seventy-six as the new decade opened. Exploiting the filmic potential of the locations in the Pennines where the visual humour could be played out by Bell on a large scale made some gruelling demands on the cast. Howard and Marina were always outdoors, the ladies were often on the road in Edie's car, and Wesley's madcap inventions needed space. The larger ensemble of the early 90s was not only needed to drive the action forward; it was becoming more necessary to ease the weight of carrying every episode off Sallis, Owen and Wilde, especially as the number of episodes increased. The pace of the show had quickened, though it never felt rushed; there was still plenty of time for the three men to dawdle down a lane, lie in the heather and look at the sky, or lean back against a tree, but each half-hour fairly flew by as the plot moved from them to the café, to Pearl's house, to Wesley's shed, to Auntie Wainwright's. By comparison, the episodes of almost twenty years earlier that were now being issued on video seemed to proceed at a snail's pace.

Less and less was being done in front of a studio audience. Bell said: 'Sometimes the film ran for twenty-four minutes and the audience came in to watch six minutes in the studio, which they'd queue up for. They didn't mind, and they laughed as much. And Bill Owen was getting a bit old, and the actors would hang around in the studios all day from eleven in the morning until nine-thirty at night just to do six minutes.' Bell was approached by Kodak with the suggestion he use some new stock they had available to make an episode on film for posterity. 'I thought, that's a good idea, and then we costed out how much it would be to do the whole series on film, and it turned out to be, with careful planning, the same as to hire a studio every week, so that's what we did.' *Summer Wine* would be all on film from 1992 onwards, and the show would later embrace a couple more technical innovations, becoming the first BBC series to be recorded in stereo sound and the first shot in high-definition. The studio scenes were filmed either at Shepperton or Pinewood, and there were those among the cast who missed playing to an audience. 'Bill was a performer, he loved the sound of an audience,' said Bell. 'That was the one thing he missed when we went to all film, he missed the sound of the laughs for the lines. All right, he got them in the end.'

Jane Freeman missed the audience for a different reason. 'We were all in the studio and much more related to the theatre. When it was done like that we were able to deliver lines and we had an audience much of the time, so you could play. Now some of the scenes drag around because we're not quite sure where they're going to laugh. Often, they laugh on the key word when it's shown to the public, and you can't hear the word that they're laughing at. In the old days, we played to an audience and when you're playing to an audience you know where you can place your lines, but with a camera, Alan gets us to pause after lines that are supposed to be funny, but if they don't find them funny, it makes a scene slow.'

The programme needed a laughter track for the viewers at home. Canned laughter, that badge of shame of so many dismal American comedy shows that used it to disguise their inability to raise a smile, let alone a guffaw, was out of the question. Bell had a cast of very experienced actors who loved playing to an audience, so he made use of them and put on a show. Audiences were invited to the BBC, later Teddington Studios, and entertained by the stars. Owen would appear and sing, Sallis would be wryly witty, Howard and Marina would serenade each other, Thora would be charm itself. By the time the lights were dimmed and the episodes shown on a cinema screen which brought out the beauty of the scenery, the studio audience was receptive and in a mood to enjoy itself. Microphones suspended above them recorded their laughter on to the soundtrack. There was no fakery. When the episodes were broadcast, what the audience at home heard was the natural, genuine reaction of people just like themselves. 'The great reward for me is to stand in that studio and watch the audience enjoying it,' said Bell. 'That is enormous reward. The cast don't just say hello, it's an entertainment and the audience loves it. "House full" signs, three shows a day with two films each. Mums and dads with three kids in the audience. They go out saying it's the best night out they've had for ages.'

What the audiences were seeing during the 1990s were episodes that featured some adventurous visual humour as well as razor-sharp writing. In 'Give Us a Lift', an armchair was bounced off the top of the police car, 'Pole Star' had Compo, Howard and Marina falling into the river outside Nora's house, 'The Self-Propelled Salad Strainer' featured a fantastic machine that deposited Compo on the roof of a house, and 'Stop That Castle' saw Bell mounting a full-scale parade featuring brass band through the centre of Marsden to escort a giant bouncy castle that is punctured by Foggy and traps the ladies as it deflates. Compo was at the centre of stunts almost weekly – trapped in a runaway tin bath in 'Stop That Bath', a bedstead hurtling down a road in 'The Sweet Smell of Excess', pitched into a pond from a giant wheel in 'Wheelies', sent thudding into Wesley's garage in 'Concerto for Solo Bicycle'. The climactic sight gags sent viewers away happy, and the dialogue made the audiences who were seeing it at the preview screenings roar with laughter:

Clegg: I used to think God invented beetles, but then Wesley Pegden said it was Hitler.

Compo: Hitler invented beetles?

Foggy: That was the Volkswagen Beetle. Hitler didn't invent creepy-crawly beetles.

Clegg: Well, I'm glad about that. That means I can go back to liking beetles.

Foggy: What's to like about beetles?

Clegg: Oh, I think they're wonderful. They look like tortoises, some of them. And yet, they can fly.

Compo: Me Auntie Meg had a tortoise.

Foggy: She had something slow and idle, and that was her husband.

The scenes between the three men were still invested with the magical quality that had first manifested itself in the late 70s; they were as conversational and quirky as ever, the classic trio rediscovering and sustaining their unique on-screen rapport. And off screen, relations were more cordial than they had been during Wilde's initial tenure as Foggy. The trio remained loyal, but it was rather less disagreeable. They still kept their distance from each other and went their separate ways at the end of each day, but Owen, approaching eighty, was less combative, as was Wilde. He had come back into the show at sixty-three having had the salutary lesson of a few years when his star had faded. At his age, a second chance at a leading part in what remained one of television's favourite shows, which brought with it good pay and a fund of audience goodwill, was not to be dismissed lightly. 'There was a classic time with the three of them in those few years before Bill died,' said Bell. 'Ronnie Hazlehurst said to me, "You know, they are now the age they should have been at the beginning. There are three old guys walking about the countryside, rather than three guys on the dole." Ronnie was right. They were very comfortable working together, too.'

The cast members who had become established in the show during Aldridge's years found Wilde to be charming, polite and modest. Juliette Kaplan fondly recalled his old-fashioned courtesy in tipping his hat to her, and Sarah Thomas would draw him out by chatting about gardening, which he loved. Jean Fergusson found that his streak of eccentricity could send the conversation in unexpected directions.

> It started to snow. So we all dived into various vehicles to shelter and I dived for this car and everybody else dived for the coach, and in the front seat was Brian. He didn't talk much, really, and because he didn't stay at the same hotel as us, we never had a social evening. All of them on the coach were saying, 'Jean's in there with Brian, what will they talk about?' Well, we were talking about all sorts of different things when suddenly – and I don't know why I mentioned it – I mentioned Sooty, and he said, 'I used to love Sooty,' and we had a Sooty conversation. So when I got back on the set, quite a few of the people on the coach watching said, 'What did you talk about?' so I said, 'Mainly, Sooty.'

The chatty, gregarious Fergusson did try to tempt Wilde away from his hotel and into the by now well-established social scene, but to no avail. 'I said, "Brian, you always stay out at the Hilton, why don't you ever come into Huddersfield and have a drink with us?" and he said, "I suppose I could, really, I quite like real ale," and I said, "Well, we go to a real ale pub on Tuesdays," and he said, "Let me know next time and I might very well join you." Well, he never did. We did invite him and he never came, which is a shame, I'm sorry he didn't.'

One of the great points of agreement between Owen, Sallis and Wilde during these years was a steadfast refusal to overexert themselves. 'Brian was very anti-effort,' said Clarke. 'Peter, it's not that he was anti, it's just that he wasn't physically terrific. I used to get shocks. I'd get somebody on the phone saying, "You know this scene where you've got them cycling, you know Peter can't ride a bicycle, and Foggy won't go into the water because he won't roll his trousers up to his knees."' The trio's definition of what excessive activity constituted could be very broad indeed, recalled Ken Kitson: 'They were spoiled, and at the end when they got old and they were ill, all you saw were close-ups because they had stand-ins that did all the walking. It annoyed me, because these stand-ins didn't even get a credit and they worked their socks off. They were good, they used to do the walks and everything, and you couldn't tell.'

If the three men were spared as much effort as possible, the supporting cast just had to get on with it. Fergusson and Robert Fyfe put up with much. 'We had to cycle down a hill very fast, and the camera was on a double-decker bus and we had to be overtaken by the bus,' said Fergusson. 'The bus had to draw level and we had to look up, and the bus driver said we were going quite fast, I think twenty miles per hour or something, which was quite fast on that hill. But because our bikes had been dismantled and put on a low-loader to do some close-ups and then put back together for the real cycling, the bolts were taken off and put back on. I'm cycling along and before we got up to speed, I look down and I said, "My God, my front wheel's wobbling," and the front wheel was about to come off.'

The climactic scene of 'Pole Star', with Howard, Marina and Compo lying in the river in the centre of Holmfirth in full fishing gear, was even more uncomfortable for Fergusson: 'The river was going into our waders because of the way it was flowing, so our waders were full of water and when the crew came we couldn't stand up, we were just lying in the water saying, "Can somebody come and help?" so somebody came down and they had to tip us upside down to get the water out of the waders before they could get us out. And all the public were there looking over the bridge.

They got a wonderful view that day of us being turned upside down.'

Bell enlisted a familiar face to help him out with the more physical aspects of a show now synonymous with visual humour. Mike Grady had bowed out at the start of the 1990s on the most amicable of terms because he had so many other projects running; Barry's character had lived on in the meantime in Glenda's conversation at the ladies' coffee mornings. Six years later, Grady's phone rang. 'I got a call from Alan saying, "Would you like to come back?" and I said, "Why would you want me back?" and he said, "We miss the character, and we like working with you, and those three old bastards are so lazy they won't walk anywhere, and I can't do a tracking shot and I need somebody a few years younger and we'll pay you some money." They could have done more, but they wouldn't, that was his point, they just bloody wouldn't.'

What they did do, though, was superlative; the audiences laughed so long and loud at the previews Bell felt compelled to edit out some of the laughter because it was drowning dialogue. One such episode, 'Destiny and Six Bananas', saw Foggy setting out to capture a mysterious creature in the woods.

Foggy: You'll be perfectly safe. We'll be in hiding and I shall tranquillise it with one of these darts.

Compo: It's just an ordinary dart.

Foggy: It's not an ordinary dart, it's very far from being an ordinary dart. I've prepared it with something to make the creature sleep.

Compo: What something? Does it work?

Foggy: Listen who's talking, does it work? No, don't worry, I've seen the natives do this in the jungle.

Clegg: Yeah, they've got poisons growing in the jungle. What have you got?

Foggy: The trained soldier learns to make do with whatever's available. You have to use whatever comes to hand.

Compo: All right, what is it that you soak the darts in that's going to put it to sleep?

Foggy: Well, if you must know, it's Horlicks.

Compo: That's supposed to make it sleep?

Foggy: Well, it makes me sleep.

As the 90s progressed, viewing figures declined from the heights of the previous decade, but were still regularly hitting ten million. Audiences were falling generally due to the proliferation of new channels, not only on terrestrial television, but on satellite, as well as the younger generation's use of home computers for entertainment. The golden age of television comedy that began with Hancock and ran into the 1980s was over, but this last great survivor of those glory years was still among the BBC's most popular programmes, and the corporation relied on Clarke to provide its Sunday evening entertainment, with the show going out at 7.30 p.m., followed an hour later by *Keeping Up Appearances*, which was regularly drawing thirteen million viewers. Later in the decade, *Summer Wine* would be broadcast earlier, in the traditional 'God slot', which at least gave the audience their fix of Thora, whose *Praise Be!* was axed in 1994 after seventeen years. Bell was unhappy with the earlier timing: 'When it was number one in the ratings, it went out at nine-twenty on a Monday night. Emotionally, that's the right time. Six o'clock? Half past five? Forget it, you're throwing it away, but they say it starts Sunday evening well.' Clarke was laconic about the earlier broadcast: 'I get the chapel vote. You either go to chapel or you watch *Summer Wine*.'

Those who opted for Summer Wine Land rather than chapel were finding themselves in the company of yet more old friends, as Bell brought in guests on an increasingly regular basis who were more than happy to take a bow in what had long qualified as a comedy institution, and Clarke relished writing for them. The presence of the guests inspired a clutch of classic episodes, giving the show an added dimension; some traded on older viewers' nostalgia for great comedy of times past, others had made their mark in currently popular shows, such as Paul Bown, a visitor from a stylish ITV sitcom, *Watching*, who guest-starred in the 1993 Christmas special, 'Welcome to Earth'. This time, he was watching for visitors from space, an amiable nerd who convinced the trio that aliens were about to land. Bown's diffident oddball echoed the trio's whimsicality, and helped to make his one of the most effective guest appearances in what was one of the finest of all episodes, demonstrating that twenty years on from its debut *Summer Wine* remained one of the freshest and most inventive comedies on television. In keeping with the theme, this was a half-hour sprinkled with stardust, conceived and executed on a grand scale with crowds flocking up the moors in search of a UFO as Clarke poked fun at the era's science-fiction blockbusters, as well as prodding its lack of civility in one of his most waspish asides for Clegg as Foggy wondered about human sacrifice at a stone circle:

> Foggy: Some people had to be victims for the good of the community.

> Clegg: Same thing today. Look what's happened to God-fearing, hard-working, well-mannered people.

Bown was not the only guest in 'Welcome to Earth'. Bell reached back to the heyday of variety for a repeat appearance by two stalwarts who had first performed a walk-on in 'Crums'. Jim Casey and Eli Woods were son and nephew respectively of the great stage drunk Jimmy James, for whom they had stooged, and their appearance touched off fond recollection in viewers of a certain age who could quote verbatim James's classic routine in which he was confronted by a man claiming to have two man-eating lions in a small cardboard box, demanding to know, 'Are you putting it around that I'm barmy?' And, of course, there was Kim Bread. His appearance in the closing scene as another alien-spotter who mistakes Compo, Clegg and Foggy for extra-terrestrials, only for them to pelt him with vegetables, prompted a huge, joyously surprised, delighted laugh of recognition from the audience. 'We went up to Shepperton Studios where John Cleese was filming *Frankenstein*, and we got him at the end of the day,' said Bell. 'It's a really important little part. He used the name Kim Bread and I regret to say that during the remaking of the titles it went back to being John Cleese. We only paid him fifty pounds.' Cleese came up with his off-the-wall pseudonym for the cameo, but it did not last into the finished programme, which saw *ET* taken the mickey out of as the trio, silhouetted on a bike, sailed past a full moon and Hazlehurst deployed full orchestra to pull out all the stops for one of his most inspired pastiches in which his tender little waltz threw its shoulders back, stuck out its chest and strutted.

'Welcome to Earth' ended 1993 on a high. There would be no series in 1994, but that year marked a sad milestone. On 10 January, Michael Aldridge died suddenly at his home in London, aged seventy-three. His wife, whom he had retired to look after, survived him. Despite the popularity of the show during his time as Seymour and the quality of his best episodes, it would always be his fate to be the neglected third man of *Summer Wine*, the member of the trio who never quite fitted as well as Foggy, never quite attracted the same audience devotion, even though nobody had been held in higher regard by his colleagues.

A guest star with one of the most glittering track records in British entertainment got the marathon runs of 1995 under way in style in a New Year's Day special. 'The Man Who Nearly Knew Pavarotti' featured Norman Wisdom as Billy Ingleton, a magnificent eccentric desperate to give a piano recital, the drawback being that he cannot play. It was another triumphant special, redolent of the atmosphere of a lost age of film comedy thanks to the presence of the pint-sized Wisdom, who at seventy-nine still fizzed with energy and ego, grabbing this dazzling late showcase with both hands and attempting to elbow everybody else aside. 'I had to pull him back a bit because he kept wanting to make it the Norman Wisdom Show,' said Bell. Ken Kitson, who early in his career had worked with Wisdom, knew what to expect from a comic so brazen about stealing scenes that no jury would hesitate in finding him guilty of theft. 'He was a bugger once people were watching and he knew he had an audience, he was away. Peter Sallis hated that, nobody got a look in once Norman got started, because he was just brilliant. I loved him to bits, but he and Peter didn't get on. You see Norman's legs sticking out of a piano, and they had a stuntman to do it, and he said, "No, no, I'll do it," and I thought, why, you're only seeing his legs? But when you saw those legs you knew they were Norman Wisdom's legs, because of what he did with them, it was unbelievable. Comedy timing right down to his toes.' Bell kept Wisdom on the tightest of leashes as he mugged and suggested slides, pirouettes and falls, infuriating Sallis, who would later observe acidly: 'I developed three words to help Norman in his work. They were "Shut up, Norman".' Clarke climaxed the episode with a song-and-dance routine for Owen, just to make it clear that ultimately there was an unchallenged, unchanging pecking order for short, comic figures in *Summer Wine*. Wisdom would be brought back the following year for another special, 'Extra! Extra!' which also guest-starred American actor George Chakiris as an impresario who recruits the trio for a film, and would go on to make four more appearances, though none matched the impact of his first.

The remainder of 1995 saw another couple of guest appearances – Ron Moody, the definitive Fagin in Lionel Bart's *Oliver!*, appeared as a conman in 'Captain Clutterbuck's Treasure', and Anita Dobson, Angie from *EastEnders*, was terrorised by the thing in Compo's matchbox in 'A Leg Up for Christmas'. The guests came mainly from the traditional end of entertainment: Eric Sykes and Warren Mitchell from their own much-loved sitcoms; Tommy Cannon, Bobby Ball, Roy Hudd and Brian Conley from what was left of variety; Matthew Kelly and Ray Cooney from farce; and a couple of versatile actresses who would later join as permanent cast members, June Whitfield and Barbara Young.

The show was in fine fettle as, in 1997, it celebrated the twenty-five years since the first filming in Holmfirth with an hour-long documentary. But the milestone anniversary also signalled that time was beginning to intrude on Summer Wine Land and making claims on its ageing inhabitants that they struggled to fulfil, bringing first an upheaval in the cast, and then worse, much worse. Wilde turned seventy as the eighteenth series drew to its close that June, and he was tiring; hard though Bell worked to cosset his stars and however much Clarke spread the burden around the cast, they were getting old and the location shoots in Yorkshire became a little more draining with every new year. Wilde wanted to do less and less, and pushed for Foggy's role to be downgraded. Clarke obliged, and several of the scripts for the next series would feature only brief appearances for the character to give him more time off, with Compo and Clegg embarking on adventures by themselves. But then illness intervened; Wilde developed shingles, a painful and debilitating condition, which ruled him out of taking part in even a reduced capacity. Bell said: 'The BBC doctor said he would either recover fully within a fortnight but have terrible pains which will persist, or it will get worse, and we thought it was probably best to rest him.' Wilde's choice was made for him; it was over for Foggy after 116 episodes. The favourite third man of writer and director, the definitive tall addled authoritarian of the audience, who had made his entrance at a time of uncertainty and provided the catalyst for its vintage years, stepped aside. This time, there would be no comeback; the man of action, the restless bundle of energy and hare-brained schemes had made his last bow, his loss regretted by all. Wilde recovered fully from his illness, but turned down repeated invitations to bring Foggy back, saying: 'Although I have often been invited to return, I always refuse as I feel I have done it, and enjoyed it.'

It was game on once again for Clarke and Bell as they considered a new authority figure. Out of the blue, the name of a veteran comic actor came up. 'It's funny how these things happen,' said Bell. 'I had dinner with Trevor Bannister and he was talking about how *Are You Being Served?* was never repeated on the BBC, and it put me in mind that Frank Thornton was still around, so when Brian rang up to say it was bad news and he wouldn't be able to do the series, I checked Frank's availability and I invited him in for lunch at the BBC. That was really only to see if he could walk all right and he walked all the way from reception to the BBC restaurant, and he was fit, and we knew he could act. He was quite surprised, because he thought he was just being chatted to about playing a guest part.'

Indeed he could act. Tall, grave of appearance and blessed with pinpoint timing, Thornton had been a fixture in television comedy since an appearance in Hancock's defining half-hour, 'The Blood Donor', in 1961. He went on to work with other stellar comedians including Michael Bentine, Spike Milligan, Benny Hill and Frankie Howerd before creating the role that made him a household name, Captain Peacock, the stern and snooty floorwalker at Grace Brothers department store in Jeremy Lloyd and David Croft's broad and bawdy *Are You Being Served?* Thornton was a mainstay of the show, which, in the late 1970s as *Summer Wine* steadily ascended the viewing charts, regularly topped them, pulling in more than twenty million viewers. *Are You Being Served?* ran from 1972 until 1985, and Thornton stuck with it, reviving his character for a spin-off in 1992, *Grace and Favour*. Thornton, at seventy-six, belonged to the golden age of sitcoms and, by the time Bell asked him to lunch, shared with Thora, Jean Alexander and Stephen Lewis a bond with the *Summer Wine* audience to whom he seemed another old friend. Thornton himself would also be in the company of a friend – he and Sallis were fellow members of the Garrick Club, and they had worked together on stage in a production of *Ivanov*. 'It was a sort of Russian double act,' said Thornton, 'And I knew Peter quite well.'

Clarke set about rewriting scripts that had featured Foggy, plus a special to introduce the new boy, and created Herbert 'Truly'

Truelove, a retired policeman whose habit of command died hard. The character was a better fit than Seymour had been, more down-to-earth and closer to Foggy. Ex-PC Clarke substituted improbable tales of Truly of the Yard's crime-fighting exploits for the former corporal signwriter's stories of derring-do in the jungle, and gave him an added dimension – a dreadful, unseen ex-wife and reminiscences of a glum marriage. Truly, in his trilby, raincoat and police tie, was a doleful, sardonic figure with great comic potential, but bringing him to life would take a little time.

Thornton arrived on location to be greeted by a hailstorm, by way of his induction to Summer Wine Land, and embarked on six of the ten episodes which would follow the special, giving him the chance to work his way into the part before filming the sequences that introduced Truly. Bell said: 'This was his first starring role, and to start with, for the first few episodes, he was acting like a supporting actor, and I had to say to him, "Frank, have more presence in your performance." Everything he said, he was listening for the line rather than letting it all happen around him. It's a very subtle difference. You can tell when someone's a star or just a support. He'd never been a principal actor, or in this case one of three principal actors, and that took a little bit of adjustment.'

Sallis offered quiet encouragement. Thornton said: 'We'd been filming for a while, and Peter came over and said to me, "You know you've got it, don't you?" which was very heartening. It was quite a responsibility taking over that position and coming into a series that had been running for so long. I'd never been a leading man, rather an ensemble player as in *Are You Being Served?* where we were all equal.' Clarke's writing was also a help. 'It was much more sophisticated. There are writers who write stuff you can't act, but Roy's is dead right, which made it easy to learn. It all fell into place straight away between the three characters, because he's such a good writer and knows what to do.'

Truly was introduced in 'There Goes the Groom', broadcast on 29 December 1997. Foggy was there in spirit, if not in person, drunk and insensible beneath a table at a stag night, before Wilde's double was loaded on to a van and whisked off to Blackpool by an amorous postwoman. Love had finally claimed him, as it had Blamire all those years before. The plot centred around a nervous groom running away because Truly had terrified him with tales of how dismal married life could be. Thornton had nailed the character, and delivered some prime Clarke writing with a morose matter-of-factness that fitted the persona of the ex-bobby:

Truly: Before I became Sergeant Truelove, CID, I had to pass rigorous tests in advanced drinking. Besides which, of course, I had an additional incentive. The former Mrs Truelove always looked better under the influence of alcohol.

Compo: The former Mrs Truelove? How long were tha married?

Truly: Thirty-seven years.

Clegg: Oh well, if you're not going to give the thing a fair chance.

Compo: Tha got divorced? After thirty-seven years?

Truly: It was a painful time, I don't like to speak about it. Marriage was all right at first. I still treasure the memory of those first few minutes.

Thornton gave Truly a decidedness that brooked no argument as he returned to the subject of the wife whose recollection provoked a shudder.

Truly: No, the former Mrs Truelove had all the arrogance of an attractive woman. It's just a pity she didn't have the face and figure to go with it. Between perms, she used to look a lot like Max Wall.

Clegg: I used to like Max Wall.

Truly: Not to wake up with.

Truly's Eeyore-like reminiscences of the former Mrs Truelove were a delight. Thornton was proving himself a worthy successor to Wilde; close enough to assume the mantle of misguided leader of men, yet sufficiently different not to invite comparisons. His long experience helped him ease quickly into a warm rapport with Owen and Sallis, making this one of the most seamless of transitions. Another loss had been coped with. The next, though, never quite would be.

PART FOUR

The Long Sunset

CHAPTER 12

Second

See Ya Compo

BILL OWEN SAILED into his eighties a contented man. There was hardly a more beloved actor on television than him, and he knew it. Stardom, that most fickle of friends, had, against all the odds, embraced him for a second time, later than he could have imagined or hoped, and this time stayed as his career developed into the most blissful of Indian summers, thanks to a role he still loved. He remained smitten by Holmfirth, too, still keen to get to Yorkshire for filming, still willing to turn out on his days off to aid good causes. His eightieth birthday on 14 March 1994 came shortly before the publication of his autobiography, *Summer Wine and Vintage Years: A Cluttered Life*, which was praised for its wit and candour. It sparked off a whole new round of interviews and profiles, and he rejoiced in the publicity, deploying all the charm of the old pro that he was, plugging the programme he regarded as his own, banging the drum for Holmfirth and its people. He was taking better care of himself these days, quitting smoking after a lifetime, watching his cholesterol and, even though he looked every day of his years, he remained young at heart and busy, fired by his passions for politics, the Boys Club movement and his writing, taking himself to his study every day when at home to work up new ideas for plays.

Inevitably, he was asked how he would like to be remembered. 'My one wish, providing I'm active, is to live to a great age,' he told the *Daily Express*, 'and to be remembered as the man who tried to do his best. I want my epitaph to be, "He really tried", because I really did.' Owen knew how lucky he had been in being cast as Compo over the misgivings of those who struggled to see beyond his familiar Cockney screen persona, writing in his autobiography: 'I also reflect on the fact that if it had not been for *Summer Wine*, I might have been just another aged actor, sitting alone, forgotten, and knowing it. But I am not forgotten, I'm even spoiled a little, accorded a certain respect, even – and I'm still working.'

Respected yes, spoiled certainly; Owen still ruled the roost on location, a diminutive yet kingly figure huddled down in his chair in a capacious green anorak against the wind, being brought tributes of mugs of hot tea by a deferential crew and wearing the air of the star that he undoubtedly was, if a little more lightly than had once been the case. He was worth the effort; once in character, he continued to sparkle, investing Compo with the impish, childlike quality that had captured the hearts of several generations of viewers. On screen, he retained the dancing, jaunty quality of movement that really did make Compo Just William with a pension book, even if he recognised that it became more taxing with each passing year. He felt his age; resting up during the evenings with the restorative 6.30 p.m. whisky and easing any aches in a hot bath were more than ever necessary, yet he never once considered retirement, accepting his limitations and getting on with the job. 'I suddenly found it impossible to run, so I had an actor to do it for me. But I'd go on even if I have to appear in a wheelchair.' Those around him marvelled at how he threw off his years when the cameras rolled. Thornton said: 'We were all pretty old, let's face it, and Bill was older than us and it was wonderful to see this elderly gentleman sitting in his chair waiting to be called, and he'd be called and get up in front of the camera and then he came alive.'

The kindly soul with whom he had shared so many scenes watched over him with stern benevolence. 'Kathy Staff was marvellous with Bill, she'd always look after him,' said Bell. 'If she felt I was asking him to do too much, she'd say so, and say, "Look, he's an older man, you're asking too much." Fair enough. She was a very caring lady.' Others found him mellower, warmer, less spiky. Mike Grady said: 'When I came back to the show, he'd gone through something of a change, was incredibly welcoming, and seemed rather less tetchy about it all.' Juliette Kaplan felt he was increasingly relaxed: 'I said to him, "To you, Bill, it all seems like a game, and doesn't seem like work," and he said, "To me, it is a game, and when it stops being a game, I'll get out."'

The old fire could still flare up if Owen felt he had been slighted, however, as Bell saw when he took his three principals to lunch before filming commenced in 1999. 'The last time they met, there was Bill, Peter, Frank and myself, we met up at the Langham Hilton just to talk about filming for that series in '99, and it was quite obvious there was a degree of friction between Peter and Bill, to which Bill overreacted and it got quite nasty, which is a shame really because they worked together so well. It was about social status. Frank and Peter were Garrick Club members, gentlemen, and Bill was very much a hard worker and gave the impression of being of the people, but I'm not sure he really was.'

The series they had met to talk about would be a milestone, the twenty-first, taking *Summer Wine* into its fourth decade and the new century with a millennium special, 'Last Post and Pigeon', to be broadcast on 2 January 2000, followed by ten episodes. All appeared well; the occasional spat aside, the trio with Thornton had settled nicely, his first two series being very funny and well received, and the show's backdrop of the Pennine scenery appeared more ravishing than ever, thanks to Bell's introduction of digital wide-screen shooting.

In 'Last Post and Pigeon', Clarke had written his most multi-layered script since 'Getting Sam Home'. This was a bittersweet and affecting tale, unafraid to pause the laughter and bow its head in tribute to the fallen as it gave Compo a back-story and returned him to the beaches of Dunkirk where he had been evacuated in 1940 with the British Expeditionary Force. After all this time, it would give a glimpse of Compo as mature, sombre, thoughtful, reflecting on fear and death. It called for all Owen's experience and expertise as he moved from humour to sadness within the span of a few lines, recalling a long-lost Compo who had faint echoes of the cockiness of young Nobby Clarke in *The Way to the Stars* all those years before.

This would be a more than usually ambitious production, involving Bell taking the trio to France for scenes aboard a cross-Channel ferry, on the beach and at a pavement café and guesthouse. Long afterwards, Bell would still be moved to tears by what followed. As filming got under way that spring, it was clear that Owen was not well. He was losing weight rapidly, looked haggard and struggled to summon up the old sprightliness for the camera. The first scene was aboard the Dover–Calais ferry, with the white cliffs as a backdrop. Time would be tight on board ship to make the shot work, so Bell rehearsed at Teddington to give himself as much leeway as possible. In the studio, he became increasingly concerned. 'Bill, for the first time, was uncertain of his lines, and that wasn't like Bill. He would sometimes paraphrase, but he knew what it was about, and I thought, this is not good, I can see us not being able to do any more next year because if he's not good on the lines now, he's going to get worse in a year's time.' Nevertheless, the scene was completed on the ferry, and the company arrived in France, heading for Bray-Dunes where the exteriors would be filmed. Once there, Bell saw another worrying indication that Owen's health was failing. 'If you invited Bill out for dinner he loved it, he would always go, and we were near a big town that had some wonderful restaurants, and Bill declined to join us, which I thought was strange. His dresser said, "Bill's not very well at all," and you'd ask him if he was all right and he'd say yes, and struggle on, and he wouldn't let you down. Bill would give everything for *Summer Wine*, it was the best thing that ever happened to him in his life, and he was going to do everything he could to support it, but when we were filming it became quite obvious he was struggling, with his health and his memory. The filming was completely successful, no problems there, but we went back to Yorkshire to start doing the exteriors for before Compo went to France, and it was quite clear that Bill wasn't himself.'

There was a meal that he did attend, for the cast. Clarke was there: 'He looked very frail. Bill was there with his wife, and he was very disconnected, and it was very odd and very sad, and that was only weeks before he died.'

Owen persevered, but then one day came to a standstill at the location he had made his own. Bell recalled: 'We were filming at Nora Batty's and Bill sat on the steps and just looked up and said, "Alan, you know me, I'd do anything, but I just can't do any more work today," and we'd filmed for four episodes but the fifth one we couldn't do, so I said, "Don't worry, we'll do it some other time," and that's the first time that had ever happened. He'd be grumpy if he was kept waiting, but this was that he was physically exhausted.'

Others could not fail to notice that Owen was suffering. Grady said: 'We were filming around Holmfirth, and we were chatting away, and I was asking him about writing, and by now he was a lot easier to deal with, he'd mellowed a lot, and we were talking about plays we'd seen, and what was good and not good, and he very quietly went off and threw up in the hedge and came back and carried on.'

Sallis, like Bell, was growing ever more concerned. He knew a specialist in London and insisted that Owen should see him. Bell took the call from the doctor. It was cancer of the pancreas, so advanced that nothing could be done. Owen had only six to eight weeks to live. His decline had been shockingly rapid. This was the most distressing of predicaments for Bell, caught between sorrow at the fate of an old friend, and the necessity of finishing a special close to completion on which much money had been spent. 'I don't think they told Bill. I rather suspect that if he'd known, Bill would have thrown in the towel and gone home. That was the difficulty, trying to keep the whole production going, and at the same time being really upset about him. He would speak to Peter because they were in the same caravan, he was in a bad way but, to his enormous credit, he worked on. Although he didn't know his days were numbered, he knew he was very ill, but he never for one minute said, "I'm giving this up," and he carried on, even though he was feeling very tired.'

Owen may not have been told that he was dying, but he was a realist and there appeared to be, in the things he said to those around him, a sad acknowledgement that his life was nearing its end. He and Sallis were sitting in a car together as filming drew to a close, when he turned to his co-star. 'He said, "I don't want to go, Peter, there's so much left to do." That went right through me.'

Owen called Andrew Bray, the friend he had made twenty-seven years before when he borrowed the boy's fishing rod. 'Before he used to go home, every time, he'd pop down to the shop, and this last Friday he rang me up and said, "I'm not fit enough to come down, Andrew." He said, "I've just had it, I've really had it, but don't worry, because whatever happens, I'm coming back." And that day he rang my wife up to say goodbye to her, which he'd never done before.'

If Owen was saying his farewells, he seemed determined to say one to Compo too, and soldiered on with dignity and courage. Bell, though grief-stricken, felt compelled to think of the programme and rushed to get it finished, while at the same time concealing from both Owen and the rest of the cast his sense of urgency. He sent out a memo: 'It was a blatant lie, saying, "Because the programme's required sooner than expected, we're going to have to bring some of the schedule forward". I didn't want Bill to see that because of his illness we were having to do it earlier. Because of the determinate time, the café scene, which normally I'd film in London, I filmed in Yorkshire. We'd done it twice before, but it was done purely to get Bill while he was alive.'

Bell's designers transformed a disused quarry near Hade Edge into a French wood, complete with waterfall and pond, for the closing scene, in which Compo found the spot where he and his comrades had rested before being evacuated; a pigeon was released to fly back to Yorkshire, and the film ended with him blowing the last post on a bugle. Bell used colour separation overlay, in which Owen was filmed alone against a plain green screen so that the images could be digitally inserted into the finished film. As he did so, there was one final spark from the feisty little star, ill as he was. 'I said, "Can you blow your cheeks out?" because he was miming it, and he said, "Don't you start telling me how to play a bugle, I've been playing one for seventy years," and I said, "It doesn't look as though you're playing it, Bill," and he said, "Well, I am."' There would have to be more manipulation to complete the film, as Bell used a double for some shots of Compo entering and leaving buildings and a voice impressionist to cover gaps.

Owen was utterly spent. In those last few days in Holmfirth, he had lived out what he wished for his epitaph; he had tried, really tried, but his resolve could carry him no farther. He returned to London, where he suffered a stroke and was admitted to King Edward VII Hospital, lapsing into unconsciousness. For his son, Tom, the final few days had the most poignant of soundtracks. 'I was teaching drama at Thames Valley University and I was directing my students in *The Matchgirls*, and it was quite extraordinary really. They were very kind and asked me if I wanted time off and I said no, not through any sense of bravado, but purely because it was something that he would have liked to have known about.' Tom dashed between rehearsing his father's songs and his bedside. Bell was constantly there, too; Sallis, who was present on the final day, said: 'I do remember going to the hospital every day, and I remember being in the visitors' room when the nurse came down and said, "He's gone".'

It was the afternoon of Monday 12 July 1999, ten days after he had filmed his last scene. Bill Owen was eighty-five and, out at Pinewood, filming was still under way for the series he had so cherished. 'It didn't surprise me for a moment that he died whilst working,' said Tom Owen. 'Both he and I knew that would probably be the case.' The tributes to him were fulsome and sincere, the obituaries full of praise for his excellence as an actor, not just in *Last of the Summer Wine*, though it had defined him for most people, but also reminding them of the length and breadth of his career as playwright, songwriter and activist for causes dear to him. The day after his death, the BBC repeated his favourite episode, 'From Wellies to Wet Suit', the finale to that inspired 1982 series that had established *Summer Wine* as the country's most popular sitcom.

His passing came as no surprise to his colleagues, who had seen how ill he was, but even so they were jolted by the loss of a man who was, more than anyone else, the face of the series. His fortitude in soldiering on to the very end and the remembrance of his love for the show gave some comfort. 'He didn't make a big deal out of his illness,' said Grady. 'You have to admire his courage, or acceptance, because there was no kicking and screaming. I thought, good on you, you went out well. He was eighty-five, still heading up a TV series, making pots of money, still railing against the Tories, having a bloody good pop at everything, adored by the nation, so hats off, God bless him.'

His performance in 'Last Post and Pigeon', broadcast six months later, would have brought a lump to viewers' throats even had Owen lived. Though desperately ill, he found depths in Compo he had never previously plumbed, and played these delicately balanced scenes flawlessly. Not a single note in his performance jarred as he stands on the sands and looks seawards:

Compo: There were a sunken ship out there, and lines of blokes, and four crazy chuffs sitting in a bomb crater playing cards for money.

Clegg: How much did you lose?

Compo: I won nearly two quid. Mind you, I don't think this RASC bloke were concentrating. I think his family were chapel. He didn't know what to do with two pairs. Makes you wonder why bits of kids should be sent into situations where they're liable to end up in ruthless card games.

Truly: You didn't feel sorry enough for him to give him his two quid back.

Compo: I were tempted, but then I thought, supposing he gets drowned on the way home?

Clegg: You'd have felt responsible, him struggling in the water with all that change in his pocket.

Compo: Precisely, Norm.

There was even greater emotion swirling about the climactic scene when Compo rediscovers the wood where he awaited rescue.

Compo: This is where we spent the night. We was knackered, and talk about hungry. We risked a fire because I'd caught a rabbit.

Clegg: (HORRIFIED) You killed a rabbit?

Compo: We were starving! People were killing each other!

Clegg: I know – but a rabbit.

Truly: Maybe it was an enemy rabbit.

Compo: Tha would have eaten two rabbits if tha could. I were well in with this sergeant though, he really appreciated me keep coming up with this food.

Truly: I've only ever seen you demolishing it.

Compo: It didn't go far with five, and I tell thee what, it tasted great.

Truly: Five? I thought you said there were six of you.

Compo: The young gunner, he were dying. We kept on telling him he weren't, but he knew he were. He weren't hungry.

He hangs a wreath on a tree, before the three men stand to attention together, and Compo raises the bugle to his lips. As the soundtrack plays the last post, not just for the story, but for Owen as well, Bell brought the camera closing in on his gaunt face, focusing on his eyes, wide, still bright with life and very, very blue as he stares straight ahead and the screen fades slowly to black. Owen could not have made a more noble or affecting curtain call; it was not, though, the audience's last sight of him. That came in the series that followed three months later; Owen had managed to do enough for three episodes, albeit in a much-reduced capacity as his condition had worsened. His final appearance came in 'Magic and the Morris Minor', virtually a cameo since most of the location work was done while he was seeing the specialist in London. The last glimpse of Owen in his signature role came in the closing scene as he recites Nora Batty's name to a car hubcap supposedly possessed of magical powers. It was a quintessential moment in Summer Wine Land, absurd, funny and beautifully played; if 'Last Post and Pigeon' bade farewell with quiet dignity, this waved him the most affectionate of goodbyes with the audience laughter he had so loved to hear.

The days after his death were hectic. Ever since the early 1980s, Owen had said he wanted to be buried in Holmfirth, and Sallis telephoned Bray asking for help with local arrangements. Tom Owen said: 'When his will was opened, there was a little piece of paper saying that his wish was to be buried in St John's Church, Upperthong, Holmfirth. And Peter Sallis knew this because they'd actually filmed many years ago in the churchyard and I think Bill had said to Peter, "If I go first, just make sure I'm in this plot here," and there was just this little reminder in his will. He wouldn't want to be anywhere else, overlooking his Holme Valley and the place he loved so much.'

When he heard of the funeral arrangements, Bell could not get out of his mind a curious little incident from two years before, when he had been making the twenty-fifth anniversary documentary:

Because I knew the actors very well and knew their thoughts, I wrote a script. When it came to doing it, I said, 'Whatever you do, say it in your own words.' Anyway, it got to Bill and I'd written, 'I feel at home here, in fact, when I die I want to be buried up at the local church,' and Bill said, 'I'm not saying that,' and I said, 'Why not?' and he said, 'I don't want to be buried here.' That was in my script, but he wouldn't say it. I said, 'You've said it before,' and he said, 'I just say that,' and it came out of the episode.

It was to be a private funeral on 19 July, a week after his death. The only representatives of the show were Clarke and Sallis. The night before, when the casket was taken into church, Bray went to say his farewells. The flag atop Holy Trinity Church, in the centre of Holmfirth, was lowered to half-mast, and a small crowd of local people gathered at the gates of St John's to pay their respects. After the service, Sallis reflected how Owen had first come to the place he now rested. 'It's twenty years ago now that we sat up here, Brian Wilde, Bill and me, and he said this is where he wanted to be buried, and it's interesting that he said it so long ago. I think we'd only been going seven years. It wasn't a whim, or a deathbed wish. His heart was in Yorkshire.' Wilde, too, reflected in *Last Of The Summer Wine – The Finest Vintage* (BBC Books, 2000) on that same day when he paid tribute to an actor he admired, even though they clashed: 'He was a wonderful actor to work with, and I treasure the memory of us sitting in the churchyard where Bill is now buried. It was a nice sunny day and Compo was looking around at the tombstones and their inscriptions. He asked, "I wonder what they'll put on my grave when I'm dead?" and Foggy replied, "Something very heavy I hope!" We all laughed then and it helps ease the sadness now.'

St John's stands a mile above Holmfirth, its churchyard an oasis of calm, screened from the town below by woodland. There is only a single break in the line of trees, and through it is a breathtaking view down into the Holme Valley; Owen's grave has sight of it. He has two headstones, at right angles to each other, one in marble that bears the inscription, 'Wm J Owen Rowbotham', the other in Yorkshire stone with the words, 'Bill Owen MBE'. There is something else, too – a stone plinth topped by a pair of immaculately clean, most un-Compo-like wellies; they are unlikely vases, but even so always have fresh flowers in them. Owen loved Holmfirth, and his feelings are still reciprocated.

Show business got its chance to pay tribute to Owen at a memorial service at Broadcasting House on 19 November at which Sallis was the main speaker. The two men had never really grown into friends, despite their long and close working relationship, but Sallis remained lost in admiration for Owen's abilities, telling the audience that Compo was: 'The finest comic creation of its time. No one presented anything, certainly not on television, to match it. Year after year I waited for it to be recognised, but it never was. You could rank that creation against the best of them – including Chaplin. I always thought it was an injustice that he never won an award for best comic performance.' There had been an award for it of sorts the previous month, when *Last of the Summer Wine* had been named by viewers as their favourite comedy series in the National Television Awards, an event at which the memory of Owen loomed large as Sallis and other cast members collected the trophy.

He cast the longest of shadows, his presence so ubiquitous over so many years that both cast and crew felt it even after he was gone. Jean Fergusson said:

Certainly after he died, and for a couple of years after he died, you thought you'd seen him in the car park, because he always used to wear this green anorak over his costume, wandering about in the car park, and you actually thought you could see him, and then a couple of times I thought I could hear him whistle. He did this funny whistle, all the time. Sometimes I'd be sitting in the car park and I could swear I could hear Bill, and it was just weird. Robert and I were together when this happened. Bill had a dresser called Bob, who was with Bill throughout the whole series, near enough, and he really adored Bill. This dresser, who was now quite old, said, 'I want to go to his grave, I think we should go to his grave,' so we went, and some person had put a pair of child's wellies on the grave. And the dresser, Bob, got down on his knees and turned over the tops of the wellies, and then suddenly they were Compo's wellies, where they weren't Compo's wellies before, just because he'd turned over the tops. Well, I was in tears because it was done with such affection, because he always used to turn over the tops of Bill's real wellies.

There had been uncertainty over *Summer Wine* previously, but never anything to compare with this. The loss of Bates, Wilde and Aldridge had all been blows, but Sallis and Owen had remained throughout, Clegg and Compo grounding the new arrivals with wit and ridicule, providing the comfort of familiarity as they bedded in the new third man, the unchanging philosopher and scamp of the trio to ease transitions; but to lose the show's most talismanic figure, there since the beginning and the driver of much of its comedy, left a hole so gaping that continuing seemed inconceivable. *Summer Wine* might die with Compo. What kept it going was economic necessity; the BBC simply could not afford to write off a series on which so much had already been spent. It would have to be finished, sad and uncertain though everybody was. Clarke said: 'Had he died between series, I'm sure we would all have said we can't possibly go on. I'm sure we would have, I'm positive in my own mind, and it's only the fact that Bill died when five were in the can and another six were in preparation that we had to continue or throw the money away, so we survived because of that. Everybody was saying, "You can't carry on," including me. I thought it was impossible, and as it happens I got three superb episodes out of his death, bless him, they were written so quickly they had to be. There's something about pressure. For a while, under pressure, you do good stuff, but it's only for a while.'

The pressure on Clarke to write a fitting end for Compo was intense, but it seemed to stimulate him. Within weeks, he came up with a trilogy of episodes, 'Elegy for Fallen Wellies', 'Surprise at Throstlenest' and 'Just a Small Funeral', that covered the loss. He would then write four more that took the series forward with a bold stroke.

Once again, Clarke astonished all those who had worked with him. After twenty-seven years of scriptwriting, there was a general agreement that this was the finest work he had ever done. Sallis said: 'What was extraordinary is that they were funny. Roy knew what he had to do, and we spoke on the phone, and I said, "This is not easy," and he said, "The trouble is, Peter, they're supposed to be funny," and it was. Those three episodes were the best he wrote.' Bell said: 'Everything had to stop, and he wrote three brilliant episodes, all within about three weeks. They're superb, because they're touching, funny and you'd think he'd sweated for a whole year to do them, but he just writes, it just flows naturally, and you just have to stand back in admiration. It was extraordinary, I couldn't believe how good they were, never changed anything in them, not a word changed. It was all great sentiment, great emotion.'

'There were two people present in those episodes really,' said Clarke. 'It was a goodbye to both of them, Bill and Compo. The time constraints did help, because there wasn't the time to get too philosophical and deep about it, thinking about what should I do, tribute here, tribute there, there was no time for any of that, you just had to convey some sense of respect for the guy. And at the same time people don't want to tune in and weep, they want to laugh. I wanted to give the guy some kind of ceremony, really.'

He did. 'Elegy for Fallen Wellies' started with a huge laugh as Nora, Ivy and Pearl rehearsed a dance routine in flapper dresses and black stockings as they sang 'Cabaret', that celebratory anthem to living for the moment before time's heavy hand descends, with Edie at the piano. On the way home, Ivy coaxes Nora to tease Compo by turning up in the costume.

Nora: I don't think I could make my living just making myself attractive to men.

Ivy: No, I don't think you could either.

Nora: There's one who thinks I'm attractive.

Ivy: I bet he would in that outfit. He'd think he'd have won the golden welly or something.

Nora: I wouldn't dare let him see me in this outfit, not on a one-to-one basis.

Ivy: I'll come with you for security purposes, oh, go on, call his bluff, I'd bet he'd run a mile.

Nora: Probably, but I don't feel like being chased that far tonight, thank you very much.

Ivy: Oh, go on, give him a surprise.

The next shot is of an ambulance racing to hospital, where Clegg and Truly arrive to join Nora and Ivy.

Truly: I wonder what put the smile on his face?

Nora: (COVERING UP LEGS) Never you mind!

Clegg: He never used to ail anything.

Truly: Even at school. We'd be coughing and sneezing, frog in your throat. He'd have one in his pocket.

Ivy: Ready for dropping down girls' blouses.

Nora: Took his time getting it out, though.

Ivy: I wonder who's going to look after his ferrets.

Nora: He can look after his own ferrets.

Truly: That's right, let's stop talking as if he's going to die. People like him don't die. It's people with creases in their trousers, collars and ties, they die.

Clegg: You think scruffy is better than insurance?

Truly: Every time.

But then, a doctor walks into the room and sadly shakes his head. The camera closes in on Clegg, who is bereft. The scene moves to Nora's kitchen, where she is talking about giving Compo the kiss of life:

Nora: I thought he'd almost gone and then this little voice whispered.

Ivy: What did it say?

Nora: That's the best kiss we've ever had, it said, but can you save it until I feel a bit better?

On the hillside, Clegg and Truly are thinking about their friend:

Truly: You think he was heavenly material, do you?

Clegg: Certainly. To be as little children. Never lost it, did he? I just wish we could have said goodbye.

The emotional weight of the episode falls on Sallis, who plays to perfection. Clegg is agitated, sad, remorseful that he was not with his friend at the end; if Owen's final performance reached into all his reserves as an actor, Sallis also drew on everything he had to pay tribute. 'It was difficult for Peter,' said Bell. 'I could tell he was moved by the whole thing.' The finale of the episode proved equally moving for the rest of the cast as it was played out on an epic scale; 200 extras were deployed across a hillside above Marsden dressed in white overalls to spell out the words 'See Ya Compo', which were echoed by Clegg as the entire company drove up the road to be confronted by the display. 'That took a lot of doing,' said Bell. 'We had to get the scouts and people like that to walk down a valley and climb up the other side, and by walkie-talkie say, "Can 'O' move over a bit to the right?"'

Even though the cast knew what the scene held, the impact of the figures on the hillside moved many to tears. Jean Fergusson said: 'When it was being set up, we didn't see it, and in real terms it was huge, it was the whole hillside, and we were all in this procession, and I was on the bike and Thora was in the car and when we came round the corner and saw it, it was a lump in the throat. On telly it was moving enough, but to actually stand there and watch it was just so touching.' 'All of us were crying,' recalled Ken Kitson. 'That was one of the most moving things I've ever seen in my life. What a powerful piece of writing that was, superb.'

There was more to come. In the second of his trilogy, Clarke turned back to a tried-and-tested device to bring Compo's voice into the farewell. Nora hands over a letter he has left for Clegg and, just as he had with Blamire and Foggy, he reads it aloud, but only after an initial reluctance.

Clegg: This is a first. He's never written to me before.

Truly: He's never been so far away before.

Clegg: Do you think he is far away?

Truly: No, not really. The dead you care about are only next door.

Clegg: Well, I'll drink to that.

Truly: Well, get it opened.

Clegg: I'll get round to it.

Truly: You're making a meal of it.

Clegg: It makes me nervous.

Truly: What's to be nervous about?

Clegg: He's spelt Clegg with only one 'g'.

Truly: Just be thankful you're not Greek.

Clegg: Maybe he didn't have the strength for two 'g's.

Truly: Oh, give over, he never could spell.

Clegg: Well, not when he was alive, but somehow you expect dead people to spell better.

Truly: He's only just got there. Wait till they've had him for a while.

Clegg: I can't get used to him being dead.

Truly: I know what you mean. Never seemed the type, did he? I mean, if he can die, nobody's safe.

The letter is opened, and it is another masterful performance, as Sallis catches Owen's cadences without ever diminishing Clegg's grief.

Clegg: Keep an eye on Nora. She doesn't know it yet, but she'll miss me. There was only ever the thickness of a bedroom wall between us, so tell her if I ever get the hang of this haunting lark and learn to pass through walls, she'll be in trouble. Good luck to both of you, you were good mates. Must close now before they cut my electric off one last time. If you're at my funeral, I don't want anybody going home sober. Good luck to both of you. Compo.

Truly: Is that it then?

Clegg: That's it. No forwarding address.

There was a twist in the plot, as Compo is revealed to have a secret girlfriend, Reggie Unsworth, to whom he bequeathed his ferrets.

Bell brought in another audience favourite, comedy actress Liz Fraser, for the role, and her presence lit up the third episode as Compo was laid to rest. There were nods to Owen's memory throughout – Andrew Bray's children were seen playing on a hillside and Bell's camera roved over favourite locations as a choir sang a revamped set of lyrics by Clarke. It was only right that Clegg should have the last words, and he did, as Compo's coffin, with wellies on top, was placed into the hearse before the cortege set off through the countryside: 'We thought you'd like another wander through the hills, old son.'

It had been the most touching and funniest of send-offs for both Owen and Compo, in which the audience's emotions had been wrung; Clarke had taken them from laughter to sadness and back again, as love had been expressed and respects paid. The trilogy had plainly struck a chord with the audience – letters poured into the BBC's audience feedback programme, *Points of View*, in their hundreds.

Now came a stroke of audacity to keep the show going and complete the remaining four episodes. Clarke decided to keep the Compo connection by using Owen's son, who bore a striking resemblance to his father. Bell said: 'Everybody said to me, "Bill was irreplaceable," and he was. It occurred to me that to bring in someone like Brian Murphy, he would be ripped to pieces, so I said to Roy, "Bear in mind that Bill has a son, Tom, who doesn't look unlike his father," and Roy then rang me and said, "Do you think Tom would be up for it?" and I was sure he would, so I rang him and the good thing was that there was now no longer any comparison. So Roy rewrote all the three episodes that covered Compo's death, and the last four episodes which introduced Tom went well because there was no question of him being critically panned because he was the son.'

Tom Owen had played a cameo opposite his father in 'The Bandit from Stoke-on-Trent' in 1978. His character would also be called Tom, and introduced in 'From Here to Paternity', which again used the device of a letter arriving, this time from Compo's long-lost son announcing that he would be arriving in town that day, leaving Clegg wondering how to break the news of his death to him. Owen leaped at the chance of continuing his father's legacy in the show. 'I would come in and do four episodes just to finish that series off. I never quite became part of that trio because there was an initial problem of the age difference. They were all meant to have known each other at school, and Frank and Peter were much older than me. The second issue was, and Alan was quite right, that if I went in as one of the trio I would inevitably have been compared with Bill, and there was no way you should put an audience in that sort of position, or me in that sort of position, because that wouldn't be fair.'

It was a bold way of providing continuity of sorts. Tom would not arrive alone; there would be a female companion, Mrs Avery, and a daughter, Babs, in a creaky old van and a dilapidated bus. Not only that, the two new female characters would be hippies of sorts. This was a radical new departure for Summer Wine Land, and it soon became clear that the audience did not like it.

CHAPTER 13

~~~

Carrying On

I T COULD NEVER be the same again, not really. *Summer Wine* would be expertly played by a cast of veterans as it more than ever became a convivial home for favourites of a certain age, and Clarke's writing remained as quirkily individualistic as ever, but the show had changed irrevocably, and never quite recaptured the magic of Owen's years in the one hundred episodes across the decade left to it. The central concept of the trio, with its ideal balance between the scamp, the leader and the timid go-between, that had propelled the laughs for more than a quarter of a century was lost, and even when revived in modified form almost ten years on, the show would never have the same focus. *Last of the Summer Wine* without its three ageing schoolboys would always feel a little uncertain, a little lacking, somehow no longer complete. This was like *Dad's Army* without Corporal Jones or *Porridge* without Lenny Godber. Duncan Wood had asked for something with three old men, and his instinct had proved spectacularly successful in Clarke's hands. 'One for all and all for one, we were the Three Musketeers,' said Sallis as he reflected on what had made it all magical. Badger, Ratty and Mole; George, Harris and 'J'; Compo, Clegg and Blamire, or Foggy, or Seymour, or Truly; the trio had been as much the heart and soul of Clarke's comic world as it was for Kenneth Grahame or Jerome K. Jerome. 'Where one goes, we all go,' Foggy had said as he and Compo arrived to accompany a gloomy Clegg setting off to see the widow in 'Getting Sam Home'. It was just another line, but encapsulated what Summer Wine Land was all about, the adventures of three mismatched friends who stuck together no matter what. Even in the episodes that bade farewell to Compo, his presence so saturated the mood that Clegg and Truly had hardly seemed to be without him.

But now there were just the two of them, and even the opening titles looked odd without a third name sharing star billing. What followed looked no less odd to the audience, and they were both quick to make their feelings plain and demonstrate the proprietorial feelings they had for this comedy institution. 'Introducing Tom, his son, and a bunch of hippies, went down like a lead balloon with the audience,' said Clarke. 'I got some angry letters saying, "This is not acceptable," and they were right, they didn't belong, and so it was trial and error to find my way back into the mainstream. I'm conscious, and have been for many years now, of the faithfulness of the audience. It means they keep me within bounds of things I can't do, or never dare do, in *Summer Wine*, not because I couldn't get it through the Beeb. They don't say they don't like it, they say, "Not acceptable, you can't do this in *Summer Wine*," and they're right, actually, you can't and I respect that.'

It was the 22nd series, broadcast in 2001, that was bringing in the complaints. The prevailing wind in television comedy was blowing in heavy irony, social satire and a world-weary air of cynicism, and while none of these were present in Clarke's writing, the letter-writers clearly felt that the characters of Mrs Avery and Babs with their hippie lifestyles were a little too close to those currently fashionable stances for the fantasy world that was Summer Wine Land. Tom would remain, but the female companions with whom he had arrived would be dropped. Clarke said: 'I'd always assumed that if Bill went, the whole thing had gone, because he was central, and we did wonder. The series that followed was an attempt to see if it was possible to continue, and the first few episodes, it seemed like no, until it pulled itself round a bit. What saved us was by this time there were so many characters about, each of whom had their following, so I got a lot of mileage from them.' The reliable, even comforting, presence of the ladies with their simultaneously raised cups, Barry and Glenda, Auntie Wainwright and Smiler, Howard, Pearl and Marina were more important than ever, and Clarke would bolster the familiar by gradually building up his two inept policemen – but that still left Clegg and Truly without their third man. Tom was used to plug the gap on occasions, and so was a character who had been introduced in a 1999 episode, 'How Errol Flynn Discovered the Secret Scar of Nora Batty'. Billy Hardcastle, played by Yorkshire character actor Keith Clifford, was another characteristically outlandish creation, a man who believed himself to be a direct descendant of Robin Hood and spent his time stalking the woods or trying to recruit a band of merry men. This was more like it, a splendid eccentric whom Clegg and Truly could wonder at but not resist, and the series began to settle after the grievous upheaval it had suffered. So did the audience. Although the figures had sunk below the six million mark, the show remained among the BBC's most popular comedies and was drawing more viewers than a clutch of newly minted sitcoms.

Plainly, it still had the most loyal of followings; equally plainly, it was becoming clear that there were elements within the BBC that thought it had stood and admired the scenery for too long and was overdue to wander off into a Pennine sunset. From the mid-1990s onwards, there had been mutterings within Television Centre that it was time to call a halt. There had been a very hurtful and very public snub when the BBC celebrated sixty years of television in November 1996 at a gala evening attended by Owen and Sallis. Viewers had voted for their favourite programmes across all genres, and awards were presented to the winners. Clips were shown of all the great hit comedies to laughter and applause – except *Last of the Summer Wine*. Owen was livid, telling the *Sunday Express* in December that year:

I was very angry that we weren't recognised. I wasn't looking for an award myself, but I would have liked the programme to have been nominated. But we weren't even mentioned. As we sat there for the whole evening and I realised that they'd passed over us, I was trying to work out just why we were there – it seemed quite pointless. Then I realised that my role for the night was to be part of a celebrity audience and fill up a chair. That was quite wounding. When a programme has been going twenty-five years though, and has even topped *Gone with the Wind* in the Christmas ratings, you know that you must have done something right. So a little respect, a word of acknowledgement, would have been very nice.

There was more to come early the following year, when word leaked out of the BBC that it was felt the programme risked looking out of place in the 'Nasty Nineties'. Alan Bell heard these sentiments for himself: 'I was at a symposium and sitting next to this young guy, and they were playing Ronnie's music, and this young guy said to his people in front, "Whenever I hear that *Summer Wine* theme, I could be sick. It's awful, it should be taken off the air." I didn't say who I was. They're young, they have no sympathy with it. It's also got something to do with the fact that they didn't have anything to do with its success. There's a slight inner resentment at this programme running for thirty-seven years and anything they do is likely to run for two, and I think that's what it must be.'

Clarke, who would still be sitting at his desk dreaming up storylines for his ever-expanding family of oddball creations in his eightieth year, was laconic about the BBC's attitude:

I always peddled the theory that they didn't know it was there, so I always said we survived because they think ITV's doing it. I don't think they've known what to do with it for years, and as executives get younger and younger, they've no idea what the thing's about, and unless, I think, the thing's hurting them, I think they've just ignored us and left us alone. I can imagine all these executives around their dinner table in Hampstead, and even if they like *Summer Wine* they're never going to confess it, never, ever dare confess it, and a lot of the decisions back at the BBC will be made on the back of the conversational code around the dinner tables because like's meeting like, and these days that means a very narrow spectrum and that goes back and percolates down, and the rest of us have that shoved down our throats whether we want it or not.

His was a belief shared by the cast, which as the new decade wore on saw the arrival of actors with very long histories in television comedy who found in *Summer Wine* an attitude towards humour that they were comfortable with. Everyone involved with the show had grown to believe that they were now creating comedy watched by older people and perhaps their young grandchildren. The mail that arrived from viewers seemed to confirm this. The letters to Clarke had spelled out their discomfort with his hippies; Robert Fyfe and Jean Fergusson had long grown used to replying to letters from children who found the antics of Howard and Marina hilarious. Nobody was under any illusions or indeed perturbed in the slightest by the picture of the audience that had emerged; just as long-serving cast members had grown older and greyer over the course of thirty years, so had their viewers, and devoted fans now sat down with grandchildren at teatime on Sundays, safe in the knowledge that this would be wholesome family entertainment they could trust not to offend. *Summer Wine* was not only the great survivor of television comedy because of its longevity; it was the last in a line of great family sitcoms that had once been the bedrock of popular entertainment, and if young BBC executives considered it a dinosaur, then so be it.

New cast members were quite at home with the ethos of the show, which chimed with their outlook on what comedy should be. Among them was Brian Murphy, a veteran farceur, whose role as the chippy George Roper opposite Yootha Joyce as his frustrated wife in two hit ITV sitcoms, *Man About the House* and *George and Mildred*, during the 1970s had made him into one of the most popular actors on television. He arrived in Summer Wine Land in

2003 to play the cheeky, freewheeling Alvin, sometimes teaming up with Clegg and Truly, sometimes acting as foil to Nora, having been moved into Compo's house. The show's family appeal attracted Murphy.

> As television has changed, particularly over thirty-five years, it's still watchable by a family, because the humour is innocent, even when there are any sexual overtones, it's still innocent, and there's no swearing and we live in our own world. The outside world doesn't impinge on it, so it's quite escapist, and that is a guarantee for an audience of a certain age group. It isn't offensive, it's still very funny, the crazy, silly things they say, the observations, without being aggressive, in your face and swearing, which sadly is what a majority of television has become. I don't think that's just being an old fogey. I think it's an insult to the memory of comics like Tommy Cooper, Morecambe and Wise, Les Dawson and many others, that they were able, with their humour, to command a big audience without any swearing, being aggressive or in your face. And I hate this description of being 'cutting edge', because cutting edge means you lose all sense of proportion and you just insult people, and if that's cutting edge, I think we should blunt the bloody knife. I think in some cases, we've lost the plot in humour.

Yet for all the reservations within the BBC, nobody dared wield the axe, simply because the show earned its keep, consistently remaining in the top ten comedies across all channels as its fourth decade wore on. Even if its audience had grown old, it was unshakeably loyal, paid its licence fee and had every right to expect to be entertained without offence. And so it rolled along, being recommissioned every year with Clarke usually delivering ten or eleven episodes, which more often than not were broadcast in the spring or summer. His writing was as serenely surreal as ever:

Clegg: You're looking very thoughtful, Truly. You look like a man who's thinking about death and what it's all about.

Truly: Well, actually, I was thinking about how much I used to like a kipper for my breakfast, but they tend to repeat.

Clegg: Well, there you are, why do kippers repeat? It's one of your fundamental philosophical problems.

Truly: What did Bertrand Russell say about it?

Clegg: Well, he mixed with the left as you know, so naturally he blamed the Americans.

Truly: Did you ever have a kipper for breakfast?

Clegg: Yes, I did once. It was on honeymoon, we were at an hotel. I thought, why not, everything else is weird.

Truly: I used to have a digestive system like an incinerator, I could consume anything, well, you had to in the police, I mean you grabbed a meal when you could, first week in the vice squad, you lost your appetite, but after that I could digest concrete, which was just as well as that was what the former Mrs Truelove did best.

Such dialogue indicated that those at the BBC dismissing the show as old hat were simply not listening; there was not another sitcom writer active to whom it would have occurred to introduce kippers, Bertrand Russell and anti-Americanism into a brief exchange between two old men sitting on a bench in the Yorkshire countryside. Clarke's writing was no less off the wall when he introduced another new character in the twenty-fourth series in 2003. Unusually, he wanted to bring in a specific actor and write for him. He'd long admired Burt Kwouk, another audience favourite thanks to his appearances as Cato, the maniac Chinese manservant of Inspector Clouseau in the *Pink Panther* films who tested his master's alertness with constant ambushes, and created for him the character of Entwistle, electrician and purveyor of eternal truths.

> Entwistle: Any of you lads in the market for a bit of ancient eastern wisdom?
>
> Truly: What's your name?
>
> Entwistle: It's on the van.
>
> Truly: Electrical?
>
> Entwistle: Entwistle.
>
> Clegg: Don't think I'm being nosy, just because I'm being nosy, but how come you've got a name like Entwistle?
>
> Entwistle: I changed my name, didn't I? From MacIntyre. I was forever being mistaken for a Scot.
>
> Truly: What are you then?
>
> Entwistle: I'm a Yorkshireman, what else?
>
> Clegg: So where does all this ancient eastern wisdom come from then?
>
> Entwistle: Hull. I was born in Hull. As far east as you can get. Any further, you're in the Humber.

Clarke found himself harking back to the show's beginnings as the show's budget was repeatedly cut; the stunts, as well as the fantastic machines that rolled out of Wesley's shed and down hillsides were consigned to the past. It was coming full circle. 'You needed to listen as well as look,' said Clarke. It could never go back to its beginnings with three men around a library table, but it was once again becoming a talking show, even if the conversations were taking place against the backdrop of the Pennines. 'There wasn't as much physical humour, and I missed it,' said Jean Fergusson. 'It's the budget, because stunts cost money, and it's the health and safety thing, and it's the age of the people as well.'

Time was catching up with the cast, however loyal to their roles they remained. 'You forget how long it's been going,' said Freeman. 'It's a lifetime really. I've gone from being a young woman to a middle-aged woman to an old woman, and yet in my mind's eye I'm still doing the third episode.' If it had become a show for an ageing audience, so it had developed into a home for actors who had a long and affectionate history with those viewers. 'They're used to having us in their living rooms,' said Kwouk. 'We're not big movie stars, we're very familiar players.' And Murphy observed wryly: 'If somebody ever says to you, "I wonder what happened to so-and-so," first of all check the obituary columns and then check the cast list of *Summer Wine*. Hopefully, you'll find some of them there.'

Owen's death had, inevitably, been an uncomfortable reminder of how old some of the cast were getting, and it also heralded more upheavals, the first of which came in the autumn of 2000 when Kathy Staff announced that she was leaving. This was another severe blow. Publicly, her reason was that she missed Owen; there was nobody to shoo off her immaculate steps any more, and Nora was a little adrift. Besides which, Staff had been offered star billing in a revived series of *Crossroads* for Carlton Television. She had always harboured a soft spot for the much-derided soap, and was excited about the opportunity of reprising her role as cook Doris Luke.

Privately, though, Staff was leaving because she had become disenchanted with what she saw as the second-class status of the women cast members, an issue that had bothered her for years. Bell said: 'She did feel a bit undervalued, and when this *Crossroads* thing came along she took it, and I thought it was a big mistake and so did she in the end. It had no standing, no prestige, and people on our show said they couldn't understand why she did it because it wasn't worthy of her.' Her departure saddened Freeman, even though she understood its reason. 'She just got disillusioned a bit with the programme. She did miss doing her things with Bill, but she really only needed a bit of cosseting. There are times when people need to be told that they're really important in the programme.'

Staff quickly realised what a mistake she had made. The revamped *Crossroads* was risible, and in an attempt to grab an audience now used to lurid soap storylines, introduced themes that this devoutly Christian woman with firm views of what was and was not acceptable in drama or comedy found to be anathema. She criticised what she saw as its reliance on 'sex for the sake of sex', and quit after less than a year, telling the *Yorkshire Post* in 2002: 'I was disappointed when I saw the scripts/storylines. A girl of sixteen pregnant right away, didn't know who the father was. Makes it even worse.' Clarke had provided the required cosseting: 'I did speak to her on the phone, and said I quite understood if she'd had enough, but I used to say things like, "You know damn well it's there if you want to come back, please if you do, give us a shout," and kept it like that.' Her unhappiness with *Crossroads* was public, and when Bell approached her agent to ask if she would be interested in returning, she accepted without hesitation, arriving back for the series of 2003, the same year that, without her, Crossroads motel shut its doors for the last time. A year later, Staff had the gratification of seeing herself billed as one of the *Summer Wine* stars alongside Sallis and Thornton.

As Staff prepared to return to the padding and wrinkled stockings, the company suffered another loss. On 18 May 2002, a few days before filming was scheduled to begin on the new series, Gordon Wharmby died aged sixty-eight. He had been suffering from lung cancer and died in hospital near his home in North Wales after being admitted with an infection. This funny, warm, likeable natural actor had grown into one of the best-loved of all the supporting cast thanks to his portrayal of the grimy Wesley. His had been an extraordinary journey, from the gauche painter and decorator that Bell took a chance on to popular comedy actor across the course of twenty years, and not without a harrowing personal cost. His death, and the filming that got under way shortly afterwards, were to mark the end of another era in Summer Wine Land. Wesley had gone; his on-screen wife would soon follow.

Indomitable, garrulous, driven, loveable Thora was nearing the end of the road. She remained unshakeably loyal to the series, and determined to carry on, but, as had been the case with Owen, resolve could carry her only so far. She was ninety-one now, and her powers had been fading for the previous couple of years in the wake of two last magnificent swansongs, a second Alan Bennett monologue, 'Waiting for the Telegram', and an exceptionally moving drama by Deric Longden, *Lost For Words*, in which she played a stroke victim regretting a lost love. She had won Baftas for both and an Emmy for the latter. Bell, who directed *Lost For Words*, was also awarded an Emmy. These were unparalleled achievements for an actress so late in her career, and bathed her final years in a warm glow of admiration from both the public and her profession. She was, though, plainly flagging, even at Thora's Table in the Huddersfield Hotel where once she had effortlessly swept all conversation before her. Jean Fergusson said: 'Towards the end, she would be talking and then she'd stop and somebody else would be saying something and she'd fall asleep immediately they started talking, and then as soon as they stopped, she woke up and came out with another story. We often used to help her, take her up to bed. I know that Jean Alexander very often went up and put her rollers in for her before going to bed, so there were two legends, one putting the rollers in and one getting ready for bed.'

Work was everything to Thora, and those around her did all they could to help her, on set as well as off. 'As one fades away, another comes in,' said Mike Grady. 'As Thora was rather fading in her abilities, Dora Bryan was there to shore it up, and she would shore Thora up as well, because they were old friends and she would spend a lot of time with her.'

Bell knew how much playing Edie meant to her, and was solicitous of her welfare. He had witnessed Thora's determination to keep the show on the road, to never let her public down, even in a crisis, a few years earlier when he called at her flat to escort her to an event, only to find that she had fallen and was unable to get up. She was rushed to hospital, where doctors wanted to amputate a leg. Thora had never lost many arguments, and she didn't lose this one. She kept her leg. And then she started arguing again, over the timing of surgery. Bell said: 'She got very heavy with the doctors at St Mary's Hospital, because the doctor was saying, "We've got to do this operation in a fortnight and by that time your condition will have stabilised," and she was saying, "I want to do it now, because I've got to get to the studio, because they're waiting for me." And he said, "You must understand, it's not every day we get an 85-year-old asking us to work fast so she can get back to work." But that was her. Thora thrived on work.'

She was hospitalised yet again during that last series. Sarah Thomas said: 'She had to put up with quite a lot of discomfort, but the work was the most important thing in her life really. She was in hospital, and she hadn't completed her filming and she was really upset about it, and Alan obviously wanted to complete it, and Jan worked terribly hard to get the doctors to allow Thora out of hospital to come to Pinewood and do the filming.'

'It was like with Bill,' said Bell. 'We had a lot of the ladies' scenes to do, so I shot everything without Thora, and it was agreed with the doctors that she would be released from the hospital to do an afternoon's filming. Jan, her daughter, said Thora was really down, but the moment the car drove through the gates of Pinewood, it was as if someone had put a shot in her arm.' Working again, however briefly, was a boost for her, but even so, those last few scenes had a poignancy about them because of Thora's frailty. On-screen she looked as tiny and fragile as a bird. Her lines, though, were delivered with all the old firmness, even if the process of getting them on camera was painstaking. Thomas said: 'She'd be sitting on the settee and she'd be asleep against my shoulder, and Alan would work round her, and he'd say, "We need to wake Thora up now, because we need her lines," and so she'd wake up and he'd give her the line and she would say it back beautifully, and that's how she had to work in the very last series she did and it was quite an effort for her. I think it was fantastic that Alan kept her working as long as she did, it was lovely that she was able to do that.'

Work was on her mind to the last, even when a few months later she was no longer able to manage in her flat and moved into a retirement home for actors in southwest London. Bell visited daily. 'She said to me two or three weeks before she died, "You know, Alan, I wake up every morning and I think it's only two weeks before we go filming again, and I look forward to it so much."' Thora was a couple of months away from her 92nd birthday when she suffered a stroke and died on 15 March 2003. The following day, her final episode, 'All of a Florrie', was broadcast, bringing the series to a close. She had enlivened every episode in which she had appeared since her first in 1986, bringing with her a unique relationship with the audience that had been forged over the course of a career so long that it seemed as though nobody could remember a time when she had not been part of the comedy landscape. It was a show the public already loved when she arrived; her presence only served to deepen their fondness for it. That year held yet more sadness; a month after Thora, Danny O'Dea died aged ninety-two, having made his final appearance as the myopic, bumbling Eli in 2002, and then in October Tony Capstick, funny and vulnerable as one of the cowardly policemen, died aged only fifty-nine.

As ever, the large cast, bolstered by new arrivals and guest appearances, provided Clarke with the means to cover the absence of Thora. Her last episode had been the first to feature Alvin, and Murphy's character would play an increasingly important part. Entwistle and his van filled the role of Wesley and his battered Land Rover in ferrying the characters around the countryside. A couple of expert hands from well-loved sitcoms also began popping up from time to time, and would eventually become regulars – Trevor Bannister from *Are You Being Served?* was a pompous golf club captain, and Christopher Beeny, who had played opposite Thora in *In Loving Memory*, played a nervy debt collector. As the decade drew to a close they would be developed as Toby and Morton, a double act of disgruntled divorced husband and his put-upon friend.

Staff had, meanwhile, settled back in. Nora's exchanges with Compo had been one of the fixed points of the show for more than a quarter of a century, and establishing a new next-door neighbour would not be easy. He could not be a would-be suitor – that gag belonged to Owen alone – so Clarke turned the relationship on its head. Murphy remarked: 'I said, "I don't want to take over from Bill Owen, I don't want to impersonate Bill," and they said, "Oh no, it won't be that," but it would be somebody for Kathy to spark off of, because at the moment she's a bit in limbo, so I moved in and Roy did a wonderful twist because instead of, as Bill did, pursuing her, I teased her and said she was in love with me, which drove her mad of course, and it meant I was nothing like Bill.'

Alvin: Have you ever thought of changing that pinny?

Nora: It's a clean pinny.

Alvin: I'm not querying its condition, it's the style.

Nora: What's wrong with the style?

Alvin: In a nutshell – it hasn't got any.

Nora: My mother wore this kind of pinny. I've always worn this kind of pinny.

Alvin: And while you keep wearing it, I have to tell you it does absolutely nothing to inflame my senses. I'm never going to lose control at this rate.

Nora: I know what you have lost – most of your marbles.

Murphy and Kwouk's comic expertise steadied the show as the decade reached its mid-point, but more departures were to come. Dora Bryan called it a day after completing the 2005 series because of illness in her family, and the following year Keith Clifford decided to move on and bowed out. Family illness as well as budgetary pressures on Bell accounted for the departure of Stephen Lewis, whose character was doing less and less, in 2007. Despite the loss of favourite characters, viewers plainly still loved Summer Wine Land. In the year that Smiler departed Auntie Wainwright's shop, the hit sitcom was the *The Vicar of Dibley*, on BBC1, which was way out in front with twelve million viewers. Virtually all the rest hovered at about five million, including *Summer Wine* with 4.5 million.

The characters of Alvin and Entwistle fitted well with Clegg and Truly, and Clarke was writing some choice exchanges:

Entwistle: Funny how life turns out. They say at school, 'What you want to be?' I say, 'Multi-millionaire'.

Clegg: Maybe they had no vacancies?

Truly: Should have worn a tie.

Clegg: I committed suicide on leaving school. Well, almost. I became a lino salesman, which is as close as you can get without a gun or a rope.

Entwistle: You didn't like lino?

Clegg: How can you like lino? It's cold, it cracks, it smells. People used to put it in their bathrooms, which were already the coldest places on earth.

Truly: That's why we never had fridges. The English bathroom was just as good.

Here they were still, new and old together, the characters secure in their own fantasy world where Clegg and Truly could ruminate on a past summoned up out of Clarke's imagination as time drifted by. For the two senior players, though, the passage of time could no longer be ignored; their days on the hills were numbered. Sallis and Thornton were, by the time filming began in 2007, both eighty-six and beginning to struggle with location work, however much Bell spared them and made artful use of doubles. Sallis's sight was failing, and there was a worrying incident when he stumbled into a hole he had not seen. Mercifully, he wasn't hurt, but everybody was shaken. It was taking longer than it had to complete scenes, and insuring actors of their age for outdoor filming was increasingly problematic. That year's location shoot would be the two veterans' last; from then on, they would only film in the safety of a studio, their conversations against the backdrop of the Pennines created by digital wizardry. Thornton's feathers were ruffled by the decision. 'They wouldn't insure us to go falling about on the moors. I thought I was fit enough, but Peter was getting blind, which didn't help him at all, though you'd never know it from looking at him, he gets away with it wonderfully well on screen.'

Sallis was more sanguine. 'It's eleven o'clock in the morning, and the director says, "I think we'll go over there," and over there meant a quarter of a mile up and down, tramping through bogs and rocks and God knows what else. They took the step, and I think they were right to. At the time, I couldn't see why we couldn't, but looking back on it I think they were right to. You can't rely on the weather up there and the going can be pretty tough and, at eighty-eight, I don't feel a hero any more.' Nevertheless, it was a wrench; it had been thirty-five years since that midsummer's week when Sallis and the rest caught their first sight of a rain-sodden Holmfirth from the minibus that brought them from Television Centre, and even though Yorkshire had never become a second home to him as it had for Owen, there were half a lifetime's memories here of a show that had transformed his career in middle age. Certainly there had been rigours, of being dumped in water, of freezing on the hills, of refereeing arguments on windswept moors, but most of all there had been laughter, pride in the success of one of the most superbly written and crafted of all comedy series, and the satisfaction of knowing that he had all the best lines. Almost twenty-five years earlier, he had assumed his best mock-gloomy manner to recite with characteristic deadpan wit the discomforts that awaited on location, telling the *Radio Times* in 1983: 'I have become accustomed to skimming through the script and finding the ominous bit, "All we see of our three is a row of bubbles on the surface of the water".' He would miss all the associations that the location work summoned up, writing in his autobiography: 'But I cannot describe to you the pleasure that it gives me, certainly – I mustn't speak for the others – just to go back there, and climb up those hills, or be driven up those hills, more particularly, to look across that landscape; it is magical. You can stand there filming and you have a break from your scene, and I find myself standing or squatting, sitting and just looking at it and thinking, you lucky sod to be here doing this with a great writer behind you, a fine director, and let's call it a ripping cast, very, very lucky indeed.'

Once again, as it had needed to do so often before, *Summer Wine* had to reinvent itself; as it turned out, it would be for the final time.

CHAPTER 14

❧

Goodbye to the Hills

S O MANY OLD friends were falling by the wayside, and the length of their tenure with the show only deepened the sense of loss. Even as the *Summer Wine* family looked to the future, it lost another who had been there from the start. On 1 October 2007, Ronnie Hazlehurst died at the age of seventy-nine after suffering a stroke at his home in Guernsey. He was still composing for the show, still applying all his wit and craftsmanship to the incidental music. His contemplative little theme tune, dreamed up in minutes but so perfect for the show it introduced, had become part of the fabric of British television. He was, quite simply, irreplaceable, and his presence would live on, not only in the sound of the harmonica over the titles, but also in the passages to underline the comedy that he had left behind over the course of more than three decades. 'I was so sorry when he passed away,' said Bell. 'I brought it to other composers who were brilliant in their own right, but it just wasn't Ronnie's music, so I went through some tapes that had survived of the music recordings and we used them. It's a lot of work to make them fit, but I think we did all right.'

A little over six months later, there were more tears shed. On 20 March 2008, Brian Wilde died in his sleep aged eighty, seven weeks after suffering a fall at his home. This delicate, subtle, supremely talented comic actor had achieved what very few of his profession had the ability to do; creating an indelible, unforgettable characterisation so vivid, touching, funny and, for all its absurdities, real, that a nation had taken him to its heart. Foggy was one of the most finely drawn of all sitcom characters, and in Wilde's hands one of the most impeccably realised. *Summer Wine* owed him an eternal debt. His arrival had coincided with Clarke finding his best form and propelled the show into its glory years; he became and always would remain the definitive third man of whom viewers would automatically think whenever the show crossed their minds. The show crossed his, too, not just because it was his greatest role; there was the closest of family connections since his son, Andrew, had become its film editor. Bell also kept in touch; after the uncomfortable start to their relationship, a warm friendship had developed, and for years he tried to coax Wilde back, recognising the unique flavour he brought, and coming within an ace of succeeding.

> We were very good friends right up to his death, and I asked him to come back. I said to Andrew, 'Could you not have a word with your dad and try to persuade him?' and he said, 'I'll have a few more words, but you know what he's like.' Brian did agree about three years before he died, and said, 'OK, I'll do an episode,' and I said, 'Good, I'll get Roy to start writing.' That night I went to a restaurant with a couple of friends of mine and the phone rang and it was Brian, and he said, 'I've been thinking about it, and I'm very sorry but I think I've done it. I really enjoyed working on *Last of the Summer Wine*, but looking back, I'm not sure it would be the same and I'd like to remember it as one of the happiest periods of my life.'

When Wilde had first joined, frailty was forcing change on the show, and so it remained all these years afterwards. Confining Sallis and Thornton to the studio in a programme that had location filming at its heart meant that their roles would be drastically reduced. A new direction needed to be found, and it came via a star long on the minds of Bell and Clarke. 'I'd thought about Russ Abbot for a guest spot, because if you've got certain parts you've got to have certain types of people,' said Bell. 'There was one episode where there was a fitness fanatic, and the first person I went to was Russ, because I thought he'd be good for it, but he wasn't available and I ended up using Brian Conley, who was marvellous. But when it got to the series where Peter was struggling a bit, I thought the answer was to bring in somebody like Russ and bring up Brian Murphy and Burt.'

Abbot was an excellent choice, from the points of view of writer, producer and viewers, as well as his own outlook. He had a long history with the mainstream comedy audience, having dominated light entertainment during the 1980s with his sketch shows for both the BBC and ITV; their blend of quick-fire gags, loopy characters and end-of-the-pier humour had been ratings winners. Adults got the jokes and children got the pratfalls. Tall, gangling and blessed with a gift for physical comedy, Abbot was an entertainer of the old school, a versatile performer who could do stand-up, impersonations, play the drums and sing. Like *Summer Wine* itself, he was the last of a line; a star comic in the grand variety tradition. It was no coincidence that audiences always expected of him his joyously accurate evocation of Tommy Cooper; they saw in Abbot not only an echo of the zest of that greatest of all front-of-cloth comedians, but the abiding spirit of an age when there was a surer, more trusting bond between performers and audience, when comics were expected to make everybody laugh, not just niche groups. There was much more to Abbot than the jokes, the sight gags, the slapstick; he had never stood still, proving his mettle as an actor in a fine series for ITV, *September Song*, and developing a busy theatre career that saw him starring in the West End. And he had a cordial history with Clarke – at the height of his sketch show, one of the most popular characters was a suave but idiotic secret agent called Basildon Bond. It was the seed of an idea, and Clarke subsequently wrote a pilot for a show called *008 – The Real James Bond*, to star Abbot, which they took to the BBC. 'It was a great giggle, I thought,' said Clarke. 'Russ loved it, but no response from the Beeb. But I was delighted when he came on board, I think he's great, a total natural.'

The abortive spy spoof was not wasted as Clarke created one of his most offbeat characters. Luther Hobdyke – Hobbo to his friends – was a former milkman convinced he has a secret past as a spy, which he can't quite remember. Abbot said: 'I wonder if this is a spin-off of the 008 character that he had in mind originally, and because it was extended to the series, I thought, right, let's give it a crack, because this is good, and they let me read a couple of episodes, and I thought, I like this.'

The series was returning to its roots after almost a decade of assorted combinations that had sometimes misfired. A trio would once again drive the action: Hobbo, Alvin and Entwistle. Clarke said: 'Swapping about, we'd always been looking for a trio to emerge, and when we brought Russ in, that was a conscious attempt to find it again.' Hobbo would be introduced in a special on New Year's Eve 2008, 'I Was a Hitman for Primrose Dairies', followed by ten episodes beginning in April that would mark yet another milestone along what had become an epic journey, the thirtieth series, a tally no other British comedy had come even close to rivalling.

Clarke's output had been astonishing in comparison with the other classic sitcoms. By the end, *Summer Wine*'s 295 episodes outstripped all its contemporaries by a huge margin; *Dad's Army* had 83 episodes, *The Liver Birds* 89, *Steptoe and Son* 59, *Porridge* 21 and *Fawlty Towers* only 12. A few American series beat it, among them *The Simpsons*, charging effortlessly past 450 episodes, *My Three Sons*, starring 1940s Hollywood leading man Fred MacMurray, that racked up 380, and deadpan stand-up Jack Benny's show, which scored 343, but none spanned nearly as many years as *Summer Wine* – and all were the work of writing teams. It is testament to Clarke's extraordinary talent that he never allowed quantity to compromise quality. In the entire canon, there are few indifferent episodes, let alone stinkers. The great sitcoms are most often recalled primarily for one or two defining episodes, shining, inspired moments when writing, direction and performance are all so perfectly attuned that the comedy takes on a joyous weightlessness, when lines or visual humour become instantly and permanently memorable. This is the magic that elevates the very best series, and *Summer Wine* had it too, but there was no single quintessential episode, not even two or three; it had many more than that, at a very conservative count at least a couple of dozen where it achieved that divine state of comedic grace. There was a definitive *series* – the matchless 1981/82 season, eight flawless episodes, but other gems are spread across the course of decades.

Its run had been, by any standards, extraordinary. By the time of its twenty-fifth anniversary, it had been a fixture of the schedules for much longer than any other comedy show in Britain or elsewhere. Misfortune had proved *Summer Wine*'s friend. The difficulties that the show had faced ultimately worked in its favour; as actors died or became too elderly to continue, the changes forced on writer and director constantly helped rejuvenate it.

Now renewal was working its magic once again. There was a mood of optimism around the show. Clarke and Bell were enthused by their new leading man, and he in turn was equally keen. It felt like a fresh start that opened up exciting possibilities – and that did not just apply to the casting. Bell had been making a case for the series to be moved from the Sunday teatime God slot, and the then Controller of BBC1, Peter Fincham, was sympathetic. There was talk of prime time on a Monday or Thursday evening, the sort of scheduling that had sent *Summer Wine* to the peak of its ratings success in the 80s. But in 2007 Fincham resigned amid a scandal over the botched editing of a programme about the Queen that appeared to show her storming out of a photo-shoot when in fact she had done nothing of the sort. The show stayed where it was. Worse, another old friend would soon be lost.

Kathy Staff, approaching eighty, was not well. The signs that something was wrong had appeared during the filming of the 2008 series, when this most conscientious, well-prepared actress who had always been word perfect was suddenly uncertain of her lines, which upset her deeply. Bell had long grown accustomed to coping with the occasional fluffs of ageing actors whose grip on dialogue was no longer as secure as it had once been, and moved to reassure her. 'It really hit her, she said, "I'm so sorry," and I said, "Don't worry Kathy, I couldn't remember lines twenty years ago, and you're doing these long speeches."' Her close friend Jane Freeman was concerned. 'She did have problems remembering the lines, and that worried me, because Kathy was always rock-solid.' The two joked about growing old together in the show, and hanging on to the very last. 'We used to say, "Well, I'll do it next year, because that'll be the last," and Kathy and I, having been in the first, wanted to be in the last one, and so we thought if it was only going on another year, that's all we were going to do.'

Staff would not have the chance to stay until the end. A brain tumour was diagnosed. As had been the case with Owen, the seriousness of her condition was kept from the cast, even though it was apparent she would not be well enough to take part in the next series. 'It was terrible, because I think Alan and I were the only two that knew Kathy was terminally ill,' said Freeman. 'I would get people coming up to me and saying, "Oh, I hear Kathy's not doing it because she's fallen out with someone, or she wasn't asked in time, or she was on holiday, or she was fed up with so-and-so," and it was awful because I couldn't say, "No, the only reason is because she's poorly."'

She rallied a little, briefly sparking hopes that she may be able to appear, but it was not to be. Kathy Staff died on 14 December 2008. 'I was devastated,' said Freeman. 'She died a year to the day from my husband dying. It was awful losing her. She was my good friend, and I miss her terribly.' Six months earlier, the congregation of St Mark's, Dukinfield, the church she had known all her life and continued to attend, had, to her delight, organised an eightieth birthday party for her. Now they mourned. Mike Grady said: 'When I went to her funeral there were all the people that she knew in that little town, and they loved her for Kathy, for who she was, and had it been any one of them, they would all have been there as well, and she would too.'

Hers had been the most unexpected of successes; rushing for a late-afternoon audition with an initially unenthusiastic producer for a bit part in a pilot that might not have gone anywhere, barking out that first line, 'They're taking his telly again,' and the handful that followed with such conviction that it drove her briefly glimpsed character into a writer's consciousness through sheer force of personality. She developed Nora Batty so persuasively that its trappings became part of the country's vernacular, all the while retaining a down-to-earth good humour that made her beloved not just of an audience but those who worked with her. What turned out to be Staff's last bow in the series that made her a comedy icon was, happily, as fine a passage ever written by Clarke for Nora, in 'Get Out of That, Then':

Nora: Why do they need a spark when they're married?

Pearl: Because they find they're getting nowhere at home, just rubbing two sticks together.

Nora: I don't see the need, when they've got everything provided.

Ivy: Oh yes, and what's your idea of everything provided?

Nora: Clean and tidy, and all they can eat.

Ivy: They want more.

Nora: I never considered they were entitled to more. Oh, you have to relax a bit on birthdays and cup finals.

Nellie: Every cup final?

Nora: I don't wish to talk about it.

Pearl: Can you remember who won?

Nora: It wasn't me. I remember that.

She constantly longed to soften Nora, to ease her implacable, scowling, slab-faced ferocity, even though, in truth, there were plenty of episodes where she displayed a more sympathetic side, usually when duped by Compo into taking pity on him. She had eventually got her way at the very end of Owen's life; in 'Last Post and Pigeon', there was a kiss of genuine tenderness between Compo and Nora as he departed for France, and in his final three episodes, the real Staff had peeped out from behind her character's mask with a smile of unabashed affection as Owen appeared on a ladder at her window. Such moments, though, needed to be strictly rationed. Clarke said: 'I used to feel sorry for her in many ways, portraying her as this enormous bitch all the time, when she was as soft as a brush.' Bell, too, recognised the comedy gold of keeping it harsh: 'She always kept saying to me, "Can I just play this a bit softer?" and I would say, "No, they want to see this hard battleaxe."'

They were both right. Nora had to be unassailably formidable. The more she bawled and shooed and berated, the more the audience loved her. She was a caricature of the northern women of Clarke's youth, and the warmth of Staff's personality that lay beneath the padding and wrinkled stockings lit it from within, assuring the audience's affections. Comically fearsome women – matrons and headmistresses and mothers-in-law – were a staple of British comedy, and if they were hefty with it, so much the funnier as they bustled and bossed. Actresses including Hattie Jacques and Peggy Mount had made careers out of such roles, and Staff stood in the front rank of that proud tradition with her portrayal of Nora. 'The public loved her,' said Freeman. 'It was a great comfort to her husband, John, because he was so thrilled with her success. He absolutely loved it that the public loved her, and they did.'

There could no more be a second Nora than a replica Compo, but Alvin needed a female neighbour to bounce off, so Clarke once again gave the relationship a tweak with a new character. Nora was packed off to Australia to stay with family, to be replaced at 28 Huddersfield Road by her sister, Stella, a former pub landlady who, far from being a nightmare in pinny and curlers, would be a glamourpuss of a certain vintage. Though no less sharp of tongue, she also held flirtatious possibilities. Staff's last episode provided the actress to play her. Barbara Young had a long history on both television and the stage, winning plaudits for her portrayal of Agrippinilla, mother of the Emperor Nero, in the BBC's epic adaptation of Robert Graves's *I Claudius* in 1976 and going on to appear in *Coronation Street*. In 'Get Out of That, Then' she guested as Florrie, despairing wife of a hopeless escapologist, played by Bobby Ball. Clarke and Bell were impressed and discussed how to move her into Nora's house. 'I suggested to Roy that we could do a bit with Bobby going off and her saying, "Remember, we're living here and not there." He said, "Can't we just use her without Bobby Ball?" and I said I thought that might be confusing, to which he said, "Give her a different wig, she's a good actress, she can be somebody else."'

That's what they did. The dowdy grey-haired Florrie was transformed into the red-headed Stella. Nobody, though, thought to tell Young, who signed up for nine episodes and went for a fitting. 'It was only when I got there that the make-up lady said, "I thought we might have a red wig," and I said, "Why, for Florrie?" and she said, "You're not playing Florrie," and I said, "Aren't I?" She said Kathy wasn't going to do this series, so they've had to rewrite the scripts and you're going to play her sister, Stella, who's a pub landlady. And I said, "Am I? Well, it would have been nice if somebody had let me know."' Once Young had got used to the idea of who she was going to be, Bell briefed her: 'Alan did say to me, "She's not going to look anything like Nora, but she's going to have the same mouth," and that was quite useful to know.'

The cast settled, filming went ahead smoothly. This would be a different, unfamiliar *Last of the Summer Wine*. For the first time in its long history, Clegg, with Truly in tow, would not be at the centre of the plots. Sallis and Thornton were now given second billing after Abbot, Kwouk and Murphy, their roles from now on brief cameos, usually in Clegg's living room, often seated to accommodate Sallis's failing sight. On location, everything had gone swimmingly. Abbot, in the context of Summer Wine Land a mere stripling of sixty, brought a new physicality to the show, standing in the back of Entwistle's van in the manner of a tank commander, and able to do stunts. 'Diving over walls and falling over the back of trucks and the front of trucks, that's been a way of life for me over the years, all the slap,' said Abbot. 'It's not as easy now, I must admit, but that's the way Roy writes, you can't say, "I can't do that," because it means something to the episode, those bits and pieces. It just gelled, it just fell into place, and that's down to the scripts. He can write visuals, and there are very, very few writers who can write visuals, and it jumps off the page at you, and you think, yeah, I can see that.' There were shades of Foggy in Hobbo's manic restlessness. Not since Wilde's early appearances had there been such a deluded man of action fired by pent-up energy. His conversation belonged in the same mould too, as in the first exchange with Alvin and Entwistle, who in time-honoured style are busy doing nothing as they contemplate the hills.

Hobbo: I have a nose for danger. It never rests.

Alvin: Rest your nose, Hobbo. Relax.

Hobbo: What are you looking for?

Alvin: Just looking.

Hobbo: I'll tell you what I'm looking for, the tell-tale flash of sunlight on metal or glass.

Alvin: Still out to get you, are they?

Hobbo: Out there, that's sniper country.

Alvin: You used to live out there in your little cottage, all alone. Why didn't they get you then?

Hobbo: No doubt they tried. I've forgotten, but once the memory comes back … chances are, I buried them out there.

Entwistle: As you do.

Hobbo: I'm telling you this in confidence, of course. There are those who wouldn't realise I was licensed to kill.

Entwistle: You still doing the needlework?

The balance of this new trio was fundamentally different from the concept that had underpinned *Summer Wine* for so many years; where once Compo, the decrepit outsider, was the most immediately identifiable comic figure, now it was the self-proclaimed leader of men. Entwistle took on something of Clegg's role as the driest of observers on the absurdities around him, and Alvin stood in the middle, a cheeky, cheery figure. Hobbo not only had his friends to contend with; he was also the reluctant target of a love-struck spinster librarian, Miss Davenport, played by another comedy veteran, Josephine Tewson. All of which meant that an enormous weight of responsibility rested on Abbot. 'Russ was terribly nervous when he came into it, but he settled in nicely,' said Jean Alexander. 'They gave him rather a lot to do in his first year. It perhaps overloaded Russ, there could perhaps have been a bit less of him and a bit more of the other two to even it up.'

Hobbo was seamlessly integrated into Summer Wine Land. The new boy lived in the same row of cottages as Howard and Pearl, and the clothes he wore – anorak, cardigan and tie – were as resolutely remote from any era as Clegg's cap and mac, making him look as though he could have wandered into a scene at any time from 1973 onwards. Clarke was as deft as ever in introducing him, his gift for making new characters feel to the audience as if they had been part of his comic landscape for years impressing Abbot. 'The thing about *Summer Wine* is that if somebody passes on or moves out, and somebody takes over, there's barely an introduction. There's a couple of lines in the first episode explaining to the viewers who he is and what he's doing there and after that it just takes on its own format. I don't know whether the viewers have noticed it, but it's the only programme I know of where everybody looks the same in every episode, and this is why they register with people. It's that wonderful simplicity, that wonderful natural vision, they say, "Oh yes, there's Hobbo, there's Compo, there's Cleggy," they know what they're going to look like. I think it's unique, instantly recognisable.'

It was odd to see Stella in her finery emerging from Nora's house, but the character fitted comfortably into the coffee mornings. There had been a subtle change in the ladies' dialogue after Thora's death; Glenda was growing more assertive. 'She was very much under Thora's thumb,' said Sarah Thomas. 'I'm finding now that Roy is making her much more strident, she's getting more like her mother, and Alan sometimes encourages me to play it quite strongly because that feels right. Alan will often say, "You're getting more like Thora," and I think that's right.' Elsewhere, the old favourites provided reassuring familiarity around the new trio. In the café, Ivy berated Hobbo, Alvin and Entwistle as forcefully as she had given Compo, Clegg and Blamire a piece of her mind, Howard was still chasing Marina and getting caught out by Pearl, and Auntie Wainwright was still chiselling the customers.

It was a good series, rich in laughs, and went down well with the preview audiences, who reacted warmly to Abbot. And then, out of the blue, before the special that introduced Hobbo was broadcast, the BBC pulled the plug. A few days before Christmas 2008, a furious Bell told the *Huddersfield Examiner* newspaper that he had been informed that *Last of the Summer Wine* was being axed. He was incandescent, later saying, 'It really was like being hit in the face with a shovel. We'd just taken it off in a new direction, and it's stopped, without anybody having seen it. I was deeply hurt for the series' sake, because we've always worked hard to make the programme good, to give it quality. We could easily turn out one episode every three days, but it'd be rubbish, we try to put some quality in, and having got it to a very high standard with a new cast, we have it stopped before anyone's seen it.'

The will-they, won't-they saga of whether the show would continue had been running far longer than most comedy series, but now it seemed that the end had come in spite of its continued popularity. There was an outcry from viewers, and 800 letters of protest were sent to the BBC, many at the prompting of the *Last of the Summer Wine* Appreciation Society, which had been founded in 1993. The angry reaction caught the BBC wrong-footed; years of indifference, of casual slights and even the scorn of younger executives had blinded it to just how devoted the *Summer Wine* audience was. Writer, producer and cast knew – the reaction of viewers in the aftermath of Owen's death had been the most powerful reminder of that – but its masters had simply failed to realise. Just as Clarke's enduring originality had passed them by, so had the close identification of the audience with his work. The evidence had long been there for anybody who could be bothered to look; those who sat down in their thousands over the years to write in often called it '*our* show'. It was theirs, shaped and nuanced by a rare empathy between writer and the people at home, born of Clarke's unshakeable conviction that the best comedy dialogue came from the rhythms of everyday conversation. Fantastical though his plots and exchanges remained, they were expressed in the same matter-of-fact manner that had marked 'Of Funerals and Fish' as the most naturalistic and unforced entry in that long-ago *Comedy Playhouse* series. Only the very greatest of sitcoms, a tiny handful of them in the vast output of the past fifty years, truly touched the hearts of their viewers to the extent that they came to regard the characters as friends and felt the show to be theirs, and the letters that poured in to the BBC were a sharp lesson to those who would dismiss it as old hat that *Summer Wine* was one of them.

It was '*our* show' too to those who worked on it, in many cases for decades, and they were, if anything, even angrier than the viewers. It was not just the unparalleled longevity of its run that fostered passionate loyalty; it was pride in something special. There was no more experienced ensemble cast on television, no more committed crew, and these seasoned pros knew how good the work of Clarke, Bell and, yes, themselves, was. This was unique comedy, a once-in-a-lifetime classic, and being part of it was a privilege. That was what made so many of those who worked on *Summer Wine* fall under its spell, even from the beginning. Michael Bates and Michael Aldridge had wept bitterly when fate robbed them of it; if some benevolent providence could have granted Bill Owen or Thora Hird the strength for even another episode, they would surely have seized it. Jimmy Gilbert, who one far-off spring day saw in an oddly titled script that landed on his desk a germ of greatness and nurtured the show, even after he relinquished the role of producer, always kept a special place in his heart for the series that enchanted him more than anything else that he had done during a lifetime in entertainment: 'For some indefinable reason, I enjoyed working on *Summer Wine* more than any other series I ever did – the only one I feel genuinely nostalgic about. I loved it.' So too Alan Bell, touring the Pennines, scouting traces on Ordnance Survey maps for locations, preferring the privations of wind-blasted days on the hills to the comforts of a desk job. 'It's not just my work, it's my hobby,' he said. 'I look back over my time with *Summer Wine*, and I was offered some nice jobs further up the ladder and I always said no, I don't want to work in an office. I've thoroughly enjoyed it. I can't think of a time when I didn't enjoy it.' *Our* show was not about to shuffle meekly round the corner from Sid and Ivy's café into oblivion without a fight.

The BBC back-pedalled furiously as the letters poured in and the story spread, insisting that no decision had been made and none would be until after the new series had been broadcast between April and June. Luck was on *Summer Wine*'s side; the corporation found itself in a bind thanks to rumbling accusations about its attitude to older people; a succession of presenters had left or been replaced across current affairs and factual programming, and several had accused the BBC of ageism, complaining that only young faces were wanted on television. These had been acutely embarrassing charges, vigorously denied, but they stuck, and now it appeared that a comedy show enjoyed by an older audience was also falling victim to an obsession with youth that had already resulted in a painfully misguided incident.

The timing of the row could hardly have been more excruciating; a little more than a month before, the Corporation had issued a grovelling apology after a breathtaking lapse of taste on the part of two of its most high-profile stars who spearheaded the drive for a young audience. Edgy stand-up Russell Brand and chat-show host Jonathan Ross – reportedly the corporation's highest-paid performer, with a twelve-million-pound deal – had become carried away during Brand's Radio 2 show and left a series of offensive, sexually charged messages on the answerphone of actor Andrew Sachs about his granddaughter. When they became public, tens of thousands of complaints flooded in to the corporation and prompted a media debate that wondered long and loud about what was going on at the BBC. The tone was as much shocked and regretful as it was outraged. How was it possible that the organisation which for so long had set the gold standard in entertainment could descend to presiding over this? What had become of the nation's provider of laughter? How could it be that the home of the greatest of television tag-teams, Morecambe and Wise and The Two Ronnies, now fostered and showered with money two stars whose idea of humour was so spiteful, sordid, desperately, irredeemably unfunny and ill-judged that those who heard it winced in embarrassed discomfort?

It only served to aggravate the incident's offensiveness, to emphasise the gulf between inspired comedy and base worthlessness, that the victim of the prank calls belonged to that revered golden age. Sachs's performance as Manuel, the hapless, hopelessly keen, bullied, loveable Spanish waiter in *Fawlty Towers*, had won him comic immortality. A generation not born when he first obediently did the bidding of John Cleese's deranged Basil Fawlty in 1974 knew and loved Manuel thanks to frequent repeats and the issue of the show on DVD. To target an actor held in such fond regard, now aged seventy-eight, seemed especially cruel.

As the debate about its values raged, the BBC cast about for evidence to offer that it remained the home of family entertainment. Ironically, given its doubts about the most venerable of comedies, its gaze fell upon *Last of the Summer Wine*. 'It's the one programme that does satisfy all the ideals of television, to entertain and not to offend,' said Bell. 'When they had all this debacle about Jonathan Ross, the one thing the BBC kept saying was that they did *Summer Wine*. The BBC have always used it as a balance. I remember when the Head of Entertainment at the time was called to answer to the governors that the output lacked strength, and he was pulled apart for the quality of programming and originality, but at the end they said, "The fact you do *Summer Wine* is a marvellous balance to that."' Brand quit his show, and Ross was taken off the air for three months, later resigning from the BBC.

A well-aimed and painful kick came from an unexpected direction. June Whitfield's presence in BBC comedy went all the way back to Frank Muir and Denis Norden's ground-breaking radio show, *Take It from Here*, which she joined in 1953, via *Hancock*, her own hit series with Terry Scott, and one of the finest recent sitcoms, *Absolutely Fabulous*, with Jennifer Saunders and Joanna Lumley, which had won her a legion of new admirers among the young. Now she threatened that she would not work for the corporation again because it was biased against the elderly. 'I honestly think the BBC don't like old people,' she said in the *Daily Express* in May 2009. 'They are prejudiced because they are all so young themselves.' She had ventured into Summer Wine Land with a guest appearance opposite Warren Mitchell before being written in as a regular, Nellie, in 2008. Whitfield had given countless interviews over the years, and was invariably charming and funny, but never had she said anything remotely like this, at least in public. Her uncompromising bluntness came as a shock and reignited the debate about whether there was an ageist culture at the BBC. She remained unrepentant: 'I think it's barmy. They do not like older people and they do not make shows for older people to watch. It's all this thing about attracting youth and they don't seem able to recognise that the youth that they're after are either sitting with headphones on, or on their laptops chatting to a friend. I don't know what the statistics are, but for people over fifty anyway, there's nothing on the television for us. Some young person gets there at the top and says, "Oh good heavens, that's been on for years, get rid of that," and they don't know what they're talking about.' Those who had been there since the beginning agreed with her. 'I think the BBC has always had an ambivalent attitude towards us,' said Jane Freeman. 'We're not what you'd call a smart programme, but we're also not low rubbish. We've been in a quaint little category all of our own, and they don't know what to do with us, some of the smart kids who've got into TV production.'

The protests hit their mark. Without admitting that *Summer Wine* had been axed, the BBC commissioned a shorter than usual run of six in May 2009, announcing a month later that a thirty-first series was being made. The decision was taken as Abbot's first series was being shown, to respectable figures of about three million viewers. There was, though, a sting in the tail. Even as the BBC relented, it made up its mind; this really would be the last taste of *Summer Wine*, bringing down the curtain after 37 years, tantalisingly close to it reaching 300 episodes. However, it wanted no repeat of protests over its axing, still less a fresh round of accusations of ageism, so the decision was kept quiet. It would be fully a year later before the cast could be sure that there would be no more, however strong their suspicions. Clarke was under no illusions that the show had been living on borrowed time for the previous few years, and now that time was up: 'It's got to come to an end sometime, and I don't know how we justify ourselves any more, except in terms of what else is there for our kind of audience.' If this was goodbye, he would ring the changes to see it out in style; he had written two- and three-part storylines before, and now, at seventy-nine, for the first time, he wrote a serial, six episodes being a manageable span across which to string a running plot about Pearl finally losing patience with Howard over Marina, and throwing him out of the house, to which he frantically tries to return with the dubious help of Hobbo, Alvin and Entwistle. The storyline would climax by drawing virtually the entire cast together for a finale at a wedding where the groom gets cold feet and fails to turn up. Refusing to be downcast, they all board a vintage bus and head off in search of a restaurant.

The company could not fail to realise that the sun was setting on Summer Wine Land when the script for that sixth episode, 'How Not to Cry at Weddings', arrived. 'I felt that the six episodes had a kind of shape that could be a finishing-off shape,' said Sarah Thomas. Juliette Kaplan put it simply: 'We all said it was the walk-down.' Bell commented: 'It was a way of bringing it to a conclusion, not that it needed a conclusion.'

For the first time, there was nostalgia in the air, as memories of Bill and Brian and Michael and Joe and John and Kathy and Thora and all the rest who had travelled for part of this long, long journey swirled around the location shoot, recollections of laughter past, days spent sheltering from the rain or when things went wrong, and more days when everyone knew and treasured that they were creating blissfully funny shows. Even though *Summer Wine* was a series rooted in recollections of the past, albeit Clarke's heightened comic fantasy of what wartime or running a very minor public school involved, and despite long-serving actors being accustomed to fans telling them that the show had not been the same since Foggy left or Owen died, the show's durability meant it had largely escaped the warm embrace of nostalgia that had fostered and enhanced the reputations of other classic comedy series of that lost, lamented golden age of entertainment where its roots lay.

Whereas *Dad's Army*, *Porridge*, *Fawlty Towers* and the rest were decades over, their magic there to be relived via frequent repeats and neatly parcelled box sets that stood as monuments not just to their excellence but to the tastes of viewers who preferred wit, generosity of spirit and intelligence to the brassiness and vulgarity of much of what they found being broadcast currently, *Summer Wine* remained ever-present, thanks to Clarke's prodigious output and the unflagging enthusiasm of Bell. It was never favoured with many repeats on BBC1 or BBC2, though it became a staple of the subscription-only G.O.L.D. Why repeat *Summer Wine* when another series was always just around the corner? The sheer volume of episodes made it impossible to bring together in one set for home consumption, even though DVD packages each containing two series sold well.

Now, though, it was apparent that the end was at hand. Time, for so long held at bay in the fantasy of Summer Wine Land, was catching up at last. The lateness of the decision to go ahead with another series meant Bell had to scurry to gather his actors and fix his locations; a tight schedule meant that the company stuck close to Holmfirth and a few favourite spots in the hills above, including Intake Lane, which held so many memories. This would be no anticlimax: Clarke's scripts were fresh and funny, Hobbo's character was now fully integrated, the secret-agent flashbacks downplayed in favour of him engaging with Howard's travails.

For Holmfirth, it was just another summer, as cast and crew rolled into town and set up base camp at a farm; sunny days brought the visitors, as they had for the past three decades. The tour buses did their usual brisk trade, departing from outside Sid and Ivy's café, ferrying their passengers around the sights they knew so well from Sunday teatimes at home; to Hade Edge and Scholes, past the White Horse and up to the high point at New Mill where everybody could disembark, look across the valley and see the private road with its cottages where Howard, Pearl, Clegg and now Hobbo lived, taking a spin by the house Bill Owen rented for so many years, and then back into town to drop off, their drivers pointing the way to Nora Batty's house and the *Summer Wine* exhibition featuring Compo's long johns next door. The lucky ones turned up while filming was under way, and the stars smiled, waved, chatted and signed autographs. This had become a way of life in Holmfirth, as accustomed and seemingly unchanging as the presence of the hills that watched over the town. In one respect, it was just another summer for the show, too; even the sunny days could be cold, and when the rain poured, as it did, there was nothing to do except take shelter and swap yarns until it stopped. Bell watched the sky as he had for half a professional lifetime, waiting for the light to be right, looking for the consistency to complete his scenes, finishing each day on time as ever, and then the actors headed back to the Huddersfield Hotel and dinner at Thora's Table.

Except this was not just another summer. The shoot began in Yorkshire on 17 August, and would last almost a month, until 15 September, when, as everything was packed up for the return to London and the cars and caravans and trucks headed down into Holmfirth, past the café, past Nora's, past the river into which the three men had so often been dumped, and the bridge where they had mused, away towards the M1, all felt this was the last farewell, even as they hoped they were wrong.

The interiors were still to film at Shepperton, including the scenes with Sallis and Thornton that would be digitally inserted into the location work. On the final day in the studios, Clarke paid one of his rare visits, to chat, to share a joke, to join the company for the end-of-term photograph on the set of Ivy's café. As Christmas neared, a day of previews at Teddington was just how it had always been – packed out, three houses, two episodes each, Kwouk and Abbot, Fyfe and Fergusson on stage, putting on a show, the air filled with expectation as the lights dimmed and Hazlehurst's music once again floated the audience away to Summer Wine Land. They laughed loud and long, as they always had, as Howard scurried and cowered, as Ivy and the ladies pursed their lips in disapproval, as Hobbo plotted with misplaced self-confidence, as Clegg and Truly delivered verbal pokes in the ribs. Outside, it was raining hard enough to rival Holmfirth, but it didn't matter to the people who streamed out of the studios, full of praise for what they had just seen. Millions at home would hear their laughter on the soundtrack of these six episodes, laughter that was spontaneous, unforced and joyous, the laughter of people who had gone home happy.

Cast and crew went home too, to wait and see what the BBC decided. As 2010 dawned and then spring turned to summer with no word, the actors began to accept offers of other work for the months when they would usually be in Yorkshire. Rumours began to circulate that an announcement was imminent, and up in Holmfirth, business people who had made a living out of the tourist trade generated by the show for decades wondered what the future held.

The statement came on Wednesday 2 June, a few weeks short of the 38th anniversary of the minibus heading north at the outset of a journey that would make television history, and it was fulsome in its praise, even as it confirmed that the six episodes to be broadcast over the summer would be the last. Cheryl Taylor, Controller, Comedy Commissioning, said: 'It is a testimony to the wit and warmth of the characters that Roy Clarke originally created that this amazing series has endured over several decades. The BBC feels enormously privileged to have played host to its many charms for such a long time and we very much respect the affection in which it is held. It is very tough to call time on such a cherished institution, but we are very sincere in our gratitude for, and admiration of, *Last of the Summer Wine*. It is the undisputed champion of long-running comedy series.' By way of tribute, special editions of *Songs of Praise* and the rural-affairs programme, *Countryfile*, would be broadcast from Holmfirth.

The axeing severed the last remaining link to the most glorious age of comedy that television ever knew or was likely to know. Across *Summer Wine*'s lifetime entertainment had been transformed around it, and not for the better as so much of it grew progressively more coarse. The sensitivity that had made Clarke excise the word 'bloody' from his scripts rather than risk offending a family audience appeared quaint in comparison to much of what was now being broadcast. The nearest equivalent of the mass audiences transcending gender, class and age that *Summer Wine* attracted in the 70s and 80s were depressingly often being drawn by the callousness of bear-pit reality shows. Where once viewers had been invited to unite in laughter, now they were encouraged to join in voyeuristic gloating at human frailty; television was all the more tawdry for the trend, and the loss of this most quirkily individual of all sitcoms that at its peak had regularly brought together more than a third of Britain's population underlined how much had changed and been cheapened. This, in stark contrast, had been the last stand of a comic era that dealt in richness and excellence, but was now irrevocably, unarguably over. Among the *Summer Wine* family, there was sadness, but no real sense of surprise. The upheaval of the previous year had steeled them for the end. Their instincts had been correct; there would be no more summers in the Pennines, no more filming at Nora's or the café, no more excited anticipation as a new set of scripts dropped through the letterbox.

At home, tucked contentedly away at the far end of a tranquil tree-lined lane in a corner of Yorkshire that keeps itself to itself, where even the locals still got lost, and birdsong provided the soundtrack to the flights of comic imagination that touched funny bones the audience never knew they had, Roy Clarke bade his own private farewell to the show that had become a way of life. 'I miss it,' he said. 'It sort of leaves a gap; it feels a bit odd.' There was still work to do; the compulsion to write still gripped him as firmly as when he pounded the beat in Dalton as a young bobby a lifetime before, where feckless men and their battleaxe wives first worked their way into his consciousness. He carried on, developing a stage treatment of *Keeping Up Appearances* and turning back to the novel he had chipped away at for years.

There had been no question in his mind over who should have the last word. Frail though he was as he prepared for his final appearances, Peter Sallis would not have given up his involvement for the world; as he approached ninety he remained as much in love with the show as thirty-eight years earlier when the pilot script arrived and he was so determined to be part of it that he turned up for the initial reading in costume. 'To have been mixed up with something like that, you don't need much else to give you a nice going-to-bed feeling. I would hate to be left out, and while I'm alive and I can breathe and I can speak, I don't think I will be left out.' His wish was granted; he never was, nor ever could have been. A running gag in the closing episode had Clegg wondering if he had locked up the house before coming to the wedding, to Truly's mounting irritation, and it eased *Last of the Summer Wine* into comic eternity aboard the bus making its unhurried way along a country road with the loveliness of the Pennines as the backdrop for one last time. As it trundled past the camera and out of shot with the titles rolling and that most wistful of theme tunes drawing to its end, the unmistakeable, unforgettable, indispensable voice bade farewell with a quirky simplicity that brought this long journey full circle with a final laugh. All those years before, it had begun with a single, unadorned line that instantly summed up the character of Compo; now it ended with another single, no less plain, line that encapsulated the timid worrier in the flat cap and mac: 'Did I lock the door?'

Acknowledgements, Sources and Bibliography

I OWE AN immense debt of gratitude to two men without whom this book would not have been possible. The first is Roy Clarke, writer of *Last of the Summer Wine*, whose warmth, wit and candour were a joy, and whose kindness in granting permission to quote from his scripts is greatly appreciated. The second is Alan J. W. Bell, the series' long-time producer/director, whose good humour, frankness, unstinting willingness to help and enthusiasm were invaluable. I would also like to thank him for giving permission to quote from an unpublished interview he conducted with Brian Wilde.

Special thanks must also go to three men whose contributions to the show are immeasurable, and gave generously of their time and memories: Peter Sallis, the only actor to appear in every episode, and producers James Gilbert and Sydney Lotterby.

The following cast members displayed great patience and kindness in sharing their recollections and opinions: Russ Abbot, Jean Alexander, Jean Fergusson, Jane Freeman, Robert Fyfe, Mike Grady, Juliette Kaplan, Ken Kitson, Burt Kwouk, Brian Murphy, Tom Owen, Sarah Thomas, Frank Thornton, June Whitfield and Barbara Young.

The *Summer Wine* crew, especially Simone Dawson and Sylvia Kendall, went out of their way to assist, as did the following long-time residents of the Holme Valley: Ron and Ruth Backhouse, Andrew Bray and Sonia Lee.

Grateful thanks are due to Clive Eardley, president of the *Last of the Summer Wine* Appreciation Society, whose advice and aid were hugely helpful. The society can be contacted at 18 Fairfield Avenue, Altofts, West Yorkshire WF6 2NH or email clivefireflash@btinternet.com.

Trish Hayes and Louise North of the BBC Written Archives Centre, Caversham Park, Reading, gave every assistance.

My appreciation to three friends: Duncan Hamilton, author and journalist, for opening the door and wise advice; Peter Charlton, Editor of the Yorkshire Post, for his forbearance and support; and Tony Earnshaw of the National Media Museum, for his thoughtfulness. Many thanks also to Graham Coster at Aurum.

Last, but certainly not least, my thanks to Carole for her love and encouragement throughout.

This book is based primarily on interviews with the writer, directors and cast of *Last of the Summer Wine*, whose names can be found in the acknowledgements. I have also drawn on material originally published in a variety of newspapers and magazines. The BBC Written Archives Centre kindly gave permission to use extracts from minutes of the Television Weekly Progress Review meetings of 14 November 1973 and 16 April 1975, as well as Audience Research Reports of 29 November 1973 and 15 January 1974.

The following is a select bibliography:

Bright, Morris and Ross, Robert: *Last of the Summer Wine: The Finest Vintage* (BBC, 2000)

Fisher, John: *Funny Way to Be a Hero* (Frederick Muller, 1973)

Fisher, John: *Tony Hancock – The Definitive Biography* (Harper, 2008)

Hird, Thora: *Is It Thora?* (HarperCollins, 1996)

Lewisohn, Mark: *Radio Times Guide to TV Comedy* (BBC, 1998)

McCann, Graham: *Dad's Army: The Story of a Classic Television Show* (Fourth Estate, 2001)

Owen, Bill: *Summer Wine and Vintage Years: A Cluttered Life* (Robson, 1994)

Sallis, Peter: *Fading Into the Limelight* (Orion, 2006)

Staff, Kathy: *My Story – Wrinkles and All* (Hodder and Stoughton, 1997)

Took, Barry: *A Point of View* (Duckworth, 1990)

Index